Rape by the Numbers

Critical Issues in Crime and Society

RAYMOND J. MICHALOWSKI AND LUIS A. FERNANDEZ, SERIES EDITORS

Critical Issues in Crime and Society is oriented toward critical analysis of contemporary problems in crime and justice. The series is open to a broad range of topics including specific types of crime, wrongful behavior by economically or politically powerful actors, controversies over justice system practices, and issues related to the intersection of identity, crime, and justice. It is committed to offering thoughtful works that will be accessible to scholars and professional criminologists, general readers, and students.

For a list of titles in the series, see the last page of the book.

Rape by the Numbers

PRODUCING AND CONTESTING
SCIENTIFIC KNOWLEDGE
ABOUT SEXUAL VIOLENCE

ETHAN CZUY LEVINE

RUTGERS UNIVERSITY PRESS
New Brunswick, Camden, and Newark, New Jersey, and London

LIBRARY OF CONGRESS CATALOGING-IN-PUBLICATION DATA

Names: Levine, Ethan Czuy, author.
Title: Rape by the numbers: producing and contesting scientific knowledge about
  sexual violence / Ethan Czuy Levine.
Description: New Brunswick: Rutgers University Press, [2021] | Series: Critical
  issues in crime and society | Includes bibliographical references and index.
Identifiers: LCCN 2020051473 | ISBN 9781978823631 (paperback) |
  ISBN 9781978823648 (cloth) | ISBN 9781978823655 (epub) |
  ISBN 9781978823662 (mobi) | ISBN 9781978823679 (pdf)
Subjects: LCSH: Rape—United States. | Rape—Canada. | Sex crimes—
  United States. | Sex crimes—Canada.
Classification: LCC HV6561 .L45 2021 | DDC 364.15/320973—dc23
LC record available at https://lccn.loc.gov/2020051473

A British Cataloging-in-Publication record for this book is available
from the British Library.

♾ The paper used in this publication meets the requirements of the American
National Standard for Information Sciences—Permanence of Paper for Printed
Library Materials, ANSI Z39.48-1992.

www.rutgersuniversitypress.org

Manufactured in the United States of America

For Bruce, Karra-Jae, and Ivy

Contents

Rape by the Numbers

CHAPTER 1

Introduction

IN MY THIRD year of college, I made the questionably ambitious decision to take Advanced Feminist Theory with a professor to whom I'll refer here as April. The reading list was dizzying. Donna Haraway, Sarah Ahmed, Judith Butler—these and others whose work struck me as equal parts aligned with and in opposition to feminism. Or at least those feminisms with which I was familiar. And whereas other professors might have pushed us to identify a favorite theorist, or at least to claim that some were more compelling than others, April posed a greater challenge. She asked us to consider the social forces behind feminist theorizing. She asked that we approach knowledge as contingent and variable, linked with specific actors and contexts. Rather than seek out "Truth" (that is, with a capital "T"), she raised the possibility that multiple truths might coexist.

Midway through the term, having established the course as postmodern but not quite having clarified what that meant, April led an exercise in knowledge production. She read several statements aloud, each beginning with a knower and finishing with a knowledge claim. "Alan knows that it is time for breakfast." "Beverly knows that she must study for her statistics exam." My peers and I were tasked with the deceptively simple mission of guessing how these actors might have come to know whatever it was that they knew.

Most statements were handled swiftly. We might propose two or three explanations, enough to demonstrate some measure of variance, and move along. "Alan always eats breakfast at 8:00, and that's what time it is." "Alan's partner announced that it was breakfast time." "Beverly's test is next week, and she did poorly on the last one." And so we continued, until April offered the following: "Mary knows that she is pregnant."

Our tame discussion erupted. Practically everyone had something to offer. April herself had prepared more than ten explanations. "Mary's belly is swelling." "She took one of those at-home pregnancy tests." "She had a dream." "She saw an omen." "She got an ultrasound, and the doctor gave her a picture of the baby." "Mary's periods stopped." "She just knows." "One of her friends is a nurse—nurses always seem to know before anyone else, don't they?" "She took a blood test." "The angel Gabriel told her that she was with child." "She's been throwing up." "Something about her food cravings changed."

Engaging as these musings were, what happened next fixed the lesson in my memory. We transitioned from merely offering explanations to assessing their credibility. Moreover, we began to consider that credibility might vary among claims of pregnancy and might be achievable through different means by different actors in different contexts (Epstein 1996; Shapin 1995; Waidzunas 2012). Some classmates had been pregnant before. A few of them—and several of our acquaintances who were not present for the exercise—had contacted their doctors to disclose pregnancies and schedule appropriate care. In every case, patients' accounts were deemed insufficient to establish pregnancy. Doctors demanded further examination under their own supervision. One person recalled that a friend had shown up well into her second trimester—belly swollen, periods ceased—only to hear her doctor say that "you're not pregnant until my test says so." So claimants were unequal. However confident Mary might be, however many friends and relatives might believe her, she was a substandard knower in medical encounters (provided that she wasn't, herself, a doctor who engaged in medically sanctioned self-assessments before declaring pregnancy). Body fluids were also unequal. Blood carried more weight than urine. Except for menstrual blood, the absence of which was of limited value. Moreover, certain signs were rendered imperceptible in these moments (Murphy 2006; Proctor 2008). Doctors might hear Mary report missed periods and at-home tests, but would hardly entertain a discussion of angels. Restriction to established medical knowledges would necessarily produce ignorance of what medicine refused to acknowledge.

Though we did not venture here, my classmates and I might have raised more ontological questions. The very definition of pregnancy, the moment at which an individual transitions from "not pregnant" to "pregnant," is a matter of some controversy. This might occur when sperm penetrates egg, when the embryonic genome is assembled or activated, or when the embryo is implanted. It might also occur, or be felt to occur, later on in the process. It might not even be a moment so much as a gradual shift. It might even be achieved retroactively, as with my classmate's friend who was told she could not be pregnant without the doctor's confirmation. Presumably, after the requisite blood test or ultrasound, she would come to have been (medically/legitimately/credibly) pregnant for months.

These days, I find myself returning over and over to April's exercise. In my present role as a sociologist, I study those who study rape. I study the social processes that shape and are shaped by scientific research. I seek out the disciplinary conventions and external pressures that set boundaries regarding what questions may be posed and what answers given. I investigate how someone might know whether they have been raped, and how scientists might accept or challenge their self-assessment. I ask who and what "counts," and how this varies. Such questions force attention to credibility struggles, and to the making and unmaking of ignorance that occurs within and through the production of knowledge (Jasanoff 2005; Latour 1987; Proctor 2008). The knowers, in my work, are mostly scientists. The knowledges are matters of scientific fact. I am again tasked with the deceptively simple mission of asking how. There are some differences, of course. I must also ask why any of this matters, and be more accountable for my own assumptions and contributions. The subject matter, and my relationship with it, differs radically from that day in Advanced Feminist Theory. I have devoted more than a decade to anti-rape work at this point in my life, whereas then I spent mere moments contemplating each statement. I have been raped; I have never been pregnant. Perhaps the most obvious shift is that I have transitioned from an undergraduate to a career academic. My professional credentials, increased since then and increasing still through this endeavor, will no doubt expand my credibility as a knowledge producer and the gravity awarded my positions.

In the following pages, I investigate scientific research on adult sexual violence. I ask (1) how scientists have conceptualized rape and other forms of sexual violence among adults; and (2) what social mechanisms enable, constrain, and otherwise influence scientific research on sexual violence. For the first question, I embark on a comprehensive exploration of four decades of scientific research. I explore what has been and remains publishable, as well as what questions and perspectives have been dominant over time. For the second question, I turn to the insights of scientists and other scholars of rape to explore "behind the scenes" processes in research.

This project focuses on the United States and Canada. I chose these nations partially for feasibility. Although rape is a global phenomenon, the politics and scope of research on rape vary tremendously across time and space. I opted for in-depth analysis within a smaller geographic region over a general assessment of global trends. There were also reasons for looking at the United States and Canada together. Both countries have produced considerable scientific literature on sexual violence. Many scholars in the field have worked in both nations or with scholars from both nations across their careers. Moreover, overlapping priorities and trajectories in antiviolence activism and policy provide important similarities in the broader social context of scientific research on rape. Take Back the Night marches, organizing for and implementing rape law reform, and the rise of #MeToo activism occurred at similar times in the United States and Canada, to name but a few examples.

Remembering April's exercise, I approach scientific works as products of particular knowers who advance and foreclose particular knowledges. Drawing on insights from feminist science studies, I further understand my own perspective as partial, situated within the various personal experiences and dispositions, disciplinary training, professional expectations, and broader cultural and historical contexts that shape my position(s) as a researcher (Barad 1998; Flax 1992; Haraway 1988; Harding 1995). More specifically, this work is informed by my training and experiences as a sociologist, as an interdisciplinary collaborative researcher, as an antiviolence advocate of more than ten years, and as a social justice activist with particular ties to queer and transgender organizing, as well as by theoretical commitments to intersectional feminism within and beyond science studies and queer theory (Barad 2007; Butler [1990] 2006; P. H. Collins 2004; Halberstam 2011; Haraway 1997; Rubin [1984] 1993). My own conceptualization of rape is informed by these politics. I understand sexual violence as a gendered and sexualized phenomenon, but also as something that may be perpetrated by and against people of all genders and sexualities. I further understand sexual violence as entangled with innumerable dimensions of power and inequality, including but far from limited to disability, race, ethnicity, age, nationality, citizenship, and class. My own identifications and positions as White, Jewish, atheist, transmasculine, queer, middle class, a (born) U.S. citizen, and a sexual violence survivor inform my own understandings and relationship to the work. Although I have sincerely endeavored to approach scientific actors and knowledges openly, it is possible if not unavoidable that my own background and perspective(s) have enabled me to perceive some knowledges and not others. Consequently, while I may produce meaningful and engaging answers to these questions, they should not be regarded as definitive or complete.

In this book, I argue that sexual violence research in the United States and Canada has been dominated by psychological inquiries, as well as by gendered and (hetero)sexual assumptions regarding who is most capable of perpetrating and experiencing rape. Scientists have produced a tremendous body of knowledge regarding the prevalence, individual-level causes, and individual-level outcomes of cisgender men's sexual aggression toward cisgender women. Interpersonal and systemic forces remain undertheorized. Same-gender violence, women's aggression, men's victimization, and violence by and toward nonbinary individuals are less likely to "count" in scientific projects.

I further argue that scientific research on rape is shaped by a range of social mechanisms that arise when questions of social morality are interwoven with scientific inquiry. Individuals face credibility challenges from outsiders—that is, scholars who do not study sexual violence—who dispute the very notion that research on rape can be scientific. These critics often assume that such "political" matters fall distinctly beyond the realm of science (Cech and Sherick 2015). Feminization in the field, both in terms of rape's reputation as a "women's issue" and the fact that cisgender women comprise the majority of scholars who study rape, seems to reinforce these objections. Such external pressures sometimes drive people to abandon sexual violence research altogether. Others seek to boost or defend their credibility through strategic choices in study design and writing style (for example, using statistics rather than personal narratives, or avoiding overtly political statements or affiliations). Some scholars of rape simply decline to seek the validation of other scientists. However, this last approach carries risks such as decreased chances for tenure and greater difficulty publishing in prestigious scientific outlets (Bourdieu 1975; Latour 1987; Levine 2018b). Even as these scholars face challenges from outsiders, their fellow insiders— that is, people who study sexual violence and thus already accept such work as scientific or disinvest in such categorizations—often pose moral obstacles. When it comes to studying rape, social implications may equal or even surpass scientific implications. Insider pressures sometimes compel researchers to abandon controversial projects, or at least to minimize departures from what has been deemed acceptable by dominant scholars in the field. It is also possible to disinvest in insiders' approval. Again, this last approach carries career risks that compound the already considerable challenges of having one's work broadly perceived as unscientific.

Finally, I argue that the "heaviness" of this topic gives rise to collective care processes within scientific research. Mentoring takes on a particular urgency given widespread concerns about burnout and outsider criticisms. Many scholars prioritize self-care and practice collective care work within collaborative projects. Such care work is not supplemental, but rather integral to the work of doing science.

To prepare for laying out these arguments, I begin by discussing the importance of critically investigating scientific research on sexual violence. I provide a theoretical framework involving feminist science studies literature on agential realism and situated knowledges (Barad 2007; Haraway 1988), social problems literature on ontological gerrymandering and enactments (Woolgar and Lezaun 2013; Woolgar and Pawluch 1985), and sexual script theory (Simon and Gagnon 1986; Simon and Gagnon 2005/1973). I then discuss my mixed methods approach, and provide an overview of chapters.

WHY STUDY SCIENCE?

Science plays a substantial, though underacknowledged, role in shaping popular understandings of rape. Many readers have probably heard the figure "one in four women." This statistic, which came from Mary Koss, Christine Gidycz, and Nadine Wisniewski's 1987 study of college students, was game changing (Gavey [2005] 2018; Jhally 1994; Rutherford 2017). It transformed rape from a personal problem into a pressing national issue. The concept of "date rape" emerged as more and more people came to understand that sexual violence was not limited to stranger attacks. Yet "one in four women" was also a point of controversy. Even as many activists drew on Koss and colleagues' work to raise awareness of rape, critics tried to discredit such alarming numbers and (re)establish rape as a minor issue.

It's also important to recognize that scientists do not operate in isolation. Since the emergence of large-scale anti-rape activism in the 1970s,[1] scientists have collaborated with community activists, practitioners, campus staff, and state officials in raising awareness of rape and promoting reforms in law and policy (Brownmiller 1975; Gavey [2005] 2018; Spohn and Horney 1992; Whittier 2009). Furthermore, scientists play unique and important roles in producing knowledge about rape. They (we) are tasked with determining the incidence and prevalence of rape (Breiding et al. 2014; Krebs et al. 2007; Rutherford 2017; Tjaden and Thoennes 2000), identifying factors that promote or deter individual risk or communal rates of perpetration and victimization (Abbey 2011; Armstrong, Hamilton and Sweeney 2006; Humphrey and White 2000), and evaluating prevention and response efforts (Coker et al. 2011; McMahon 2014; Morrison et al. 2004; Rothman and Silverman 2007). Service providers and state officials often request, challenge, or draw from scientific research in order to improve upon their own efforts to address rape.

While many perceive scientific knowledge simply as an objective reflection of reality, research is in many ways a social process (Barad 2007; Bourdieu 1975; Epstein 1996; Fox and Alldred 2016; Jasanoff 2004; Jasanoff 2005; Latour 1987; Shapin 1995; Shapin and Schaffer [1985] 2011). Every scientific project requires scientists to make decisions. They (we) must decide whether to work alone or collaboratively (and with whom to collaborate). They must select questions, methods, recruitment strategies, and data analysis techniques. They must decide how to interpret their findings, and whether and how to publish them. Those who study rape must determine, to some extent, what rape is. They must prepare for and answer criticisms from within and beyond the field. Such matters have far-reaching consequences, often determining who "counts" as a potential victim or survivor, who "counts" as a potential aggressor, and whose research on sexual violence is recognized as "real" or "credible" science.

Decision-making processes in the study of rape can produce divergent and sometimes contradictory scientific facts. To understand why, it is worth noting that researchers are themselves subject to influence by peers, disciplinary conventions, historical events, social movements, state and other institutions, funders, and public ideals. Researchers also engage various identities, personal and collective values, and life experiences throughout the work of doing science. In the United States, for example, scientists who study social problems such as rape may face pressure to quantify them (Jasanoff 2005). Scholars who receive funding from the Office on Violence against Women may be further compelled to represent rape as a component of (men's) violence against women more broadly, and may be encouraged to focus on college campuses in light of recent federal investment in addressing sexual violence among students (Rutherford 2017; White House Council on Women and Girls 2014). Those who receive lesbian, gay, bisexual, transgender, and queer (LGBTQ)–specific grants from the American Psychological Association may be compelled to incorporate or even prioritize same-sex violence on or off campus. Those who pursue funding from the National Institutes of Health may find that success hinges on incorporating content on alcohol (specifically to obtain National Institute on Alcohol Abuse and Alcoholism funds, which are a major supporter of public health and psychological research on sexual violence). When designing, conducting, and reporting on their own research efforts, and when reviewing others' work for publication, scientists must continually decide to what extent they can and should challenge dominant perspectives (Bourdieu 1975).

The predominance of conflict, particularly regarding the study of high-stakes social problems, gives further testament to the social character of scientific work (Epstein 2006; Shapin 1995; Waidzunas 2012). When attempting to address rape, scholars may appeal to competing or entirely contradictory perspectives, and thus produce competing findings regarding the causes of rape and appropriate strategies for intervention. Scholars who assume that rape is a biological phenomenon, driven by evolutionary processes, often clash with those who assume that rape is a consequence of patriarchy. In such situations, scientists may engage in credibility struggles to strengthen their own positions and weaken those of their opponents. Academic and state credentials, professional experiences, and personal accounts may provide foundations from which to claim authority or expertise within the field of scientific research on sexual violence (Bourdieu 1975). To further complicate matters, credibility disputes within science may inform, and be informed by, broader political contexts (Epstein 1996; Waidzunas 2012). For example, feminist researchers who sought to address date rape in the late 1980s and early 1990s faced hostility from scholars outside of rape research communities who reasserted "real rape" discourses and strove to discredit findings such as "one in four women" (Estrich 1987; Jhally 1994; Rutherford 2017). Those doing such work in the Obama years enjoyed a more supportive political climate.

While scholars of rape have provided rich accounts of feminist anti-rape activism, legal reforms, and social and medical services (Bevacqua 2000; Corrigan 2013; Martin 2005; Mulla 2014; Spohn and Horney 1992), as well as the capacity of sexual violence to maintain power relations (Collins 2004), there have been few comparable investigations of scientific work (Rutherford 2017 is a partial exception, as is Gavey [2005] 2018, whose work on discourses of violence and consent critically examines historical connections between scholarly research and shifting public perceptions of rape). Scholars in the sociology of knowledge, in turn, have conducted few investigations into the production of knowledge about sexual violence. Researchers have explored popular and institutional support for rape myths (Edwards et al. 2011; Ryan 2011), and approaches to sexual communication and the interpretation of sexual consent and refusal (Muehlenhard 2011; Muehlenhard et al. 2017), without exploring their (our) own potential role in shaping these issues. Yet scientists can and do have influence (Gavey [2005] 2018).

This book contributes to the interdisciplinary field of sexual violence research as it acknowledges that scientists' own conceptualizations of this social problem, and the social mechanisms that inform their work, shape broader understandings of and responses to rape. Decisions regarding study design, recruitment, and theoretical foundations guide the production of knowledge. Published works may impact popular and institutional approaches to rape and consent (Gavey [2005] 2018; Jhally 1994; Rutherford 2017). Ongoing reliance on statistics like "one in four women" in policy and public debates ensures ongoing influence for scientists who produce and interpret statistics, and a potentially more limited impact for qualitative scholars (Espeland and Stevens 2008; Jasanoff 2005; Porter 1995). Ultimately, if the construction of scientific knowledge matters for social policy, as well as popular understandings of rape, it is necessary to investigate the social processes happening within science. It is of further importance to consider relationships between science and such external influences as social movements, state and community institutions, members of target or prioritized populations, and broader historical and cultural contexts.

In a recent paper entitled "Surveying Rape: Feminist Social Science and the Ontological Politics of Sexual Assault," psychologist Alexandra Rutherford (2017) applied insights from feminist science studies to examine the history and impacts of efforts to quantify sexual violence. She focused on two widely contested figures from surveys of college students in the United States: Koss, Gidycz, and Wisniewski's 1987 finding that one in four college women had experienced completed or attempted rape, and Krebs and colleagues' 2007 finding that one in five women experience some form of sexual assault during their college years. Both figures received tremendous coverage in popular press outlets. Supporters insisted that Koss's and Krebs's data drew attention to the real phenomenon of sexual violence against women, particularly the scope of date rape in student populations. Critics accused Koss and Krebs of overstating the real prevalence of sexual violence against women, and of embracing biased methods and data interpretation strategies in order to advance particular political (read: feminist) agendas. Koss and Krebs were both accused of using overly broad definitions of rape in order to bolster their estimates. Koss, in particular, was criticized for labeling experiences as rape when her study participants did not. These highly publicized controversies served to secure national attention for both studies, and to introduce or reinforce (contested) concepts such as "date rape" and "campus sexual assault" in popular consciousness.

Rutherford (2017) argued that instruments such as campus sexual assault surveys do not simply measure objective empirical realities, but also participate in generating ontological and social realities. She encouraged her readers to approach surveys as performative, and insisted that "in treating the rape survey not as a transparent measuring instrument, but rather as a practice that performs within a complex assemblage of implicit and explicit beliefs, attitudes, institutions, communities and politics (including, importantly, feminist politics), social scientists can be more deliberative about the social worlds they realize through their methods and, perhaps more importantly, engage more effectively in debates with the critics of these contested realities and their stakeholders" (116). Rutherford by no means sought to suggest that rape was not "real" or "important," but rather that the nature and scope of rape were unavoidably connected with methodology.

This project complements and extends Rutherford's analysis, contributing to sexual violence research and what might be termed "social histories of rape" in three distinct ways. First, rather than focus exclusively on efforts to quantify (campus) rape, I investigate scientific research on sexual violence more broadly. This enables documentation of general patterns in the field as well as differences across a range of subfields, including prevalence research, causal inquiries, and outcomes/effects research. Second, drawing on Karen Barad's theory of agential realism (1998; 2007), I approach sexual violence, scientific knowledge about sexual violence, and participants in such research as intra-active phenomena[2] (see also Fox and Alldred 2016). In addition to considering the capacity of a particular measurement tool to be "intimately involved in structuring the experience it purports to measure" (Rutherford 2017, 102), I emphasize relationships among objects of study and agencies of observation. This includes scientific researchers who are, themselves, complexly situated producers of knowledge (Haraway 1988). Disciplinary training, collaborative relationships, professional and popular expectations, funding and other resources, historical events, social movements,

personal dispositions, and other forces may influence researchers' approaches
to studying rape in ways that have philosophically and empirically meaningful
consequences.

Finally, introducing a concept I refer to as *precasting*, I consider researchers' and research instruments' capacity to set boundaries regarding which
actors are relevant to their objects of study, and in what ways. In defining
rape, for example, quantification researchers such as Koss and Krebs have not
only contributed to the ontological realization of date rape in popular consciousness, but also collective perceptions of typical (or even conceivable)
aggressors and victims/survivors.[3] They advance particular understandings
of which acts, aggressors, and victims count when it comes to rape.

In the following section, I review these theoretical approaches and contributions in greater detail. This overview is intended to be cursory; the
potential for agential realism and precasting to enhance scientific understandings of (the study of) sexual violence will be explored further in subsequent chapters.

Toward a Sociology of Sexual Violence

As will be demonstrated in subsequent chapters, scholarship on sexual
violence has been dominated by psychology and individual-level inquiries.
This is readily apparent through quantitative trends in the field over time.
Psychologists and psychology journals have produced more scholarship on
rape than any other discipline over the past forty years, and have also produced many of the most highly cited studies on the scope, causes, and
aftermath of sexual violence. While sociologists and other social scientists
have not been altogether absent, their contributions have often focused on
particular contexts and communities such as fraternity culture (Armstrong,
Hamilton, and Sweeney 2006; Martin and Hummer 1989), marital rape (Bergen 1996), same-sex violence (Girshick 2002), and institutional responses in
domains such as social services and criminal justice (Burgess and Holmstrom
1974b; Martin 2005). Much of this literature falls within the sociology of
gender and sexuality, and to a lesser extent the sociology of violence. This
project extends and complements these contributions through working
toward a broader and more comprehensive sociology of sexual violence. In-
depth assessments of rape scholarship, as well as social mechanisms within
this scientific field reveal opportunities for further sociological intervention. Moreover, the role of researchers in shaping understandings of sexual
violence and the related influence of social processes such as credibility
struggles and gender politics within science have received minimal attention
in sociological (and other) research in this field. Even within the sociology
of gender and sexuality, gendered patterns in sexual aggression and victimization are sometimes approached as settled matters rather than urgent and

challenging empirical questions. In taking a feminist science studies approach, I am able to extend sociological literature through a critical assessment of sociologists' and other scientists' role in producing knowledge about rape.

This project also contributes to the sociology of scientific knowledge through consideration of a feminized field that occupies a contested status within science. As the following chapters will demonstrate, sexual violence research is feminized in terms of participation, in that a substantial majority of scholars and study participants are cisgender women; and reputation, in that many within and outside the domain of science regard rape as a "women's issue." Moreover, rape is often regarded as an inherently political matter, which contributes to credibility challenges from scientists who believe that science and politics can and should be entirely separate (Cech 2013; Cech and Sherick 2015). These perceptions contribute to the devaluing of sexual violence scholarship within the larger domain of scientific research.

Attention toward sexual violence offers a more specific contribution to gender and sexuality research within science studies. This literature has often emphasized more masculinized—or at least masculine-coded—domains such as the scientific conceptualizations of male sexuality or homophobic responses to HIV/AIDS (Epstein 1996; Waidzunas 2015; Waidzunas and Epstein 2015), or focused on reproduction and birth control (Clarke 1998; Mamo 2007; Oudshoorn 2003; Thompson 2007). Feminist science studies scholars who emphasize gendered logics and social practices often study fields such as medicine and "natural" sciences such as physics and biology (e.g., Barad 2007; Clarke 2004; Haraway 1997; Jordan-Young 2011; Mamo 2007; Oudshoorn 2003; Pitts-Taylor 2016; Star 1989). This can make it difficult to discern social mechanisms particular to more feminized scientific fields. Michelle Murphy's (2006) study of Sick Building Syndrome offers a partial exception due to its inclusion of women's health activists' perspectives on health and disease. However, the controversy she studied was characterized by conflict between professional scientists and lay feminist activists (rather than feminists and nonfeminists within the domain of professional science). Susan Leigh Star and Anselm Strauss (1999) investigated "invisible work" within computer-supported cooperative work, particularly the domestic and background labor often unrecognized and disproportionately performed by women. Their analysis offered valuable insights regarding feminized labor within science, but not social practices within fields that are broadly feminized from the outset, such that even more conventionally visible labor is dismissed as nonscientific. When considering social processes within science, sociologists and other scholars have focused on processes such as credibility struggles, competition over resources and peer recognition, gatekeeping within and between disciplines, standards for interpreting and evaluating scientific evidence, and strategies for demonstrating superior knowledge and technical prowess (Bourdieu 1975; Jasanoff 2005; Latour 1987; Murphy 2006; Shapin 1995; Shapin and Schaffer [1985] 2011; Waidzunas and Epstein 2015). More feminized processes, such as care work, have been relatively neglected (see Acker 1990 for a discussion of similar concerns in research on labor inequality). This project thus builds on previous efforts in the sociology of scientific knowledge and feminist science studies through considering social practices within the feminized domain of sexual violence research, and specific attention toward collective care work and other feminine-associated practices within science.

Intra-active Phenomena and the Study of Rape

It is conventional, in many scientific circles and in the popular imagination, to envision empirical research as a process whereby scientists detachedly investigate the properties of objects external to them. In the context of research on sexual violence, this would rely on the assumption that something called "sexual violence" (or "rape" or "date rape" or "acquaintance rape" or "sexual harassment" and so on) exists independently of researchers' efforts. The challenge, then, would be to find effective approaches to identify and document the properties of sexual violence, and afterwards to convey/represent said properties clearly and comprehensively for peer and other audiences. In *Meeting the Universe Halfway: Quantum Physics and the Entanglement of Matter and Meaning*, Karen Barad (2007) offers an alternative perspective via agential realism. This approach builds on the work of physicist Niels Bohr, particularly his notions of phenomena and complementarity.

In Bohr's philosophy-physics, to borrow Barad's descriptor, scientists do not study external objects with preexisting determinate properties but rather intra-active phenomena. These phenomena are composed of entangled objects of study and agencies of observation. Barad's use of "intra-active," as opposed to the more common notion of "interactive," indicates the inseparability of phenomenal components. Scientific facts/findings will vary in accordance with the apparatuses employed. Such apparatuses are complexly entangled with the objects they are intended to measure. It is not until scientists enact "agential cuts" that distinct objects or findings or data points can be perceived. Barad further pointed to Bohr's argument that some objects of study were characterized by *complementary* properties that could not be assessed simultaneously. In such cases, different observational approaches would yield differently propertied phenomena. Within quantum physics, efforts to identify the true nature of light provide an apt example. It has long been known that light manifests both wavelike and particle-like properties. Bohr—and Barad, through her reading of Bohr—attributed the seemingly paradoxical nature of light to variation in experimental conditions. The documentation of light waves and light particles could not occur simultaneously; rather, these properties/entities were detected through different measurement apparatuses. Within the broader field of research on light, waves and particles were detectable within different phenomena characterized by different agencies of observation. Significantly, this entanglement of objects of study and agencies of observation indicated a similar entanglement of epistemological (ways of knowing) and ontological (ways of being) matters.

In Barad's analysis, Bohr's writings on phenomena suffered from an under-theorization of agencies of observation. He seemed to focus a great deal on laboratory equipment without necessarily considering the entanglement of laboratory researchers and broader institutional contexts. It is worth quoting her concerns in some detail:

> Apparatuses, in Bohr's sense, are not passive observing instruments. On the contrary, they are productive of (and part of) phenomena. However, Bohr leaves the meaning of "apparatus" somewhat ambiguous. He does insist that what constitutes an "apparatus" emerges within specific observational practices. But while focusing on the lack of an inherent distinction between the apparatus and the object, Bohr does not directly address the question of where the apparatus "ends." In a sense, he only establishes the "inside" boundary and not the "outside" one. For example, if a computer interface is hooked up to a given instrument, is the computer part of the apparatus? Is the printer attached to the computer part of the apparatus? Is the paper that is fed into the printer? Is the person who feeds the paper? How about the community of scientists who judge the significance of the experiment and indicate their support or lack of support for future funding? What precisely constitutes the limits of the apparatus that gives meaning to certain concepts and the exclusion of others? (Barad 1998, 98)

To address these concerns, Barad engaged Bohr's philosophy-physics through and alongside the work of feminist science scholars such as Donna Haraway and critical social theorists such as Michel Foucault and Judith Butler. She argued that observers (including but not limited to professional scientists), apparatuses (such as laboratory equipment and quantitative surveys), and objects of study (such as light and sexual violence) were all entangled. Moreover, observers were situated within and across varying material and discursive social contexts that informed phenomenal intra-actions.

In scientific research on sexual violence, differently situated scholars might favor different research questions, methodologies, funding sources, publication outlets, and more. They might engage differently with "the same" research instruments and objects of study. Individual scholars might also engage "the same" phenomena differently at different times. As identitarian articulations manifest and shift—that is, as various aspects of self, such as gender, victimization history, age, disability, feminist identity (or lack thereof), and disciplinary background come into and out of play—scholars' perceptions of sexual violence and scientific knowledge of sexual violence may shift accordingly (Vila 2017). In a sense, what it means to be human—or rather, what it means to be a particular sort of human, such as a scientist or feminist or activist or person of moral character or objective seeker of knowledge or source of objective knowledge—may be at stake within scientific research.

Precasting Assailants and Victims/Survivors

This project focuses on the scientific study of sexual violence among human adults. As noted above, I contend that scholars have the capacity to set boundaries regarding who counts. In other words, scientists may determine which actors are relevant to this subject matter, and in what ways. I refer to such boundary work as *precasting*. This concept is indebted to sociological and philosophical literature in science studies and social problems, specifically the concepts of ontological gerrymandering (Woolgar and Pawluch 1985) and ontological enactments (Woolgar and Lezaun 2013) that provide a means for theorizing exclusions built into research designs. Sexual script theory (Simon and Gagnon 1986; Simon and Gagnon [1973] 2005) further aids in exploring mechanisms whereby research might produce scripted possibilities for consensual and nonconsensual sexual encounters. Precasting provides another extension of Rutherford's (2017) analyses, which did not substantively address questions regarding who might qualify as an assailant or victim/survivor, or how such questions might be answered differently across different research efforts, including the important prevalence studies of Koss and Krebs (Koss, Gidycz, and Wisniewski 1987; Krebs et al. 2007).

Ontological Gerrymandering and Ontological Enactments

In 1985, Woolgar and Pawluch introduced the concept of ontological gerrymandering to describe a problematic trend in social science literature. They were particularly concerned with definitional work, which emphasized variations in conceptualizations of social problems. Such work consistently relied on scholars' (pre)determination that some assumptions were open to skepticism and others were not. They illustrated this argument through a critique of Pfohl's (1977) "The 'Discovery' of Child Abuse," which depicted child beating as a stable phenomenon while treating definitions of child beating as changeable: "The condition ('child beating') to which the claims-making activities refer is portrayed as fixed; by contrast, definitions of this (unchanging) condition are portrayed as highly variable—child beating has been variously the prerogative of the parent, part of the larger problem of poverty, a function of the psychopathic impulse of the disturbed parent, and child abuse; finally these variations in definition are 'explained' by reference to socio-historical circumstances" (Woolgar and Pawluch 1985, 218).

Woolgar and Pawluch questioned the assumption of a "fixed" phenomenon and scientists' predetermination of which phenomena are constant and which may vary. They further critiqued Pfohl, in particular, for assuming that the final definition of child beating was most appropriate: "The use of such words as barriers . . . reaffirms that Pfohl's article is an account not of the creation of a label but of the slow removal of one barrier after another until the parental abuse of children was finally revealed for what it was" (221). One can imagine a similar critique of studies that depict rape as a stable phenomenon with varying—and increasingly apt—social definitions (e.g., Brown-miller 1975). For example, rape might have shifted in popular discourse from the husband's prerogative to a function of the psychopathic impulse of disturbed criminal men to an unfortunate but very personal problem before being recast as a social problem and outcome of patriarchy. Yet what does not vary in these depictions is that the perpetrator is always understood to be a cisgender man, while the victim is always a cisgender woman.

Responding further to this problem, Woolgar and Lezaun (2013) theorized ontological enactments. Rather than view any objects' ways of being as fixed, they advocated viewing different statuses as achieved (or not) in specific contexts (see also Mol 2002). Texts enact varying statuses of objects in different moments, and enact the same sort of status (e.g., woman, actual/potential rapist, actual/potential rape survivor) differently in different moments. Thus, any features of texts conceptualizing social problems, including but not limited to definitional work, might be treated as socially and temporally contingent. In other words, someone's status as a rape victim or survivor might vary across time and space. It may depend on whether sexual violence seems relevant, or rather whether victimization is activated or put into play. It may depend on whether the person's experience matches others' expectations, or even their own understandings, of what constitutes rape. It may depend on whether and how consistently a particular person is considered a potential victim or survivor. Individuals' victim status (or lack thereof) is further inseparable from questions of power and social inequality, particularly but not limited to race, gender identity, social class, physical appearance, age, and disability status. Such matters may arise explicitly in a given text or encounter, or implicitly as "areas of silence and difficulty" (Clarke 2004, 74).

Sexual Scripts and the Scientific Study of Sexual Violence

While these concepts are useful for analyzing the construction of scientific knowledge, sexual script theory (Simon and Gagnon 1986; [1973] 2005) provides a means for describing the impact of scientific discourses, as well as cultural material available for the production of these discourses. This framework provides a three-tier approach to sexuality that encompasses interpersonal scripts, through which actors negotiate sexual encounters; intrapsychic scripts, which comprise individual conceptions; and cultural scenarios, the broader social frameworks through which actors learn how (not) to engage sexually. Conceptualizations of rape are available as cultural scenarios through which actors identify incidents as (non)consensual. Actors may employ different scenarios in different moments. The "same" behavior (e.g., verbally expressed ambivalence) may activate rape scripts in one scenario, thereby deterring aggression; and seduction scripts in another, in which case aggression may persist (Alcoff 2018; Gavey [2005] 2018). Boundaries can also shift or conflict. While numerous scientists have employed sexual script theory in investigations of rape, particularly in studies of rape myth acceptance (e.g., Lonsway and Fitzgerald 1994; Ryan 2011), few have assessed their own engagement with sexual scripts in the course of doing science. Consequently, many risk unintentionally reinscribing cultural scenarios from popular and academic discourses when producing scientific knowledge. If the only scenarios engaged presume that "typical" rapes occur on heterosexual dates, for example, scientists may limit analyses to such circumstances without considering the potential for violence in queer encounters. While there can be compelling methodological and theoretical reasons to limit individual studies to particular scenarios and populations, it is worth considering whether such approaches are embraced conscientiously and transparently. Sexual scripts may comprise part of the broader social/cultural context in which observers are entangled, shaping the content of research design.

Precasting in Sexual Violence Research

Scientists' conceptualizations of rape do not merely produce states of being, such as victim or rapist, that may be enacted in scripted encounters. They set boundaries regarding which actors may achieve which states. Such boundaries represent a form of ontological gerrymandering that I theorize as precasting. Precasting constitutes ontological gerrymandering (Woolgar and Pawluch 1985) because the manifestations of a social problem are limited to the actions of predetermined actors, even as other aspects of the problem are allowed to vary. Koss, Gidycz, and Wisniewski's (1987) work offers an example. In their groundbreaking prevalence study, the role of "rapist" was limited from the outset to men who targeted women. The role of "rape victim" was likewise limited to women who were targeted by men. Other pertinent details were allowed—even presumed—to vary among incidents of rape. These included victim-aggressor relationships (e.g., strangers, casual acquaintances, dating partners, spouses, and other long-term partners) and the specific acts involved (e.g., presence or absence of alcohol, use or threat of physical force, vaginal versus oral versus anal penetration). Bachman, Paternoster, and Ward's (1992) work on rape proclivity provides another example. This research relied on vignettes in which women were precast as victims and men as aggressors. Other details varied across vignettes, including victims' consumption of alcohol, victim-aggressor relationships, assailants' use of force, victims' engagement in resistance, and physical or psychological harm to victims.

When studying rape, scientists produce and otherwise engage with sexual scripts regarding typical or even conceivable violent encounters (Gavey [2005] 2018). Precasting occurs when particular actors are presumed (in)capable of enacting particular statuses (Woolgar and Lezaun 2013). Studies that precast women as victims and men as aggressors may render same-sex violence, women's aggression toward men, and any violence by or toward persons with nonbinary gender identities imperceptible or even unthinkable (Alcoff 2018; Cardi and Pruvost 2015; Murphy 2006). Rather than subject such matters to empirical scrutiny, researchers investigating sexual aggression might assume from the outset that only men can rape, and design sampling frames accordingly. Rather than openly and conscientiously limit analyses to particular actors or environments, researchers might simply assume that their theoretical and methodological approaches reflect the obvious "truth" of sexual violence—conceived as an external referent with determinate properties, rather than an intra-actively produced phenomenon—and thus require no explanation.

While my analysis will focus primarily on gendered precasting, it is crucial to note that this concept may apply to enactments of any status. Collins has critiqued controlling images that depict Black men as sexual aggressors toward White women (Collins 2004). These cultural scenarios inform popular understandings of rape, as well as institutional approaches in such diverse arenas as criminal justice, news media, and healthcare. Among friends and other acquaintances, such scenarios may inform reactions to disclosures of victimization and aggression. In a qualitative study of race and sexual victimization among women, Wyatt (1992) found that Black women expressed great "concern about how others will perceive their credibility as rape victims" due to the assumption that "real" or perhaps "sympathetic" victims were presumed to be White women (87; see also Gavey [2005] 2018; Tillman et al. 2010).

Other scholars have addressed widespread presumptions regarding victims' and aggressors' (hetero)sexuality. Relative to heterosexual women, lesbian and bisexual women experience considerable barriers to disclosing victimization experiences; racial minority lesbians and bisexual women experience additional barriers relative to their White counterparts (Sigurvinsdottir and Ullman 2015). In studies with college students, heterosexual people have often been perceived as more legitimate and sympathetic victims—and thus less at fault for the violence they suffer—than queer people (Davies, Rogers, and Whitelegg 2009; White and Kurpius 2002). In vignettes with male aggressors and victims, for example, gay victims are often perceived as more at fault than heterosexual victims. This likely reflects homophobic stereotyping as well as problematic assumptions that people who are attracted to men (including gay/bisexual men and heterosexual/bisexual women) somehow provoke or even enjoy victimization by men.

Precasting is problematic because it forecloses scientific inquiry. Empirical uncertainties are treated as settled matters unworthy of investigation. In the context of sexual violence research, this can prevent the investigation of anything that diverges from dominant rape scripts. Given the influence of scientific research on state actors and practitioners (Jasanoff 2004), precasting can ultimately inhibit the development of inclusive policy and services. Men who experience sexual violence may struggle to find support from advocates who have been trained to approach rape as a subset of violence against women. Women who perpetrate may find themselves unwelcome in offender intervention programs. Nonbinary individuals may be excluded from services for victims and aggressors. Such possibilities speak to Barad's (2007) argument that it is not merely epistemological and ontological dimensions of research that are inseparable, but rather epistemological, ontological, and ethical dimensions. It is important to note that some measure of precasting may be unavoidable in scientific research (including the present endeavor, particularly given my exclusive focus on human actors).[4] However, as the conclusion to this book explores, reflexive and transparent approaches—along with openness to other phenomenal possibilities—may go a long way toward fostering more inclusive scholarship.

In drawing attention to these cases of gendered precasting, I do not seek to downplay the pervasiveness of men's violence toward women, or the causal forces of patriarchy and sexism (Brownmiller 1975; Eschholz and Vieraitis 2004; Yodanis 2004). It is rather my intention to assert the existence of other gendered patterns in sexual violence. I further argue that the causal forces behind men's aggression toward women may not fully align with those behind same-sex violence, women's aggression toward men, and incidents involving nonbinary individuals. Such incidents of sexual violence warrant empirical investigation in their own right. Moreover, scientific research on men's sexual violence toward women can and should explicitly recognize that this gendered pattern—however dominant—is not exhaustive. The opposite of gendered precasting is not gender neutrality, so much as gender inclusivity.

METHODS

For this book, I investigated four decades of scientific research on rape. As noted above, I asked (1) how scientists have conceptualized rape and other forms of sexual violence among adults; and (2) what social mechanisms have enabled, constrained, and otherwise influenced scientific research on sexual violence. I focused on scientific inquiries in the United States and Canada between 1975 and 2015. The year 1975, though certainly not representing the dawn of rape research, was of great importance in the field. Susan Brownmiller's *Against Our Will* and Diana Russell's *The Politics of Rape* were both published that year. Collectively, these works advanced a patriarchal model of rape. According to this model, rape is not an individual or psychological problem, but rather an interpersonal manifestation of patriarchy. Societal gender inequity, or more specifically widespread male domination and female subordination, produced a rape-supportive culture. In a sense, Brownmiller and Russell provided theoretical foundations for understanding the epidemic of sexual violence documented twelve years later in Koss, Gidycz, and Wisniewski's (1987) research. The ending point of 2015 corresponded with the beginning of this project.

My efforts began with the literature. I searched for relevant scientific journal publications and developed a dataset of more than 1,300 studies. At first, I had expected to tell a chronological story, documenting the overall history of rape research decade by decade. Yet as I began to sift through the science, I determined that following the trajectory of various subfields—incidence and prevalence studies, the causes and deterrents of sexual violence, and the aftermath—would make for a more compelling story. Scholars in these subfields have produced and contested various "dominant" or "publishable" research questions and methodologies. They have also focused on different populations. When seeking to count incidents, researchers have turned most often to the general population. When seeking to account for rape, to identify causes and deterrents, researchers have turned most often to college students. When seeking to understand the consequences of rape, researchers have turned most often to victims and aggressors involved in criminal justice processes or receiving care services from hospitals or rape crisis centers. I proceeded to explore these subfields in greater depth. Finally, I turned to the scholars, themselves to gain a sense of the social processes within science. In the following sections, I describe this threefold approach in greater detail. Chapter descriptions follow, along with some suggestions for readers of varying backgrounds and interests.

Quantitative Content Analysis of Scientific Abstracts

To identify relevant studies for content analysis, I consulted the Social Sciences Citation Index within the Web of Science database. I searched for publications with any of the following terms in their titles: rape, sexual assault, sexual violence, rapist. All searches were completed between February and April of 2016. To ensure feasibility and gain a sense of knowledges that had acquired some traction in scientific communities, I restricted the search to works that had received at least ten citations among those published from 1975 to 2009 and at least five citations among those published from 2010 to 2015 (see Waidzunas and Epstein 2015). This yielded an initial pool of 1,855 records, including 1,511 and 314 from these respective time periods. All records were screened for study relevance. My aim was to identify empirical studies and reviews of empirical studies that focused on rape among adults, including (though not necessarily exclusively) within the United States and Canada. Works that did not meet these criteria—theoretical literature, historical overviews, and policy papers that did not provide, critique, or otherwise review empirical data; studies focused exclusively on sexual violence involving children; works focused exclusively on sexual violence outside of these nations; and those for which I was unable to locate abstracts—were excluded. The final pool contained 1,313 records, including 1,107 from 1975 to 2009 and 206 from 2010 to 2015.

To gain a sense of scientists' conceptualizations of sexual violence over time, I coded all records along the following dimensions: lead author, title, year, academic citations, methods (qualitative, quantitative), study aims (causes and deterrents, effects and aftermath, incidence/prevalence, policy/program evaluation, assessing theoretical and/or methodological approaches), area of focus (victims or victimization, perpetrators or perpetration, professionals in violence prevention and response, bystanders and/or the general public), gender dynamics (women as victims, women as perpetrators, men as victims, men as perpetrators, transgender inclusivity), and target population (general or community populations, colleges and universities, military, care facilities such as hospitals and crisis centers, current or former prison inmates, other actors involved in criminal justice proceedings such as complainants or defendants, demographic populations such as African American women or queer individuals). These initial codes were based on the first research question for this project regarding scientists' conceptualization of rape, with particular attention toward populations of interest and gender inclusion because of my engagement with intersectional feminist and queer theory perspectives. Most of this information was collected through a review of abstracts, though full texts were consulted regularly as needed to complete content analysis of each study. When pieces were difficult to classify along these criteria, I supplemented coding with qualitative notes.

Categories were not mutually exclusive. For example, a study that explored both the prevalence of rape and risk factors for victimization would have been classified as addressing both incidents/prevalence and causes. To limit the imposition of my own assumptions onto scientists' work, I restricted coding to the explicit content of each publication. For example, if a piece focused on college women's experiences of sexual victimization and seemed (in my estimation) to regard men as default sexual aggressors but did not incorporate such assumptions into the text, I coded that study as addressing "women as victims" but not "men as perpetrators."

Throughout the content analysis process, I wrote memos to reflect upon emergent patterns/themes and to refine the coding scheme (Emerson, Fretz, and Shaw 2011). After reviewing several hundred works, I noted a rather striking form of precasting in which authors engaged gender neutral language in abstracts to describe manuscripts with gender specific approaches. For example, an abstract might refer to "interviews with seventy-five rape survivors" when describing a study with exclusively women participants, or reference a "typical date rape scenario" that would later be revealed to concern heterosexual men's aggression toward women. In these instances, gendered assumptions were so firmly ingrained that authors presumed it unnecessary to be specific. I began to code abstracts and overall manuscripts for "gender inclusive approaches," defined as approaches allowing for the possibilities of aggression by men and women, as well as the victimization of men and women (transgender and nonbinary inclusivity were assessed separately). After completing coding, I ran chi-square tests to determine whether researchers' approaches varied significantly over time.

As systematic and comprehensive as my search and analyses were, they carried at least two substantial limitations. Neither was clear to me at the outset. However, subsequent analyses and conversations with other scholars made these limitations clear, and I believe they merit attention at this early stage before reviewing any of the data or arguments. Some publications in the field were missed by my search terms of rape, sexual assault, sexual violence, and rapist(s). Incorporating additional terms such as sexual aggression, sexual victimization, and sexual coercion would have provided a more comprehensive sample. More significantly, I found relatively few abstracts for publications focused on socially marginalized communities and/or anything that deviated from the dominant script of men's sexual aggression toward women. Very few pieces focused on racial/ethnic minority populations. Few pieces focused on people with disabilities and/or chronic illnesses. Few pieces emphasized class distinctions. Few pieces incorporated or addressed queer communities, or even included sexual orientation as a variable. Not a single piece focused on transgender individuals; as far as I could tell, none provided a clear avenue through which transgender men and women might make their transgender identities known, and none provided an option for nonbinary individuals to self-disclose. Yet there have been, and continue to be, such investigations. I ultimately came to realize that my search terms provided a sense of "mainstream" or "dominant" literature, and that this literature prioritized and constituted dominant conceptualizations of rape. Incorporating scholarship on sexual violence in marginalized communities would have required individual searches for every such community. Studies that address the prevalence, causes, and outcomes of sexual violence among transgender people, for example, appear to align more readily with "transgender literature" than "sexual violence literature" at first glance. Works such as Griner and colleagues' (2020) "The Intersection of Gender Identity and Violence: Victimization Experienced by Transgender College Students" and Stotzer's (2009) "Violence against Transgender People: A Review of United States Data" provide information on sexual victimization among transgender people; neither would have been screened in via my Web of Science search.

Qualitative Analysis of Scientific Studies

The first stage of this project helped to illuminate overall historical trends and convinced me to consider the subfields of incidence/prevalence research, causes and deterrents, and effects/aftermath separately. However, quantitative analysis of abstracts did not reveal the relative dominance of different perspectives, priorities, disciplines, or methodological approaches. To address these matters, I closely analyzed four incidence/prevalence studies that varied considerably in definitions of rape and other forms of sexual violence, sampling frame and target population, and survey design. Such matters had notable consequences for gendered precasting and the related questions of who counts as a potential victim or aggressor. To identify themes in the study of the causes and consequences of rape, which were considerably larger and more diverse areas of inquiry, I selected the ten top-cited pieces within each subfield from 1975 to 1984, 1985 to 1994, and 1995 to 2004; and the five top-cited pieces from 2005 to 2009 and 2010 to 2015. I analyzed all eighty studies closely, using the qualitative software Atlas.ti. My approach was guided by the coding scheme described above, supplemented with concepts specific to causal and/or effects inquiries and concepts too in-depth to incorporate into analysis of abstracts (e.g., sexual desire, power/control, substance use, standardization, sampling frames). After studying texts from each decade, I composed detailed memos regarding overall trends within that decade as well as differences across time periods.

Interviews

Scientific abstracts and full texts were of tremendous value in addressing my question about scholars' conceptualizations of rape. Yet they provided an incomplete and almost superficial picture. What is "publishable" does not always align with authors' perspectives. It would have been inappropriate to assume that researchers contending with word limits, theoretical and discursive conventions across journals and disciplines, and other pressures always conveyed their perspectives completely and transparently in publications. Scholars' ideas might also change in form or substance through the peer-review process. More important for this project, published texts rarely reveal the social processes behind their production. In order to understand the interpersonal, institutional, and cultural dimensions of research on sexual violence, it was necessary to speak with the researchers, themselves.

Recruitment began with my review of scientific abstracts. As I sampled publications, I developed a list of scholars whose work varied in overall focus, methodology, and discipline among other factors. I began reaching out via phone and email. On completing interviews, I asked participants for referrals for others (including, but not necessarily limited to, other scientists) who had influenced, taken part in, or otherwise affected their research on sexual violence. Finally, I networked at professional meetings and conferences. This last strategy led me to scholars who had not yet published or received many citations, as well as scholars whose publications on sexual violence were missed in my initial Web of Science search.

Whereas my content and textual analyses had offered a sense of dominant perspectives and priorities in sexual violence research, interviews offered variation. I reached out to widely cited scholars whose work had demonstrably influenced the field, and to scholars who focused on relatively marginal or neglected aspects of this work (e.g., sexual violence within intimate partnerships). I reached out to established researchers, early career scholars, and graduate students. I sought out scholars who were trained in different disciplines, employed different methodologies, and who worked in different fields within and outside of academia. Across all of these approaches, I contacted eighty-three scholars. Forty-nine (59%) responded, including forty-three (52%) who expressed interest in completing an interview. I was able to schedule and conduct interviews with thirty-one of these scholars (37% of the initial recruitment list, 72% of those who expressed interest). All recruitment and interviews took place between October 2016 and October 2017.

Interviews were semistructured (see the appendix for the interview guide). They began with broad questions about participants' work (e.g., what led you to study sexual violence?), which were often sufficient to generate rich discussions on a range of subjects including priorities for the field, collaboration and conflict among scholars, varying methodological approaches, and strategies for building and maintaining relationships with community partners. Interviews ranged in length from approximately half an hour (this occurred when researchers had severe time constraints, but still wanted to participate) to two hours. Most conversations were between fifty and seventy minutes.

Drawing from literature in active interviewing and feminist research methods (Campbell et al. 2010; Ellis and Berger 2003; Holstein and Gubrium 2003), I strove for transparency and nonhierarchical interactions in each encounter. I invited participants to ask any questions or share concerns before, during, and/or after interviews. I tried to be as clear as possible in sharing my overall research aims, as well as the logic behind various questions. When participants asked me for information, I shared as much as seemed possible without violating others' confidentiality or my own personal boundaries (though I sometimes asked that we save such questions for the end of our conversations). This ranged from providing impromptu explanations for the project and anticipated findings (and plans for sharing and acting on those findings), to discussing my own personal connections with sexual violence research and advocacy, to discussing interview and content analysis findings, to sharing interview guides and Institutional Review Board paperwork (the interview component of this project was approved by the review board at Temple University).

All participants provided oral consent to participate and, if they were comfortable with this, for me to audio record our conversations. I transcribed all recordings and removed identifying information as thoroughly as I could in order to safeguard anonymity. Although nearly all participants were visible in the field of sexual violence research through publications and/or presentations at professional meetings, many shared personal experiences and critical insights that made it necessary to prioritize confidentiality. I further encouraged participants to assist me in recognizing aspects of their work and experiences that might be difficult to write about without revealing their identities, and to let me know of any content they wished me to omit from transcripts or subsequent writings for any reason. When analyzing and writing about interviews, if I had doubts about my capacity to preserve confidentiality while discussing a particular study or insight, I either omitted that content or consulted with participants to develop a suitable approach. It should be noted here that the initial decision to safeguard anonymity was mine. I knew that I planned to ask scholars about sensitive matters, such as conflicts with graduate advisors and colleagues. Several participants explicitly shared concerns about confidentiality during our conversations. Although a few were open to being identified, I felt that it would be difficult and confusing to refer to some by name and others by pseudonym. Moreover, participants with concerns about their own anonymity might feel worried if they encountered identifying information for their colleagues in the text (all participants received a copy of the original version of this manuscript, initially prepared as a dissertation for my PhD program in sociology). For these reasons, I opted to prioritize anonymity for all. When participants are quoted in this book, they are referred to using pseudonyms, and with other identifying information, such as place of employment, omitted.

Throughout the processes of recruiting, interviewing, and transcribing, I wrote memos to reflect upon emergent patterns/themes and interpersonal dynamics across interviews. I then developed a coding scheme based on my primary research questions, previous strategies for analyzing abstracts and full texts, and concepts that seemed more specific to these qualitative data. All transcripts were analyzed in Atlas.ti.

CHAPTER OVERVIEW

Drawing inspiration from ambitious works in feminist science studies, such as Donna Haraway's *Primate Visions* (1989) and Karen Barad's *Meeting the Universe Halfway* (2007), I envision this project as speaking differently to different audiences. Some may wish to read all chapters in order; others may prefer to focus on one or two that seem particularly relevant to them and their interests. To accommodate this, I have attempted to compose a narrative without too much repetition while also ensuring that each chapter stands sufficiently alone that readers might be selective without sacrificing clarity. Based on my discussions with scholars in the field, as well as advocates who expressed interest in this project, I have also written this to be accessible to people who are somewhat unfamiliar or uncomfortable with statistics. Rather than simply present figures such as "one in four women," I engage the political context of their production. I demonstrate the capacity for different definitions, question designs, and recruitment strategies to produce different understandings of the scope of rape. As I follow rape by the numbers, I encourage readers to think about who counts as a potential victim or aggressor, what forms of violence count as rape, and why that matters. When presenting my own statistical analyses, I include some of the information one might expect in a scientific journal, while also situating the numbers in broader social and historical contexts.

Part I: Conceptualizing Rape

Readers who seek a critical "state of the field" will be particularly interested in this section. Chapters draw equally upon content analyses of scientific abstracts, close assessments of well-cited literature across subfields, and interviews with scholars who have contributed to the production of scientific knowledge concerning the scope, causes, and consequences of sexual violence. Readers who are interested in the feminist science studies application of this project may be particularly interested in chapter 2 on incidence and prevalence research, whereas readers seeking to identify areas for improvement in rape scholarship more generally may be more drawn to chapters 3 and 4 concerning the causes and aftermath of sexual violence.

Chapter 2, "Locating the Problem," concerns scientists' efforts to quantify rape and other forms of sexual violence among adults. Quantification has long been central to raising awareness of and garnering public and institutional support for addressing social problems in the United States and Canada (Jasanoff 2005). Rape statistics have been particularly effective in this regard. Scholars and activists seeking to reduce sexual violence often engage high prevalence estimates to raise alarm and to bolster demands for resources and policy reforms. At the same time, those who doubt that rape is a common or pressing issue often seek to discredit prevalence research.

I begin chapter 2 by (re)visiting a controversy over rape statistics in the late 1980s and early 1990s. In this well-publicized dispute, conservative scholars such as Neil Gilbert and Katie Roiphe challenged Mary Koss, Christine Gidycz, and Nadine Wisniewski's assertion that, based on their empirical survey of more than 3,000 undergraduate women, rape was a widespread problem in the United States. I utilize the perspective of agential realism (Barad 2007) to consider different actors' interpretations of that research, and the capacity of different survey approaches—and even of different interpretation approaches within the same survey—to produce radically different prevalence estimates. From there, I consider broader trends in incidence and prevalence research over the past forty-plus years, and explore the relevance of precasting through a close reading of four large-scale investigations that varied by definitions, survey design, sampling frames, and interpretative strategies. Finally, I explore researchers' insights on the (non) significance of consistency in definitions and the broader role of quantification in sexual violence research and activism. Gendered assumptions and tensions between scholars' investment in intersectional feminism on the one hand, and addressing patriarchal violence on the other, pose an ongoing problem in this subfield. Struggles over whether to engage predefined conceptualizations of rape and other forms of sexual violence, or to provide participants with an opportunity to name and define their own experiences, comprise another central concern (Alcoff 2018; Gavey [2005] 2018). Over-all, this chapter argues that quantification requires scientists to "locate the problem" of sexual violence through selecting specific definitions and sampling frames, and that gendered politics loom large within this subfield.

Causal inquiries consider the social forces and other conditions that promote or deter sexual violence. Much like incidence and prevalence research, this subfield has been beset with controversy. Yet the nature of disputes has differed. Quantification conflicts have been centered on the very existence of some forms of sexual violence, such as date rape, and whether sexual violence constitutes a widespread social problem. Anti-rape activists and scholars have often found themselves opposed by actors who are otherwise uninvolved with this field. In causal research, or research seeking to identify the causes of rape, insiders—that is, scientists and other scholars who study sexual violence—often challenge one another regarding what constitutes a scientifically and/or morally sound causal explanation.

Chapter 3 argues that concerns over misuse have been a central mecha-nism within causal research on sexual violence. This chapter further dem-onstrates that psychological and individual-level accounts of men's sexual violence toward women have been consistently dominant, whereas systemic investigations and additional gendered patterns in victimization and aggression have been neglected. I begin with a review of two controversial approaches to accounting for sexual violence: communication-based models, such as Charlene Muehlenhard (2011) and others' work on "token resistance" in heterosexual dating; and evolution-based models, such as Randy Thornhill and Craig Palmer's (2000) search for an ultimate causal understanding of men's sexual violence toward women. From there, I assess four decades of quantitative trends in this subfield and provide an in-depth look at the ten most highly cited works from each decade between 1975 and 2015. My analysis reveals a persistent, though declining, tendency to favor psycho-logical and psychiatric research and individual-level accounts to the detri-ment of systemic explanations. Finally, I turn to participants' insights. The scholars who took part in *Rape by the Numbers* endorsed a broad range of causal explanations; however, different approaches to discussing causation confirmed that some perspectives remain controversial or otherwise mar-ginal in the field. Participants expressed support for more interdisciplinary work, increased engagement with and from social science fields such as sociology and anthropology (in addition to, rather than in place of, psycho-logical inquiries), and greater attention toward cultural and institutional factors.

If chapter 3 explores scientific inquiries into the "why" of rape, chap-ter 4 investigates the "so what" question. Throughout my analyses of scien-tific abstracts and top-cited studies, I encountered no controversy that seemed comparable to those outlined above. Yet it was in this subfield, "Investigating the Aftermath," that interview participants expressed the most criticism and insistent calls for shifts in priorities. Many shared frustration with what they perceived as stagnation. They worried that the same disciplines, instruments, and questions continued to dominate. Many of these same participants shared excitement for novel or somewhat neglected outcomes and interventions. Several scholars who had worked on criminal justice processes called for the consideration of victims' (positive and negative) experiences with various criminal justice institutions and processes in addition to the more established outcomes of reporting, indictment, conviction, and sentencing; and for investment in alternatives to criminal proceedings such as restorative justice conferencing. After briefly reviewing these insights, I assess four decades of quantitative trends in this subfield and provide an in-depth look at the ten most highly cited works from each decade between 1975 and 2015. Echoing the trends in chapter 3, I demonstrate a persistent tendency in the literature to favor psychological and psychiatric research and individual-level considerations. I further demonstrate that cisgender men's violence toward cisgender women has dominated to the extent that the consequences of other gendered patterns in violence remain largely unknown. Finally, I bridge these observations with participants' insights to outline potential new directions for research.

Part II: Social Mechanisms

This section explores social processes within the study of rape, and draws almost entirely on participants' insights. Science studies scholars may be particularly interested in these chapters, as they consider factors that promote and sustain participation in science as well as credibility struggles and conflict among researchers. Scholars of feminism, women's and gender studies, and labor (in)equality may appreciate my analysis of the feminization of rape research, as well as my and many participants' argument that care work and mentoring are central (rather than supplemental) to the work of doing science.

Throughout this project, I welcomed questions from participants about my background, immediate and long-term hopes for this research, theoretical framework(s) and methodology, and data interpretations. The question I most often received concerned pathways into the field. Many participants anticipated a sort of standard trajectory that began with antiviolence activism or personal encounters with sexual violence and ultimately extended into academic pursuits. To put it another way, they expected antiviolence work to be a lifelong commitment that preceded and informed academic ambitions. I initially shared those expectations. To our collective surprise, the thirty-one scholars who took part shared a wide range of motivations for engaging in sexual violence research. Chapter 5, "Choosing to Study Rape," begins with those stories. After exploring pathways into the field, I turn to social mechanisms that sustain actors in this often emotionally and intellectually demanding work. This chapter argues that choosing to study rape—choosing to study anything, really—is not so much a one-time decision that determines a life course, but a decision that may be made and unmade repeatedly, and is often contingent on the presence of support and care work among peers. Mentoring and collaboration play substantial roles. Extending and departing from my own training as an advocate, I further propose that self-care is a collective process with great significance for building and sustaining scholarship in this field.

Whereas chapter 5 concerns supportive forces in sexual violence research, chapter 6, "Dividends and Detriments of Dissent," focuses on conflict and credibility struggles. The title of this chapter is borrowed from Amin Ghaziani's *The Dividends of Dissent* (2008), which considers the impacts of internal conflicts in queer activism. While it may be objected that science and social movements comprise different domains, Ghaziani's insights seem particularly productive for this area of scholarship. Many scientists who study rape have activist backgrounds, and others are drawn toward antiviolence advocacy through their research efforts. Even those who do not venture directly into social movement work are likely to contend with those who do.

In chapter 6, I argue that the heaviness of sexual violence as a research topic, and its dual association with questions of social morality and feminist activism, contributes to specific credibility and moral challenges among scientists. Some struggles involve actors to whom I loosely refer as outsider scholars, that is, individuals who are trained scientists or academics but do not study sexual violence. Many participants recalled hearing that scholarship on sexual violence was altogether unimportant or unscientific. Further conflict occurs among insiders as sexual violence researchers disagree about which research questions and methodologies are worth pursuing, and what should be published/publishable in scientific periodicals and other outlets. After considering these interpersonal conflicts, I turn to institutional forces. More specifically, I examine the role of universities, which have the capacity to influence research trajectories through hiring and tenure guidelines and other career pressures; and grant providers, which have the capacity to influence research via the hierarchical process of identifying priority and nonpriority areas for support.

The final chapter of *Rape by the Numbers* revisits the project's primary research questions (how have scientists conceptualized rape and other forms of sexual violence among adults; and what social mechanisms enable, constrain, and otherwise influence scientific research on sexual violence) and the analytical resources of Karen Barad's (2007) agential realism and my own concept of precasting. Approaching the scientific study of rape as a dynamic and developing field, I celebrate historical and ongoing achievements while calling for greater investment in theoretical and methodological inclusivity, systematic and interdisciplinary analyses, and accountability in scientific endeavors.

PART ONE

Conceptualizing Rape

CHAPTER 2

Locating the Problem

I really want people to define [rape] for themselves,
obviously. That's part of my work, thinking about how
people think about it. . . . That's a really interesting
conversation that I think qualitative and quantitative
researchers can have. Because we're all so stuck thinking
about how to get money and grants, and do good in the
world if we don't have numbers . . . and people don't want
to believe them anyway. So I don't know what the point is.
People don't even believe "one in four," "one in five," even
though the numbers say that. But again, you can't get any
public money without showing that this is a problem. So
that's a really interesting juxtaposition to think about.

—Kristen, sociologist

The prevalence estimates we get are very different if you
say, "Have you ever been sexually assaulted?" Well, that
requires somebody to interpret "what do you mean by
sexually assaulted?" . . . If you ask, "Have you ever been
sexually assaulted?" they might say no. But if you ask
them, "Has anybody ever touched you in private areas
that made you feel uncomfortable?" they would say yes to
that . . . the more specific event-based questions that you
ask, people will be able to say yes or no, that that specific
event happened to them. But not necessarily conclude that
that was a sexual assault. So I don't want them concluding, based on a very fungible definition, what physical or
sexual assault is. I want to be able to make that determi-
nation based on whether something specific happened to
them against their will.   —Karen, criminal justice scholar

QUANTIFICATION—THE CALCULATION of incidence and prevalence rates—has long been central to the work of addressing rape (Gavey
[2005] 2018; Rutherford 2017). Particularly within the United States, the
recognition of rape as a social problem has been and arguably remains

33

contingent upon numbers over and above personal stories and high-profile cases. A single claim of #MeToo can perhaps be ignored. One or two survivors may be dismissed or discredited. Tens or hundreds or thousands of survivors may drive a film director or physician or actor or politician or coach or clergyperson from power. Statistical figures like "one in five college women" may force attention to campus sexual assault, even among reluctant legislators and administrators.

This chapter concerns scientists' efforts to quantify rape and other forms of sexual violence. I begin with a controversy over rape statistics in the 1990s. Drawing on the science studies concepts of credibility struggles and environments (Epstein 1996; Shapin 1995; Waidzunas 2012) and the insights of agential realism (Barad 2007), I delve into the politics and value conflicts behind the numbers. I demonstrate that prevalence surveys—including those that yield such as explosive figures as "one in four women"—can render some survivors visible while rending others invisible, particularly when it comes to gender and sexuality.

Ultimately, I demonstrate that quantifying rape requires scientists to make a series of decisions, each of which may shape the perceptibility of different acts, victims, aggressors, and bystanders as well as prevalence estimates. One must determine what rape is in order to count it (Espeland and Stevens 2008; Gavey [2005] 2018). Having defined rape, scientists must then determine where and with whom rape happens (or might happen) in order to refine research questions and develop sampling frames. In other words, quantification entails locating the problem. Rape and other forms of sexual violence are not external referents awaiting documentation by detached scholars, but rather intra-active phenomena made intelligible by agential cuts within research. The scientists who produce such research are complexly situated and entangled with disciplinary conventions, scientific and nonscientific communities, historical events, social movements, state and private institutions, and public ideals (Bourdieu 1975; Epstein 1996; Epstein 2006; Jasanoff 2004; Latour 1987; Shapin 1995; Shapin and Schaffer [1985] 2011) and draw in varying ways upon their own personal values, identifications, and dispositions (Vila 2017). There are no innocent or clean scientific truths, statistical or otherwise (Flax 1992).

Later in the chapter, I explore four decades' worth of efforts to quantify sexual violence in the United States and Canada. I review 125 incidence and prevalence studies to explore overall trends across time, and look closely at four studies to better understand how differences in definitions, sampling, and survey design determine who and what will "count." Consistent gendered precasting, characterized by emphasis on cisgender men's sexual aggression toward cisgender women in study design and interpretation, has located the problem predominantly—and, at times, exclusively—in heterosexual contexts. Experiential criteria—particularly those aligned with legal and other state conceptualizations of rape and other forms of sexual violence—have been favored over criteria such as self-assessment in prevalence studies. Notably, this second pattern is not reflected in research on the causes and consequences of rape, as will be seen in later chapters.

In the final sections of this chapter, I present insights from scientists. Participants reinforce the social significance of prevalence research. Their experiences as scholars and, in some cases, as antiviolence advocates speak to the politics of varying strategies for locating the problem. As noted by Kristen, quoted above, institutions such as universities and state agencies are more inclined to support research for social problems with established quantitative reach. Social processes in the production of knowledge produce statistics that ultimately shape policy and interventions, funding and other resource distribution, and collective understandings of sexual violence.

MAKING AND UNMAKING AN EPIDEMIC

In 1987, the popular image of sexual violence shifted from a rare and personal concern into an epidemic due to a new and startling statistic. According to psychologists Mary Koss, Christine Gidycz, and Nadine Wisniewski, one in four of the more than three thousand college women they surveyed reported experiencing a completed or attempted rape (1987; see also Gavey [2005] 2018; Jhally 1994; Rutherford 2017). The "one in four women" statistic received tremendous attention in mainstream news outlets, and continues to influence activists and state officials to this day.

Whereas years of organizing protest marches, providing education and support through rape crisis centers, and advocating for legal reform had fostered incremental changes in dominant perspectives (Bevacqua 2000; Matthews 1994; Spohn and Horney 1992), Koss, Gidycz, and Wisniewski had a greater and more immediate impact on public perceptions for at least two reasons. First and foremost, they commanded credibility as scientists. Activists might face challenges from public audiences, politicians, journalists, and scholars for their presumably vision-clouding agendas. Scientists, on the other hand, were largely expected to possess a detached objectivity as knowledge producers (it should be noted that science has faced considerable credibility challenges since the 1980s, both from rightwing skeptics who doubt knowledge that conflicts with their political goals and postmodernist critiques of science as a master narrative, and that "one in four" might thus fare differently were it produced and published today). Second, as statistical researchers, they appealed to a way of knowing that wields considerable power in the United States. Public perceptions of scientific objectivity are socially and historically contingent. Whereas public audiences in other nations, such as Germany and the United Kingdom, often emphasize other factors such as scientists' credentials and consensus among experts when evaluating scientific claims, quantitative knowledges have been regarded as particularly credible in the United States for more than a century (Jasanoff 2005). Moving scholarship on rape from the realm of personal and historical narrative (e.g., Brownmiller 1975) into "the language of numbers" ensured broader reach (Espeland and Stevens 2008; Jasanoff 2005, 265; Porter 1995; Waidzunas 2012; Woodward 1999).

The early 1990s gave rise to a "backlash" in which critics sought to reframe anti-rape activism and scholarship as manufacturing a false problem (Gavey [2005] 2018; Jhally 1994; Rutherford 2017). "One in four women" was subjected to immense scrutiny. Neil Gilbert (1991; 1992), a professor of social welfare (and therefore perhaps an outsider to the world of professional science), accused Koss and colleagues of using an overly broad definition of rape. He noted that a majority (73%) of women whom the researchers classified as rape victims did not self-identify as such. These arguments gained considerable ground when echoed by literature graduate student and self-identified feminist Katie Roiphe, who dismissed Koss and her supporters as "rape crisis feminists" whose politics were detrimental to women's sexual autonomy (1991; [1993] 1994, 70). What followed was in essence a trial of strength (Latour 1987) in which critics attempted to sever Koss's alliance with the women who had participated in her study and arguably with college women more broadly. Actors on both sides further contested the nature of feminism, and thereby also their relative claims to feminists as potential allies. Through insisting that rape was a threat to women's welfare, Koss positioned her research as inherently feminist. Drawing attention to women's assessments of their own experiences, Gilbert and Roiphe also appealed to discourses of feminist activism. They (re)presented Koss's work as disempowering through its negation of participants' narratives.

April's exercise is useful here. The controversy over "one in four women" might be (re)envisioned as a centering on a few key actors who promoted and disputed particular matters of scientific fact:

> Mary knows that one in four college women have experienced completed or attempted rape.
> Mary knows that rape is a common and urgent threat to women's welfare.
> Neil knows that far fewer than one in four women have experienced completed or attempted rape.
> Neil knows that rape is rare.

In the 1990s, disagreements over such big-picture claims directed attention to quantification strategies. A more thorough approach might thus begin with more foundational knowledges. Before counting prevalence rates, Mary must have determined what rape is, and must have developed a strategy for identifying college women and asking after their experiences. She must have determined how to identify rape victims. Neil's critique might thus extend to, or perhaps emerge from, these theoretical and methodological decisions. Consider, then, the following:

> Mary knows that Participant Y is a rape victim.
> Neil knows that Participant Y is not a rape victim.

So how might Mary know? And how can readers, as modest witnesses to Mary's scientific endeavors (Haraway 1997; Shapin and Schaffer [1985] 2011), make sense of this matter of fact? This particular Mary relied on two resources in producing a definition of rape: Ohio criminal statutes and the Federal Bureau of Investigation's (FBI) Uniform Crime Reports (Koss, Gidycz, and Wisniewski 1987). Ohio took a broad approach. Penile-vaginal penetration, penile-anal penetration, oral assaults, and penetration by objects might all qualify as rape provided that assailants used physical force and/or administered intoxicants to victims in order to subdue them. Statutes embraced a gender inclusive approach, such that male and female actors might both qualify as assailants or victims. In contrast, the FBI (then) restricted rape to forcible acts of penile-vaginal penetration with male assailants and female victims.[1] Combining Ohio's range of criminalized acts with FBI gender restrictions, she used the following questions to document experiences of rape (Koss, Gidycz, and Wisniewski 1987, 167):

> Have you had sexual intercourse when you did not want to because a man gave you alcohol or drugs?
> Have you had sexual intercourse when you did not want to because a man threatened or used some degree of physical force (twisting your arm, holding you down, etc.) to make you?
> Have you had sex acts (anal or oral intercourse or penetration by objects other than the penis) when you didn't want to because a man threatened or used some degree of physical force (twisting your arm, holding you down, etc.) to make you?

Participants who received these questions were also asked, directly, whether they had ever been raped. All questions were administered in reference to participants' adult lifetimes (operationalized as age fourteen and above, for lifetime prevalence), and to the previous calendar year (for twelve-month incidence).

If Mary (Koss) knows that Participant Y is a rape victim, it is because Participant Y answered "yes" to at least one of the three questions listed above. Fifteen percent of surveyed women did so—approximately one in seven. An additional 12% reported one or more attempts (i.e., incidents in which penetration did not occur). Together, these findings produced a lifetime prevalence of 27% for completed or attempted rape among college women—just over one in four. Notably, Participant Y's answer to the more direct question about experiencing rape would not have affected her categorization. Those data served to distinguish among established rape victims who did (27%) and did not (73%) classify themselves as such (Koss, Gidycz, and Wisniewski 1987). In a previous publication, Koss had theorized the latter group as "hidden" or "unacknowledged" victims whose experiences were rarely captured in federal victimization surveys (Koss 1985; see Gavey [2005] 2018 for a critique of this categorization).[2]

What, then, of the counterclaim? How could it be that Neil (Gilbert) knows that Participant Y is not a rape victim? Perhaps she answered "yes" only to the first question. This would disqualify her if Neil rejects the premise that nonconsensual sex constitutes rape if the means of force is involuntary intoxication. Indeed, Neil Gilbert was insistent on that point (1992; see also Roiphe [1993] 1994). Alternatively, Participant Y might have answered "no" to the direct question. This would disqualify her if Neil believes that self-identification as a rape victim supersedes other classification criteria. In either event, Neil might dispute her individual history as well as the broader claim of "one in four women." As Mary Koss has noted, eliminating involuntary intoxication measures would shift the lifetime prevalence of completed or attempted rape to "one in five women" (see Jhally 1994). Relying on direct measures would shift the lifetime prevalence of completed rape from 15%, or one in seven, to approximately 4%, or one in twenty-five (15% multiplied by the 27% of documented victims who were not "hidden").

Rape Statistics and the Struggle for Credibility

In this well-publicized controversy—covered in such high-profile news outlets as the *New York Times* and *Wall Street Journal*—actors on both sides faced credibility challenges as producers of scientific knowledge (Shapin 1995). In responding, they endeavored to defend the validity of their perspectives (Epstein 1996) and discredit those of their opponents, even while claiming to engage in dispassionate and detached analyses of the true nature of rape. As a major figure in the anti-rape movement (in addition to being a scientist), Koss was likely mindful of the challenges feminist activists had faced in raising awareness about sexual violence. Many had been accused of promoting "sex wars" by prioritizing emotion and anecdotes over empirical data (Whittier 2009). In response to Gilbert's criticism, Koss turned neither to personal narratives nor to the emotional trauma suffered by some victims/survivors. This is not to say that she was unmoved by women's experiences of rape—far from it—but rather, that she may have recognized their limited strategic use in the credibility environment (Waidzunas 2012) of scientific communication and publishing. Instead, Koss noted that she and her colleagues had consulted FBI and state policy in developing their definition of rape. Doing so, she presented the law as authoritative in distinguishing rape from consensual encounters, and bolstered her credibility as a scientist through indirect appeals to state authority (Jasanoff 2004). She had this to say in regard to women's self-assessments:

> Let me just give an analogy. If I went to a chemical dependency treatment program and administered an alcoholism screening test to one of the clients there and I said, "Do you drink in the morning to get rid of a hangover? Do you hide liquor around your house?"—and the person responds "yes." "Have people in your family complained that your drinking is interfering with your life?"—and the person responds "yes." "Do you have periods when you can't remember what you've been doing because you were drinking?"—and the person responds "yes." And then I turn around and say, "Do you consider yourself an alcoholic?" and the person says, "Absolutely not." Do I then turn them out of the chemical dependency program because they don't think they're an alcoholic, or do I pay attention to the characteristics of their behavior as they're describing them, which qualify that person to be an alcoholic? And it's the same thing with the rape victims. The fact that they had intercourse against their consent because a man threatened bodily harm or used physical force means that they qualify as rape victims, and the fact that they don't realize this does not disqualify the experience from happening. (interviewed in Jhally 1994)

In this instance, Koss appealed to scientific expertise—her knowledge and skills as a professional researcher in psychology—over and above women participants' accounts.

Gilbert, on the other hand, faced challenges as a man critiquing feminist efforts to address violence against women. By insisting that women study participants be treated as experts on their experiences and further enlisting Roiphe, a feminist-identified woman, as an ally, he guarded against accusations of being antifeminist. His rejection of involuntary intoxication relied on notions of common sense. Allowing that women might be raped by men who employed (physical) force, he asked what "having sex 'because' a man gives you drugs or alcohol signif(ied)" (1992, 5), as though faulty logic were self-evident there.

Rape Statistics as Phenomena

How can an agential realist framework help us understand this controversy (whoever "we" happen to be)? Rather than viewing Koss and Gilbert as engaged in a dispute over the true nature of an external referent called rape, we might approach rape as phenomenal. We might consider the possibility that rape is not reducible to specific experiences or self-assessments, or engagements with prevalence surveys, but rather manifests differently across entanglements with different agencies of observation. This approach provides a means of rethinking the dispute over which survey items come to matter.

In the previous chapter, I briefly reviewed Barad's discussion of complementary properties, which she draws from Bohr's philosophy-physics (Barad 2007). Wave-particle duality provides an example in physics research. Light manifests wavelike properties under particular experimental conditions, and particle-like properties under other conditions. However, it is not possible to observe both simultaneously, as their perceptibility relies on different agencies of observation. What if rape is similar? What if rape has both experiential and identitarian properties, or rather experience-identity duality? What if Koss and Gilbert simply enact agential cuts differently within the "same" phenomenon? And if this is the case, how might an agential realist approach serve to account for those differences, and the "ethico-onto-epistemic" possibilities therein (Barad 2007, 364)?

Barad wrote extensively of other physicists' use of thought experiments to explore and contest scientific questions. Following their lead, I theorize possibilities for identifying rape victims and nonvictims across different measurement approaches in my own thought experiment with a hypothetical sample. To be consistent with (the logic of) 1980s prevalence research, I envision a sample of cisgender undergraduate women. Importantly, these seven hypothetical women are not intended as a "representative" sample, but are rather envisioned for variation in experience and identity regarding their victimization (non)histories:

Participant A: no history of unwanted sexual contact; does not identify as rape victim/survivor

Participant B: history of nonconsensual digital penetration and oral-vaginal contact by a cisgender woman, achieved through the use of force; does not identify as rape victim/survivor

Participant C: history of nonconsensual digital penetration and oral-vaginal contact by a cisgender woman, achieved through the use of force; identifies as rape victim/survivor

Participant D: history of nonconsensual penile-vaginal penetration by a cisgender man, recalls verbally protesting and then "freezing";[3] does not perceive of the incident as forced; does not identify as rape victim/survivor

Participant E: history of nonconsensual penile-vaginal penetration by a cisgender man, recalls verbally protesting and then "freezing;"

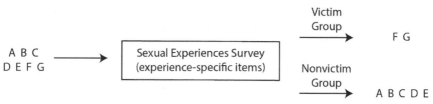

2.1. Apparatus One: Legally Defined, Gender Restricted (experiential)

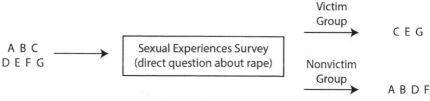

2.2. Apparatus Two: Self-Assessment (identitarian)

does not perceive of the incident as forced; identifies as rape
victim/survivor

Participant F: history of nonconsensual penile-vaginal penetration
by a cisgender man, achieved through the use of force; does not
identify as rape victim/survivor

Participant G: history of nonconsensual penile-vaginal penetration
by a cisgender man, achieved through the use of force; identifies as rape victim/survivor

Figures 2.1 and 2.2 predict the intra-active classification of these women,
based on different agencies of observation—not merely in terms of which
survey items they receive, but how those items matter for their ontological
status as victims or nonvictims (i.e., where/how agential cuts are made). In
each hypothetical research scenario, this sample of seven women is divided
into "victim" and "nonvictim" groups through intra-action with a particular measurement apparatus. These apparatuses are drawn from different sections of the Sexual Experiences Survey.

In the first approach, rape is assessed as experiential. Women participants are classified as victims or nonvictims based on their responses to the
three survey questions that Koss, Gidycz, and Wisniewski (1987) used to
identify rape victims, which specify men as assailants and otherwise align
with Ohio criminal statutes. The two women who have experienced forcible penile-vaginal assault by a cisgender man both emerge as rape victims,
even though only one of them self-identifies as such. In 1987, Koss favored
and reported on this approach. This was likely connected with her training

and commitments as a feminist researcher invested in raising awareness of the pervasiveness of sexual violence. She did not seek simply to raise awareness of the struggles of women who thought of themselves as victims, but to draw attention toward all sexual violence perpetrated by men and against women. At the same time, the original Sexual Experiences Survey rendered same-sex violence imperceptible (Murphy 2006), and further excluded incidents in which assailants did not rely on force or involuntary intoxication to subdue their victims.

The second approach prioritizes personal narratives of victimization. Women who consider themselves rape victims/survivors emerge as such; others do not. Criminality is a nonissue. The perceptions of researchers, police, bystanders, strangers, media consumers, and others are likewise nonissues. Note that this identitarian property is complementary to experience. Numerous scholars have documented that variation in question design produces variation in prevalence estimates (Cook et al. 2011; Fisher 2009; Koss 1993; Wolff et al. 2006). Consistent with Koss and colleagues' 1987 study, individuals who have experienced assaults that legally qualify as rape or sexual assault infrequently say "yes" to questions that use those terms. However, these same individuals may answer "yes" to a question that describes their experiences without labeling them. While it is now uncommon for prevalence research to rely on identitarian measures for these reasons, other areas of sexual violence research often do so indirectly. For example, evaluations of medical and therapeutic treatments tend to rely on participants who seek out support in these arenas—that is, people who desire and see fit to pursue services for sexual assault survivors.

In their criticisms of Mary Koss's work, Neil Gilbert and Katie Roiphe made repeated references to study participants' identities. Yet they would not likely have accepted the outcome of apparatus two as theorized here. In my hypothetical sample, two women whom even Koss and colleagues would have described as nonvictims were empowered to self-categorize as such—and surely the authors of such works as "Date Rape Hysteria" (Roiphe 1991) and "The Campus Rape Scare" (Gilbert 1991) would be loath to facilitate an increase in prevalence estimates, or to encourage any ostensible nonvictims to shift into victimhood. Indeed, both authors expressed dismay that incidents they rated as trivial or nonsevere might ever be called rape in scholarship or advocacy (Gilbert 1992; Roiphe [1993] 1994). They disputed the very existence of date and acquaintance rape and sought to (re)establish rape as a rare, if serious, occurrence. So how might these actors make use of data from the Sexual Experience Survey? Where would they make their agential cuts to distinguish victims from nonvictims?

While I argue here that identitarian and experiential properties are complementary, this does not mean that both cannot be assessed within the

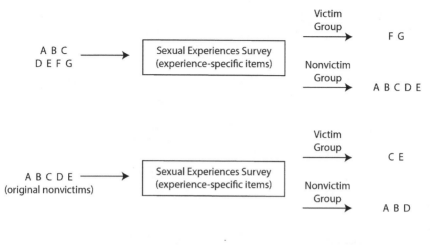

Final Victim Group: C E F G
Final Nonvictim Group: A B D

2.3. Apparatus Three: Two Steps, Broad Approach (experiential *or* identitarian)

boundaries of a single psychological study. Researchers might perform a two-step analysis to broaden or narrow the criteria for victim status. In the former case, it would be productive to use an *or* approach: after participants answered experiential questions, for example, established victims could be set aside. Those who emerged as nonvictims might then receive experiential questions and potentially be reclassified.[4] In the latter case, it would be productive to use an *and* approach: after participants answered experiential questions, established nonvictims could be set aside. Those who emerged as victims might then receive experiential questions and potentially be reclassified. Figures 2.3 and 2.4 illustrate these potentialities.

In figure 2.3, a two-step process ensures that women who identify as rape victims/survivors are included in the victim sample, even if their experiences do not match legal definitions of rape (or researchers' operationalizations of those definitions). The two women initially classified as victims retain this status. Of the five women initially classified as being nonvictims, only three retain this status at the end of analysis. Nancy Wolff and colleagues took a similar approach in a study of sexual violence among incarcerated people (Wolff et al. 2006).

In figure 2.4, the five women first classified as nonvictims retain this status. Only one of two in the victim sample retains that status at the end of analyses. This thought experiment is particularly useful for exploring the Koss/Gilbert dispute. For Koss, the agential cut that disentangles object (participant) from measurement apparatus (survey instrument) occurs after the experiential questions. The second part of apparatus four serves to

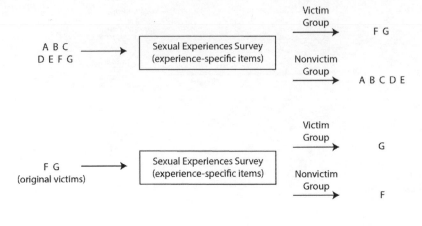

2.4. Apparatus Four: Two Steps, Strict Approach (experiential *and* identitarian)

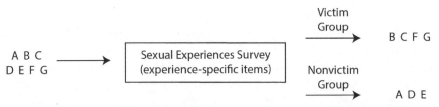

2.5. Apparatus Five: Legally Defined, Not Gender Restricted (experiential)

distinguish between acknowledged victims (G, in this example) and unacknowledged or hidden victims (F, in this example). For Gilbert, the experiential questions serve, at best, to identify women who might potentially have experienced rape. It is not a definitive assessment tool. Only at the second step, when this prescreened sample is asked directly about (non)histories of rape, may credible victims be identified.

These models do not exhaust the possibilities for identitarian or experiential phenomena. Within the realm of experiential measures, Koss and colleagues' initial approach might be read as conservative in spite of the criticism they received. Inconsistent with Ohio state legislation (though, as they pointed out, consistent with FBI definitions at the time), they embraced strict gender criteria for victims and assailants. An analysis more consistent with state laws—that is, without restriction to men as aggressors—would produce the outcome depicted in figure 2.5.

Notably, this is more consistent with the revised, gender-inclusive Sexual Experiences Survey (Koss et al. 2007), introduced by Koss and several other established scholars in the field twenty years after the first publication

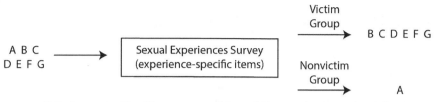

2.6. Apparatus Six: Nonconsensual Sexual Penetration (experiential)

of "one in four women." This shift in measurement apparatuses is entangled with broader shifts in research, community activism, and other domains toward an understanding of sexual violence as a gender inclusive—though, as discussed in the first chapter, not necessarily gender-neutral—issue.

Yet even this approach might be read as conservative. Some criminal statutes, scholars (including several participants in the present study), and antiviolence advocates define rape as encompassing all nonconsensual penile-vaginal, penile-anal, oral-penile, oral-vaginal, and oral-anal incidents, as well as penetration by other body parts or objects. These may loosely be characterized as incorporating all nonconsensual sexual penetration. Importantly, it is not necessary to associate penetration with perpetration. For example, a cisgender woman may perpetrate penile-vaginal assault against a cisgender man by such means as force or threats, persistence despite his refusals or lack of expressed consent, exploiting his intoxication, or assaulting him while he is asleep or unconscious. To return to thought experimenting, the nonconsensual sexual penetration model has striking implications for estimating prevalence in this hypothetical sample, as demonstrated in figure 2.6.

Of course, these models may also be combined with identitarian measures in broad or strict approaches. Table 2.1 provides an overview of all apparatuses described here, including classification criteria and the consequent victim/nonvictim breakdown among these hypothetical seven women.

In these six hypothetical approaches to distinguishing rape victims from nonvictims, only two participants are consistent in status. Participant A, who has never experienced unwanted sexual contact and does not identify as a victim/survivor, is consistently classified as a nonvictim. Participant G, who has experienced nonconsensual penile-vaginal penetration achieved through the use of force and also identifies as a victim/survivor, is consistently classified as a victim. The remaining five women vary in status based on the measurement apparatus, including emphasis on identitarian or experiential criteria; the specific nature of experiential criteria where applicable; and whether the apparatus involves a single measure, a two-step assessment of complementary properties designed to broaden the classification of victims (i.e., an *or* approach), or a two-step assessment of complementary properties designed to restrict the classification of victims (i.e., an *and* approach).

TABLE 2.1

Rape Prevalence Counts in a Theoretical Sample of Seven Cisgender Women

Apparatus	Criteria	Victim-Nonvictim Ratio	Victim Participants
One	Identifies as victim/survivor	3:4	C E G
Two	Original Sexual Experiences Survey (SES)	2:5	F G
	(Ohio definition of rape, aggressor must be a man)		
*Three**	Meets criteria for apparatus one or two:	4:3	C E F G
	Identifies as victim or meets experiential criteria in SES		
*Four**	Meets criteria for apparatus one and two:	1:6	G
	Identifies as victim and meets experiential criteria in SES		
Five	Ohio definition of rape	4:3	B C F G
Six	Nonconsensual penetration	6:1	B C D E F G

*Apparatuses three and four employ two-step processes.

It gets more complicated from there. Even these hypothetical phenomena fail completely to involve transgender and nonbinary identifications, and while some incorporate sexual aggression by both cisgender men and cisgender women, none incorporate aggression toward men or masculine-identified people. Several important dimensions of the agencies of observation are also omitted (see Fisher 2009; Koss 1993). Survey administration procedures, including but not limited to the setting in which participants receive questionnaires and whether they provide spoken, handwritten, or computer-based responses may all impact results. The order and precise wording for experiential questions will affect participants' self-assessments and reporting decisions, as will the terminology chosen for broad/direct questions (e.g., participants may report differently when asked about experiences of rape, sexual assault, sexual violence, sexual harassment, sexual coercion, and unwanted sexual experiences, to name but a few possibilities). It is also possible for participants' narratives to shift across time and space in a way that may impact their responses within or across research encounters. Understandings of forceful contact, and of what does and does not constitute rape, are variable. Understandings of the motivations, actions, and interpersonal dynamics within sexually violent encounters are variable. Identifications are variable. Understandings of and labels for personal experiences change over time. Participants' willingness to disclose victimization to researchers, even among those who identify as victims or survivors, cannot be assumed in general or within specific research efforts. These important points are often missed in much literature on reliability testing for survey instruments: inconsistency in responses may be connected with shifts in participants' identitarian articulations and intra-active engagements with questionnaires. Rather than interpret inconsistencies solely as indicative of "faulty instrumentation" or participants' "self-contradiction," they may be (re)envisioned as—at least in part—indicative of variation within and across phenomena.

What does this mean for prevalence research? There is no call here to end such work. The stakes are simply too high, given continued reliance on and credibility awarded to statistical knowledge in arenas such as social policy (Jasanoff 2005; Porter 1995). Moreover, the recognition/assumption that scientific research entails social processes, and that varying approaches produce different matters of fact within and across phenomena, need not be discouraging. Such interpretations would stand in stark defiance of insights from numerous scholars in feminist science studies (Barad 2007; Haraway 1988; Haraway 1997; Harding 1995; Murphy 2006). The preceding analyses do not tend toward a relativist framework in which all potential apparatuses and estimates appear equally valid, nor an objectivist framework in which one apparatus is somehow deemed the sole arbiter of scientific truth. Rather, they demonstrate a need to consider the inseparability of ethics, epistemology, and ontology within science. Quantification projects informed by agential realism will prioritize transparency, including detailed descriptions of measurement approaches and the logics behind them. Scholars engaged in such work might understand themselves as intra-acting within phenomena, and enacting agential cuts that might have been made differently.

FORTY YEARS OF QUANTIFICATION

The controversy over "one in four women" looms large within the history of rape research (Gavey [2005] 2018; Rutherford 2017). Public and scientific disputes between Koss and her supporters on the one hand, and Gilbert and his supporters on the other, speak to broader historical trends in public understandings of science, sexual violence, and sexual and gender politics; as well as the various markers of credibility and ethics within scientific domains. But what about the larger field? How dominant was Koss's approach in the 1980s, and has this shifted over time? Was her emphasis on college men's violence toward college women typical of prevalence research, and has it remained so? How else have scholars located the problem? To answer these questions, I turn to a historical overview of scientific efforts to quantify sexual violence.

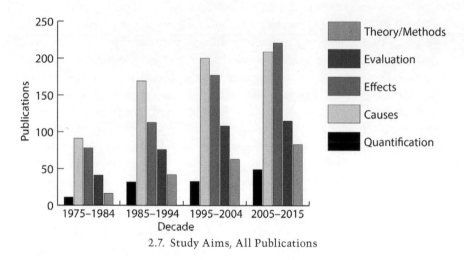

2.7. Study Aims, All Publications

Figures 2.7–2.14 present patterns in the overall field of sexual violence research and the subfield of quantification. This is based on my review of scientific journal abstracts (see chapter 1 for a detailed description of this process, including strategies for finding relevant abstracts and analyzing them). Among other characteristics, I examined the overall aims of each study (e.g., whether quantification was the sole purpose, or whether researchers were also interested in the causes of rape), major areas of focus (e.g., victimization, perpetration), incorporation of various gendered patterns in violence, and target populations. In order to observe changes across time, I separated results by decade: 1975–1984, 1985–1994, 1995–2004, 2005–2015.

While these figures offer a visual representation of scientific inquiries, table 2.2 provides data in the form of frequencies (raw numbers, such as the total number of studies addressing women's victimization in each decade), percentages (the percentage of sexual violence studies that focused all or in part on women's victimization), and significance as determined by chi-square tests. For those who are less familiar with statistical analyses, significance does not refer to the social or scholarly import of data. Significance testing provides a way to determine whether any changes or differences are substantial enough to comprise a mathematical trend. For this project, a statistically significant trend would indicate that something about sexual violence research has changed over time. A statistically insignificant finding would indicate that the field has remained stable, even if the graphs (or our own personal observations) seem to show otherwise.

Out of the 1,313 studies assessed, only 125 sought to quantify sexual violence through the calculation of incidence and/or prevalence rates. This was somewhat surprising, given the cultural significance awarded to statistics

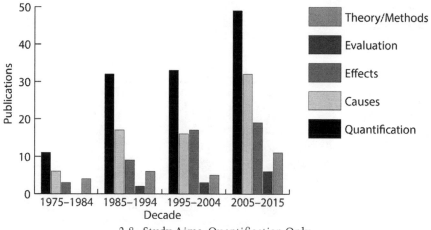

2.8. Study Aims, Quantification Only

in the United States (Jasanoff 2005; Porter 1995; Waidzunas 2012; Woodward 1999), and the attention given Koss and colleagues' 1987 study—with more than 1,100 citations to date, it was the second most-cited piece across all four decades. As figure 2.7 shows, quantification studies have been consistently outnumbered by inquiries into the causes and effects of sexual violence, as well as by evaluation studies and critical assessments of theoretical frameworks and methodologies. Theoretical/methodological refinement studies have grown significantly more common over time, and the relative prominence of effects research has ebbed and flowed significantly. Prevalence research, causal inquiries, and evaluation studies have comprised roughly the same proportions of rape research over time.

As figure 2.8 shows, many studies in this area have embraced multiple aims. Researchers frequently paired incidence/prevalence estimates with data for risk factors (causes) or health outcomes (effects). There were no statistically significant trends in the incorporation of additional study aims within this subfield. In other words, it has not become more or less common for prevalence researchers to incorporate additional study aims.

Figures 2.9 and 2.10 concern researchers' attention toward victimization, perpetration, professionals who prevent and respond to rape, and bystanders or the general public. In the overall field of research on rape, scientists have consistently prioritized victims/victimization. These trends have intensified over the past four decades, as evidenced by significantly increasing attention toward victimization and declining attention toward perpetration and bystanders/general publics. Quantification researchers have also emphasized victimization. As evident in the graphs in figure 2.9

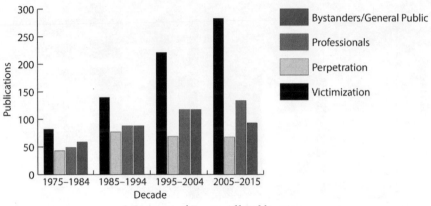

2.9. Areas of Focus, All Publications

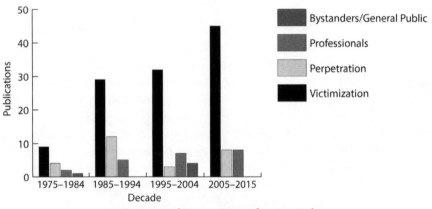

2.10. Areas of Focus, Quantification Only

and figure 2.10, emphasis on victimization is even more pronounced in this subfield. There has been a notable decline in perpetration studies over time. Research with bystanders (e.g., studies investigating the number of known victims/survivors in participants' social networks), while a consistently minor aspect of quantification, has varied significantly in scope.

Gendered approaches in quantification appear relatively consistent with the broader field. As shown in figure 2.11, sexual violence scholars overall have devoted the most attention to women's victimization, followed by men's aggression, men's victimization, and women's perpetration. While there has been a significant increase in studies of men's victimization over time, it remains a relatively small concern in rape scholarship. Although attention toward men's aggression has declined significantly, it remains the second most-investigated gendered dimension of sexual violence among those considered here. The sort of precasting assessed in content analysis—in

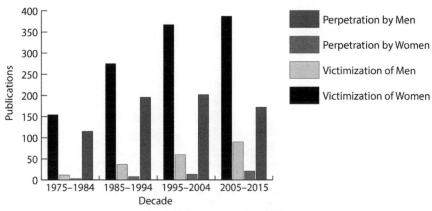

2.11. Gendered Patterns, All Publications

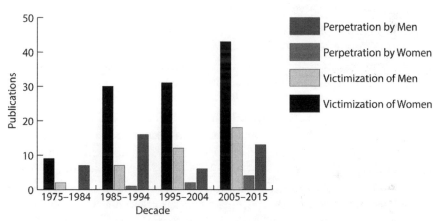

2.12. Gendered Patterns, Quantification Only

which authors utilize gender nonspecific language in abstracts for gender specific approaches—declined significantly in the broader field from 30.11% of all studies between 1975 and 1984 to 21% of those from 2005 to 2015 (not shown in a graph, but noted in table 2.2). Within quantification (figure 2.12), women's victimization and women's aggression have again received the most and least attention; men's victimization and aggression have alternated between second and third. Also consistent with the broader field, men's perpetration has received less attention over time. Gender precasting varied considerably across decades.

In the broader field, researchers have prioritized student populations (figure 2.13). This is likely due to numerous factors, two of which I will tentatively outline here. For several decades—certainly since the emergence of "one in four women"—college women have been regarded as a priority

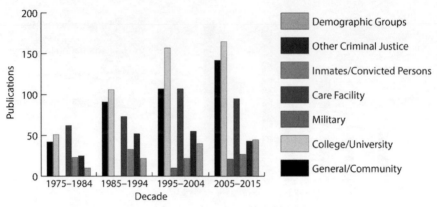

2.13. Study Populations, All Publications

population for sexual violence prevention (Anderson and Whiston 2005; Krebs et al. 2007; Krebs et al. 2009; Morrison et al. 2004; White House Council on Women and Girls 2014). Additionally, a substantial proportion of scientific research on rape has been produced by psychologists, whose discipline relies heavily on undergraduate study participants (Henrich, Heine, and Norenzayan 2010). Studies targeting the general population and/or community samples ranked consistently second. Practically nonexistent from 1975 to 1994, research with military populations emerged in the following decade and appears to be on the rise. Over time, scientists have conducted proportionately fewer investigations with care facility and inmate/convicted populations. Research specific to demographic populations, such as studies of rape among people with disabilities, has comprised a relatively minor proportion of publications (single-gender studies were not classified as "demographic" unless they were also explicitly focused on other demographic populations).

Quantification studies depart considerably from these patterns (figure 2.14). Scientists seeking to count incidence/prevalence rates have most consistently turned to the general population. Research specific to demographic populations has been far more prominent in this subfield, particularly over the past two decades. Investigations with military and convicted populations show a more striking increase. As with the emphasis on college students in the larger field, some of these patterns may be connected with researchers' characteristics. Quantification tends more toward collaborations between scientists and state institutions, such as the Centers for Disease Control (CDC) and the Department of Justice (e.g., Black et al. 2011; Tjaden and Thoennes 2000). It would be unsurprising if state (or state-funded) scientists were particularly invested in populations employed by or under the

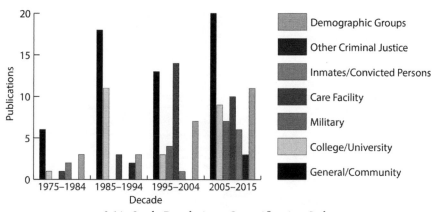

2.14. Study Populations, Quantification Only

care of state institutions (e.g., military and incarcerated populations). More-over, such agencies are often tasked with monitoring and ensuring the welfare of the general population, and may therefore be more inclined to approach sexual violence as a community problem. Even the comparative emphasis on demographic-based studies might be understood through the idiom of coproduction. This concept emphasizes the simultaneous production of scientific knowledge and social order (Jasanoff 2004). Within research on rape, agencies such as the Office on Violence against Women regularly receive grant applications for community-specific services and must be prepared to assess populations' relative need and/or worthiness of state support. In this sense, state actors would be invested not only in supporting state institutions but in determining and (re)inforcing state-approved understandings of which populations were most "in need" of scientific attention. For the most part, quantification scholars have been consistent over time in terms of study population. The only exception I found concerned research with care facilities such as rape crisis centers and hospitals, which rose and fell significantly over time.

Four Approaches to Locating the Problem

After completing content analysis of scientific publications, I selected four pieces for closer review. Considering overall trends in prevalence research, I chose studies that addressed victimization and varied in target population and space. To gain a sense of their relative impact, I then investigated each study's institutional and popular reception, including academic citations, press coverage, and other less formal coverage in various agency websites and online communities. In this section, I present an overview of study design, major findings, and reception for these four studies. I further

TABLE 2.2
Descriptive Statistics for All Publications and Quantification Pieces, by Decade

	All Publications				Quantification Pieces			
	1975–1984	1985–1994	1995–2004	2005–2015	1975–1984	1985–1994	1995–2004	2005–2015
Precasting[ac]	53 (30%)	91 (30%)	102 (26%)	90 (21%)	2 (18%)	9 (28%)	1 (3%)	6 (12%)
Study Aims:								
Quantification	11 (6%)	32 (10%)	33 (8%)	49 (11%)	–	–	–	–
Causes of Rape	91 (52%)	169 (55%)	200 (50%)	209 (49%)	6 (55%)	17 (53%)	16 (49%)	32 (65%)
Effects of Rape[b]	78 (44%)	113 (37%)	177 (44%)	221 (51%)	3 (27%)	9 (28%)	17 (52%)	19 (39%)
Evaluation	41 (23%)	76 (25%)	108 (27%)	115 (27%)	0 (0%)	2 (6%)	3 (9%)	6 (12%)
Theory/Methods[b]	16 (9%)	42 (14%)	63 (16%)	83 (19%)	4 (36%)	6 (19%)	5 (15%)	11 (23%)
Overall Focus:								
Victimization[b]	82 (47%)	140 (46%)	221 (55%)	283 (66%)	9 (82%)	29 (91%)	32 (97%)	45 (92%)
Perpetration[bc]	43 (24%)	77 (25%)	69 (17%)	68 (16%)	4 (36%)	12 (38%)	3 (9%)	8 (16%)
Professionals	49 (28%)	88 (29%)	118 (30%)	134 (31%)	2 (18%)	5 (16%)	7 (21%)	8 (16%)
Bystanders/General Public[bc]	59 (34%)	88 (29%)	118 (30%)	93 (22%)	1 (9%)	0 (0%)	4 (12%)	0 (0%)
Gendered Patterns:								
Victimization of Women	154 (88%)	275 (89%)	367 (92%)	387 (90%)	9 (82%)	30 (94%)	31 (94%)	43 (88%)
Victimization of Men[b]	12 (7%)	37 (12%)	60 (15%)	90 (21%)	2 (18%)	7 (22%)	12 (36%)	18 (37%)

TABLE 2.2 (*continued*)

	All Publications				Quantification Pieces			
	1975–1984	1985–1994	1995–2004	2005–2015	1975–1984	1985–1994	1995–2004	2005–2015
Perpetration by Women	3 (2%)	8 (3%)	14 (4%)	21 (5%)	0 (0%)	1 (3%)	2 (6%)	4 (8%)
Perpetration by Men[bd]	115 (65%)	196 (64%)	202 (51%)	172 (40%)	7 (64%)	16 (50%)	6 (18%)	13 (27%)
Study Population:								
General/Community	42 (24%)	91 (30%)	107 (27%)	142 (33%)	6 (55%)	18 (56%)	13 (39%)	20 (41%)
College/University	51 (29%)	106 (34%)	157 (39%)	165 (38%)	1 (9%)	11 (34%)	3 (9%)	9 (18%)
Military[b]	0 (0%)	0 (0%)	10 (3%)	21 (5%)	0 (0%)	0 (0%)	4 (12%)	7 (14%)
Care Facility[bd]	62 (35%)	73 (24%)	107 (27%)	95 (22%)	1 (9%)	3 (9%)	14 (42%)	10 (20%)
Inmates/Convicted Persons[b]	23 (13%)	33 (11%)	22 (6%)	27 (6%)	2 (18%)	0 (0%)	1 (3%)	6 (12%)
Other Criminal Justice	25 (14%)	52 (17%)	55 (14%)	43 (10%)	0 (0%)	2 (6%)	0 (0%)	3 (6%)
Demographic Groups	10 (6%)	22 (7%)	40 (10%)	45 (11%)	3 (27%)	3 (9%)	7 (21%)	11 (23%)

[a]p<.05, [b]p<.01 for full sample of publications in chi-square analysis; [c]p<.05, [d]p<.01 for quantification pieces

NOTE: Categories for study aims, overall focus, gendered patterns, and study population are not mutually exclusive. For example, a study may address both victimization of women and victimization of men.

discuss markers of scientific credibility within manuscripts and assess gendered precasting in study design and data interpretation.

Establishing the Scope of Rape

Given its historical significance, I began with Koss and colleagues' 1987 study from the *Journal of Consulting and Clinical Psychology*, "The Scope of Rape: Incidence and Prevalence of Sexual Aggression and Victimization in a National Sample of Higher Education Students." Researchers focused on postsecondary institutions in the United States and took a range of criteria, including region, racial/ethnic minority representation, proximity to urban settings, and type of institution (private, public, religious), into account when choosing schools. The final sample included 3,187 women and 2,972 men from 32 schools. Participants completed written surveys in classroom settings. In addition to gender and sexual violence histories, they were asked to disclose religious affiliation, family income, and race/ethnicity.

As mentioned above, Koss and colleagues drew on Ohio legislation to distinguish between rape and other forms of sexual violence, and on FBI definitions to identify women solely as potential victims and men solely as potential aggressors. When calculating incidence and prevalence rates, they classified participants according to the most severe incident reported (e.g., a woman who reported two incidents of unwanted sexual contact and one attempted rape was classified as a victim of attempted rape). Women reported lifetime rates of 54% for any sexual victimization, including 12% for attempted and 15% for completed rape. Men reported rates of 25% for lifetime perpetration, including 3% for attempted and 4% for completed rape. Study authors calculated six-month incidence rates of eighty-three victimizations per one thousand women (including thirty-eight rapes, as per FBI definitions) and thirty-four perpetrations per one thousand men (nine rapes, as per FBI definitions). The highest rate of victimization was reported by Native American women, followed by White, Hispanic, Black, and Asian women. The highest rate of perpetration was reported by Black men, followed by Hispanic, White, Asian, and Native American men. There were no statistically significant differences by family income or religion.

"The Scope of Rape" featured several identifiable markers of scientific credibility. Researchers appealed to state authority in justifying definitions of rape. They utilized the previously established Sexual Experiences Survey (Koss 1985; Koss and Oros 1982) to document violent incidents and conducted independent reliability and validity testing, adding a sense of standardization and replicability to their work (Timmermans and Epstein 2010). Perhaps anticipating critiques about generalization, they provided an extensive discussion of sampling and recruitment along with comparisons between the study sample and broader population of U.S. undergraduates.

Even the tone of the piece may be interpreted as strategic, or at least pro-ductive, within the credibility environment of professional scientific publi-cations (Shapin 1995). Whereas many investigations of rape blatantly approach readers' affect as an object-target (Anderson 2014), seeking to mobilize alarm and emotional investment, Koss and colleagues' writing was straight-forward and unemotional, and thus less vulnerable to critiques of being overly political (Whittier 2009).

Finally, Koss, Gidycz, and Wisniewski (1987) sought to preemptively identify and discredit potential opponents. Their literature review offered a thorough critique of prior quantification studies, casting doubt on other sci-entists' definitions, survey designs, and sampling frames. Their manuscript directly confronted discrepancies between researchers' and participants' assessments, insisting that some rapes are not "acknowledged as rape by the [woman] victim" and speculating that "some men fail to perceive accurately the degree of force and coerciveness that was involved in a particular sexual encounter or to interpret correctly a woman's nonconsent and resistance" (169). This established self-reports of experiencing or perpetrating rape as less authoritative than self-reports of experiences that met researchers' (and legislators' and federal officials') definitions of rape.

As noted above, these scientists conceptualized rape as a heterosexual phenomenon characterized by cisgender men's aggression toward cisgender women. Gendered assumptions were so firmly engrained that data for women and men appeared alongside one another in tables; readers were simply expected to recognize that women's reports concerned victimization (by men) and that men's concerned perpetration (against women). Women's aggression and men's victimization were rendered imperceptible through omission in survey questions and data tables. Sexual orientation and gender variance were rendered "area[s] of silence and difficulty," omitted from the narrative altogether (Clarke 2004, 74). Additionally, although findings var-ied significantly by race/ethnicity, the narrative presented rape as a gen-dered phenomenon without calling for a theoretical model that engaged both racism/White supremacy and sexism/patriarchy as causal forces (see Collins 2004; Combahee River Collective [1977] 2006; hooks [1984] 2000). Finally, in seeking "the scope of rape" through a study of college students, these scientists implicitly located this social problem among undergraduates and, to a lesser extent, on campus.

It should be noted that Koss has since moved toward approaches that incorporate the possibility of sexual victimization toward and sexual aggres-sion by people of all genders. Twenty-five years after introducing the Sexual Experiences Survey and twenty years after publishing "The Scope of Rape," she collaborated with an accomplished team of sexual violence scholars to revise the instrument (Koss et al. 2007). Revisions included "conversion to gender neutrality" (357), with options to (re)adopt gender-specific approaches "with minimal wording substitutions or deletions" (360). For example, one item now asks participants to indicate whether "someone had oral sex with me or made me have oral sex with them without my consent" under a range of coercive and forcible circumstances. It is difficult to assess the impact of such changes to date. Researchers may easily reintroduce gender-specific items or administration procedures to the SES, as encouraged by Koss and colleagues, or employ restrictive sampling frames that negate the more inclusive approach of revised measures. Nonetheless, researchers now have the option to utilize the SES without relegating men's victimization, women's aggression, and incidents involving nonbinary persons to a "lost realm" (Proctor 2008).

Koss, Gidycz, and Wisniewski's 1987 study received immense attention within and beyond the scientific field. To date, it has received more than 1,100 academic citations. Initially published in an academic journal, findings were quickly expanded and repackaged for general consumption in Robin Warshaw's *I Never Called It Rape* ([1988] 1994). At the time of this writing, a Lexis-Nexis search for "Mary Koss" and "rape" uncovered more than eighty pieces from multiple nations including the United States, Canada, the United Kingdom, and Australia. A substantial majority seemed to reference the 1987 study, including several published in recent years.

Study findings were controversial, and this was evident in the press coverage. Works alluding to an epidemic of violence gave way to more skeptical pieces within a few years. This shift was even the subject of an academic documentary, *The Date Rape Backlash* (Jhally 1994). More recently, particularly post-2000, there seems to have been a return to more supportive press coverage. It is also worth noting that Mary Koss's affective engagements in journalistic texts differed sharply from the academic manuscript. When quoted directly, she made consistent efforts to mobilize support for social change. Such approaches were likely better suited to the credibility environment of news media, in which overtly political and emotional narratives—including emotional calls to alarm in response to statistical knowledge—might hold equal or greater sway than dispassionate rhetoric (Epstein 1996; Woodward 1999).

Koss, Gidycz, and Wisniewski's work has also received a great deal of attention among bloggers and in activist communities. A Google search, using the same terms, produced more than eleven thousand hits. Many individuals and institutions have drawn supportively on the 1987 study, engaging its findings to (re)establish rape as an urgent problem. Others have drawn critically on this work, either to discredit anti-rape activism writ large or to pose specific criticisms concerning the researchers' theoretical and methodological approaches. Overall, though, "one in four women" remains a rallying point for antiviolence work. Numerous authors within and beyond academia continue to cite this statistic. "One in Four" is even the name of a national campus-based sexual violence prevention organization in the United States, despite subsequent studies' having produced different estimates (e.g., Krebs et al. 2007).

Sexual Violence and Incarceration

Controversy notwithstanding, Koss and colleagues' work helped to establish date rape as a concept in popular consciousness, and to garner institutional support for addressing rape on campus (Gavey [2005] 2018; Rutherford 2017). With the publication of *No Escape: Male Rape in U.S. Prisons*, the Human Rights Watch (2001) achieved something similar for rape among incarcerated persons. The report provided numerous case studies of men who had been assaulted by fellow inmates, a thorough consideration and critique of conditions that promote sexual violence in prison, and a call for better prevention and care services as well as rigorous investigations into the scope of inmate-on-inmate sexual violence. Institutional support followed through coverage in news and fictional media, and the passage of the *Prison Rape Elimination Act (PREA)* in 2003.

As its title suggests, *No Escape* did more than extend the problem of rape to prisons. This report located that problem among inmates in men's facilities. Authors stated that they had declined to consider staff-on-inmate violence. Regarding women's facilities, they claimed that data for staff-on-inmate violence in these spaces had been published elsewhere, and that they had discovered no information regarding sexual violence among women inmates: "if the problem of prisoner-on-prisoner sexual abuse exists in women's institutions—a possibility we do not exclude—it is likely to take somewhat different forms than in men's prisons" (6). While the Human Rights Watch was upfront about gendered assumptions in the introduction to *No Escape*, much of the remaining text obscured this through nonspecific references to "inmate-on-inmate" violence. The problem of inmate-on-inmate rape, if not rape in prison more broadly, was rendered practically synonymous with rape among incarcerated men.

Answering the call for quantification and funded by *PREA*, Nancy Wolff and colleagues set out to determine the prevalence of sexual violence in a state prison system. This system included one women's prison and twelve men's prisons. They invited all inmates in the general population and 10% of those in segregation units to complete a survey about the quality of life in prison; 6,964 men and 564 women agreed to participate. Victimization items addressed inmate-on-inmate and staff-on-inmate violence. Measures for sexual violence were separated by perpetrator (inmate-on-inmate versus staff-on-inmate) and time frame (prior six months versus the present bid/conviction). Given variation in bids/sentences, I focus here on data for six-month incidence rates. Other measures addressed gender, age, race/ethnicity, incarceration history, substance use history, and mental and physical health. The resulting study, "Sexual Violence inside Prisons: Rates of Victimization," was published in the *Journal of Urban Health* in 2006.

Like "The Scope of Rape" (Koss, Gidycz, and Wisniewski 1987), "Sexual Violence inside Prisons" employed two approaches to documenting victimization. Participants were asked directly whether they had ever been sexually assaulted by an inmate or member of staff. Ten additional questions addressed specific experiences, and were intended to document histories of nonconsensual sexual acts (forced oral, anal, and vaginal sex acts; the closest equivalent to "rape" in this study) and abusive sexual contact (unwanted sexual contact that did not qualify as forced sex). Participants reported lower rates of victimization through identitarian measures than through experiential measures. In other words, many would have been classified as "hidden" or "unacknowledged" victims by Koss. Wolff and colleagues calculated prevalence rates using unduplicated positive responses to general and specific measures. In other words, they employed a combined "narrative/identity as victim *or* qualifying experience" approach to quantification.

Women reported significantly higher rates of inmate-on-inmate sexual assaults for all measures (21% versus 4.3% for any sexual violence, 3% versus 1.5% for nonconsensual sex acts, and 20% versus 3.5% for abusive sexual contact in the previous six months). There were no significant gender differences in reported staff-on-inmate sexual assaults (7.6% versus 7.6% for any sexual violence, 1.7% versus 1.9% for nonconsensual sex acts, 6.6% versus 6.6% for abusive sexual contact). Overall, women were more likely to be assaulted by inmates than staff; the reverse was true for men. Younger inmates were also more likely to report victimization than older inmates.

Wolff and colleagues' manuscript featured several notable markers of scientific credibility. General victimization questions were adapted from the DOJ's *National Violence against Women and Men Survey*, and experience-specific items were based on definitions from the National Center for Injury Prevention and Control (housed within the CDC). These choices, along with repeated references to *PREA*, engaged state authority and scientific standardization (Timmermans and Epstein 2010). Perhaps anticipating skepticism, given the extent to which findings contradicted common understandings of prison rape, study authors offered a thorough critique of prior quantification studies with inmates. They argued that their approach would produce "more accurate estimates" (836) due to improvements in representativeness (sampling frame included all state prison inmates), validity (improved question design), and reliability (improved administration procedures, including computer-assisted methods). Acknowledging overreporting as a possibility, they tied this to credibility issues among participants in not-ing that even the most reliable methods would "not correct for bias moti-vated by custody officers or the prison system" (843). This point stood out within the broader field of quantification, as researchers tend to note under-reporting but not overreporting as a concern.[5]

In designing this project, Wolff and colleagues seemed to begin with the understanding that sexual violence was a problem inside prisons, and with recognition of two common perceptions about gendered patterns in aggression and victimization: first, that sexual violence was often conceived as a matter of noninstitutionalized men's violence toward noninstitutional-ized women, and second, that the concept of prison rape was largely con-fined to men's violence toward other men in the popular imagination. Their research suggested a relocation, or at least a broadened location, of the prob-lem of rape. Wolff and colleagues drew on preexistent structures of feeling (Anderson 2014; Woodward 1999)—collective senses and expectations of fear, concern, and hope for a less violent world—and redirected these affec-tive resources toward incarcerated women. Regarding violence against women more broadly, they pointed out that the "percent of inmate-on-inmate rape in women's prisons was over ten times higher than rape rates of adult women in the total population, and the rates for staff perpetrated rape is almost six times higher" (844). Regarding rape in prison, they noted that studies with incarcerated men outnumbered studies with incarcerated women at a rate of three-to-one. Regarding rape in men's prisons, they called for greater attention to staff-on-inmate violence.

In the decade since its publication, "Sexual Violence inside Prisons" has received nearly thirty academic citations. Wolff has been interviewed and referenced numerous times before and since, though not clearly in reference to this particular study. The only nonacademic reference I located was a 2006 article from the *New Jersey Star-Ledger* (Schwaneberg 2006), no longer accessible through the periodical's site. The journalist referenced Wolff and colleagues' data to argue that New Jersey had relatively low rates of prison rape, and repeated concerns about potential over-reporting of staff perpe-tration. The piece also quoted a Department of Corrections spokesperson who described women's reports as "surprising" and shared plans to increase surveillance in women's prisons.

Quantifying Gay, Lesbian, and Bisexual Victimization

Quantification rarely occurs in isolation. Scientists often include a series of demographic measures as a means of assessing relative risk, and to improve multivariable models by controlling for selected characteristics. This dimen-sion of study design entails heavy demands in methodological decision-making. Once scientists have selected variables for inclusion (e.g., race/

ethnicity), they must develop strategies for operationalizing them (e.g., which categories to include, whether to provide an "other" option, or to allow for multiple identifications). Subsequent decisions concern approaches to model building (e.g., whether to incorporate race/ethnicity as a predictor for sexual victimization), data interpretation (e.g., whether to approach racial variation in victimization as a consequence of racism), and presentation of findings (e.g., whether to call for a theoretical model that incorporates race/racism, or for further studies with particular race/ethnic populations, or simply report racial variations without further explication).

Rothman, Exner, and Baughman (2011) began with a demographic focus. Noting the widespread conceptualization of rape as a heterosexual phenomenon, but also recognizing a growing body of research concerning sexuality and victimization risk, they conducted a systematic review of literature quantifying sexual violence against gay, lesbian, and bisexual (GLB) individuals in the United States. The review was published in *Trauma, Violence, and Abuse* in 2011. Studies were selected for inclusion if they documented the incidence or prevalence of lifetime sexual assault, adult sexual assault, childhood sexual assault, intimate partner sexual assault, or hate crime sexual assault among gay, lesbian, and/or bisexual persons in the United States; had response rates of 30% or greater; and stratified findings by gender (i.e., did not combine data for men and women). After finding 4,511 potential works in an initial search, study authors identified 71 articles with data for 75 studies that met all inclusion criteria. Sample sizes ranged from 29 to more than 60,000, with a mean of 499. One-third of the studies utilized probability or census-based sampling, whereas the remaining two-thirds utilized nonprobability or convenience samples. I focus here on findings for lifetime and adult victimization.

Different studies employed different approaches to defining sexual violence, question design, recruitment, and survey administration. There was also striking variation in prevalence estimates. Among gay and bisexual men, estimates ranged from 12% to 54% for lifetime sexual assault and 11% to 45% for adult sexual assault. Among lesbian and bisexual women, estimates ranged from 16% to 85% for lifetime sexual assault and 11% to 53% for adult sexual assault. Overall, nonprobability samples yielded higher estimates than probability samples.

Study authors devoted considerable attention to methodological critique, which served to advance analyses and establish scientific credibility. More specifically, they drew attention to widespread reliance on nonprobability samples and variation in definitions of sexual violence, definitions of sexual orientation, recruitment strategies, and survey design. They compared estimates from GLB prevalence studies to data from established, highly cited studies with heterosexual or general populations in order to justify their claim that GLB communities faced higher risks.

More than any other publication selected here for close analysis, Rothman, Exner, and Baughman's (2011) review contested assumptions underlying the production of scientific knowledge. The most central of these was frequent omission of sexual orientation measures. Even among GLB prevalence studies, the authors noted a lack of data concerning assailants' gender and sexuality.[6] Overall, Rothman, Exner, and Baughman described GLB individuals as "vulnerable" to sexual victimization (63) and insisted that quality data were "urgently need[ed] in order to proceed with funded initiatives" (56). In making this argument, the authors notably connected scientific inquiries with service provision and resource distribution.

"The Prevalence of Sexual Assault against People Who Identify as Gay, Lesbian, or Bisexual in the U.S.: A Systematic Review" received nearly seventy academic citations in the five years since its publication. The study has received modest nonacademic attention. Boston University, Rothman's home institution, published a short overview. Boston's NPR station also quoted Rothman regarding sexual violence toward GLB individuals, in connection with a case at Brandeis University. While she has been quoted or consulted in several other news pieces, most concerned different work.

Surveying the General Population

By the start of this project, the CDC had conducted and published data from two rounds of the *National Intimate Partner and Sexual Violence Survey* (*NISVS*, Black et al. 2011; Breiding et al. 2014). Researchers employed random digit-dialing to survey English and Spanish-speaking members of the noninstitutionalized adult general population. Data for the second round were collected in 2011 and published by Matthew Breiding and colleagues in 2014. The final sample included 6,879 women and 5,848 men. Victimization measures addressed sexual violence, intimate partner violence, and stalking; I focus here on data for sexual violence. Other items addressed demographics, contextual factors (e.g., age at first assault) and outcomes (e.g., police contact) for violent experiences.

The *NISVS* defines rape as completed or attempted forcible penetration by an assailant, or completed drug-facilitated penetration by an assailant. Penetration may be oral, anal, or vaginal; and committed with a penis, other body part, or object. Other measures for victimization included being made to penetrate an assailant, coerced unwanted penetration, unwanted sexual contact, and unwanted noncontact sexual experiences. Participants were asked to report lifetime experiences, as well as any victimization within the previous twelve months. Women reported lifetime rates of 19%

for rape and 44% for other forms of sexual violence (including 1% for being made to penetrate an assailant), and twelve-month incidence rates of 2% and 6% for other forms of sexual violence (case count for being made to penetrate was too small to estimate incidence). Approximately 99% of women rape victims and 95% of women victims of other forms of sexual violence had exclusively male perpetrators. Men reported lifetime rates of 1.7% for rape and 23% for other forms of sexual violence (including 6.7% for being made to penetrate an assailant). The case count for rape was too small to calculate a twelve-month incidence rate; however, 5.1% of men reported other forms of sexual violence, including 1.7% who reported being made to penetrate an assailant. Approximately 79% of men who reported rape had only male perpetrators, whereas a majority of those who reported other forms of victimization, including 83% of those made to penetrate an assailant, had only female perpetrators.

CDC researchers emphasized racial patterns in victimization. Among women who reported rape, multiracial persons reported the highest rates, followed by Native American/Alaska Native, Black, Whites, and Hispanic persons; case counts were too small for other racial/ethnic groups to determine relative estimates. Among women who reported other forms of sexual victimization, multiracial persons reported the highest rates, followed by Native American/Alaska Native, White, Black, Hispanic, and Asian/Pacific Islander respondents. Among men who reported rape, counts were too small to determine relative prevalence estimates. Among men who reported other forms of sexual violence, multiracial persons reported the highest levels of victimization, followed by Hispanic, Native American/Alaska Native, Black, White, and Asian/Pacific Islander respondents. Researchers called for investigations into risk and protective factors that might vary by race/ethnicity and greater attention toward multiracial persons and American Indian/Alaska Native women.

The introduction and discussion of Breiding and colleagues' publication aimed to raise alarm and motivate action. This may indicate shifts in popular and scientific approaches to rape since the late 1980s. Whereas previous researchers were likely pressured to appear detached or apolitical in the earlier decades of anti-rape research and advocacy (Whittier 2009), researchers working in the 2010s perhaps had more freedom to present rape as an urgent, emotionally weighted, and widespread social problem entangled with systemic inequalities.

The narrative also featured several markers of credibility over and above that conveyed by the scientific and governing authority of the CDC. Prior to survey launch, study authors noted that data from 1995 to 1996 provided the best national prevalence estimates (see Tjaden and Thoennes 2000). The first

NISVS thus provided a noteworthy update with data from 2010. For the 2011 round, Breiding and colleagues pointed to improvements in survey design (e.g., dividing an item that addressed multiple forms of victimization into several items that each addressed a single form). This served to establish the scientific value of the *NISVS* in general and the second round of data in particular.

Even ostensibly gender-inclusive projects may adopt definitions, research instruments, and/or sampling frames that draw heavily from dominant rape scripts. In the cultural scenarios often designated as "typical date rapes" in research, cisgender heterosexual men assault cisgender heterosexual women, and commit acts of penile-vaginal assault. Scientists who engage these scenarios may incorporate those elements directly into vignettes or survey guides. Others may reject some components, such as the notion that only women can be raped or the restriction to penile-vaginal acts, but assume that other dimensions of sexual violence are otherwise relatively consistent. This occurs in vignette studies that incorporate male and female victims, while featuring only male aggressors who engage in penile penetration (e.g., Ford, Liwag-McLamb, and Foley 1998; McCaul et al. 1990; White and Kurpius 2002). Such work modifies the ontological gerrymandering evidenced in other forms of precasting: the sex assignments and gender identities of victims are allowed to vary, while those of aggressors are fixed as male/masculine. Studies that prioritize inclusivity, that embrace openness toward all gendered patterns in sexual violence, may precast even more subtly if aggression is presumed synonymous with penetration. Such was and remains the case with the *NISVS*.

In the first and second rounds of data collection, researchers restricted rape to the penetration of a victim by an assailant. In forcible contexts, even an attempt at penetration was sufficient to constitute rape. To put it more bluntly, a forcible penile-vaginal assault qualified as rape if and only if the person with the penis was the assailant; if the person with the vagina was the assailant, this incident constituted a "lesser" form of sexual violence. This distinction put CDC definitions at odds with numerous state criminal statutes (Levine 2018c; Whitman 2012), though it was consistent with FBI definitions and the Campus Sexual Assault Study (Krebs et al. 2007).

The restriction of aggression to penetration has distinct consequences for documenting (or producing) gendered patterns in rape. Figure 2.15 depicts the prevalence of rape reported in the 2011 *NISVS* (Breiding et al. 2014) using both the CDC definition and an expanded definition that includes being made to penetrate (the former is consistent with federal definitions including that of the FBI, while the latter is consistent with many state-level criminal statutes). Values for the latter represent upper estimates (i.e., sum of reports for both forms of assault). Figure 2.16 provides the same comparison for twelve-month incidence rates.

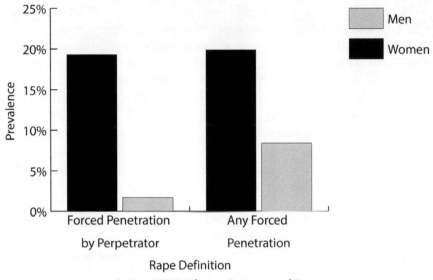

2.15. *NISVS* Lifetime Estimates of Rape

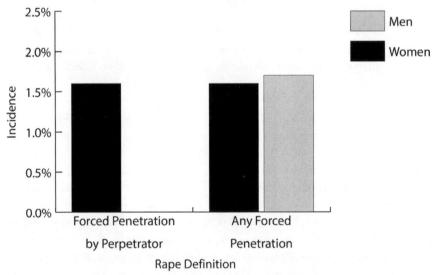

2.16. *NISVS* Annual Estimates of Rape

Data for women are minimally affected by this definitional shift. Lifetime rape estimates increase from 19.3% to 19.9%, whereas twelve-month incidence rape estimates remain at 1.6%. Data for men change substantially. When being made to penetrate is classified as rape, men's lifetime prevalence increases nearly fivefold from 1.7% to 8.4%. Men's twelve-month incidence moves from 0% to 1.7%. Gender differences in lifetime prevalence narrow considerably, though women continue to report substantially higher rates of violence. Gender differences in twelve-month incidence essentially vanish.

Rape definitions have further consequences for data on sexual aggression. Based on victims' reports in the *NISVS*, men comprise nearly the full population of rapists provided that rape is restricted to forced penetration by an assailant. If the definition expands to include forced envelopment/being made to penetrate an assailant, women comprise more than 80% of the aggressors who rape men.

The *NISVS* has received a great deal of academic and nonacademic attention. Breiding and colleagues' piece in the *Morbidity and Mortality Weekly Report* received more than thirty academic citations in the first two years after publication. Breiding also published an abridged version of this paper in the *American Journal of Public Health* (Breiding 2015). Outside of academic contexts, it was challenging to distinguish between references to the 2010 and 2011 surveys. A Lexis-Nexis search for the *NISVS* produced more than eighty relevant works from multiple countries, including the United States, Canada, New Zealand, Turkey, Ireland, India, and England (approximately one quarter seemed to draw specifically on the 2011 round). A Google search for "National Intimate Partner and Sexual Violence Survey," using quotation marks, produced more than thirty thousand hits. Most engaged CDC data to establish interpersonal violence as a widespread problem. The "one in five women" figure for lifetime prevalence of rape, reported in both rounds, was often cited as evidencing an epidemic.

Not all press coverage was supportive. After the 2010 round, Christina Hoff Sommers of the American Enterprise Institute accused CDC researchers of vastly overstating the prevalence of rape in the United States, going so far as to argue that the study demonstrated "the devastating impact that careless advocacy research can have on truth" (Sommers 2012). Her critique was published in the *Washington Post* and *St. Paul Pioneer Press*. Much like backlash critics in the 1990s, she did not dispute the CDC's implicit assumption that, of all gendered manifestations of sexual violence, men's violence toward women was most worthy of being called rape. Instead, she accused the researchers of political bias and poor methodology in order to challenge the accuracy of "one in five women."

PARTICIPANTS' INSIGHTS

Few participants in this project had worked directly on incidence and prevalence research. This seems unsurprising in retrospect, given that only 125 of the 1,313 abstracts identified concerned quantification. Nonetheless, most if not all were quite familiar with this literature and the cultural power of rape statistics. Participants and I also engaged in numerous discussions of definitions (see the appendix for the interview guide). Scholars shared personal and professional definitions of rape, sexual assault, sexual violence, and consent; and often spoke at length about the need (or lack thereof) to standardize definitions across scientific inquiries. Several individuals addressed the politics of defining rape, and the promise and limitations of quantification as a scholarly and activist project.

When asking directly for definitions of rape and other forms of sexual violence, I encountered varied and complex responses. Several individuals spoke of legal definitions as a reference tool, though no one seemed to endorse any particular federal or criminal statute(s) as comprehensively capturing these phenomena. Several participants restricted the notion of rape to penetrative assaults, which is consistent with most legislation in the United States and Canada. Others endorsed further-reaching definitions. Madeline, a sociologist, commented that "I work with a broad definition of rape—I use it interchangeably with sexual assault. It is bodily violation of a sexual nature, and it is not about sex, but about power." Stacey, a psychologist, shared that "with my participants, I talk about sex they didn't agree to, because I know that most of them don't call it rape or sexual assault, even if it legally qualifies." Stacey was also critical of the term "sexual violence," which I use most often in this project, based on concerns that such language "contributes to stereotypes of all sexual assault as physically violent and forceful."

Some participants declined to provide definitions altogether, or instead emphasized the complexities of sexual consent and violence. These scholars described a tremendous range of factors that might exert pressure or coercion, alongside what seemed to be an ever-growing scope of possibilities for sexually violent behaviors. Audrey, a public health scholar, shared that "these definitions change as we think about . . . new ways of committing violence." She was worried that sexual aggression in social media and other online spaces was increasingly prominent, particularly in students' and other young people's lives, but had not yet been adequately addressed in scholarly work. Julia, a social work scholar, struggled to incorporate alcohol and other substance use into prevalence measures due to variation in individuals' tolerance as well as concerns about mitigating aggressors' culpability:

> I do think the area where we still need some more work done is trying to understand alcohol and incapacitation, especially within the context of college campuses. These are the questions that have come up sometimes. Like exactly when is it that you're unable to give consent when you're drinking? And it's really hard to put that into a quantifiable formula, since everybody's different. It becomes really challenging to talk to students about these issues in a way that will meet the reality of what

their socializing and their drinking behaviors are. So I think that's an area where we still have a lot of work to do.

When I asked whether this complexity informed her approaches to study design and interpretation, she elaborated: "Yes. And also the concern that I think sometimes alcohol becomes a focus, and takes away from the fact that there's still accountability for someone's behaviors. So if the person who is the offender was drinking, that needs to be understood as something we need to address with prevention, but it also doesn't necessarily excuse the behavior. So I think it's really tricky." Participants whose work included alcohol and other substance-related sexual violence repeatedly echoed these concerns. Audrey, quoted above, commented that "we want one definition that fits every situation, and I don't know if we can ever get there."

As my interview research progressed, I found that participants' investment in defining rape and other forms of sexual violence—as well as their political and methodological concerns about such efforts—varied along several dimensions including discipline, project aims, and institutional context. Those with experience in quantification emphasized the value of experiential questions. Karen, a criminal justice scholar quoted at the beginning of this chapter, was insistent on this point. Margaret, a public health scholar, went so far as to say that her personal definitions were unimportant for her research, and that it might not even be necessary to produce standardized definitions for various forms of sexual violence. What mattered, instead, were methodological clarity and rigor in "capturing sexually coercive behaviors that range from what we might call 'nonsevere' or 'noninjurious' to the 'most severe' or 'most injurious.'" In contrast, Julia suggested that some hierarchical approaches to quantification "reflect this sort of lack of understanding that something that may not involve penetration, but is still a form of sexual violence, can still have really negative consequences." However, she shared Margaret's investment in clearly defining and documenting a range of sexually violent acts that reflected the tremendous variation in study participants' experiences.

Whereas quantification scholars emphasized precise and experiential questions, others focused more on individuals' self-identification and personal narratives of (non)victimization. Kristen, quoted at the beginning of this chapter, found value in encouraging people to "define it for themselves." Susan, a sociologist, worried that self-definition might be a prerequisite to seeking support services: "If you don't call it rape, you're probably not going to call rape crisis. So language is incredibly important. And you know, it's just as important to a person that you might study as it is to the person who is doing the studying. That's why survey construction is so important. You might be saying the wrong thing. People might misunderstand you. And I'm sure it happens, even in the best survey." Significantly, Susan tied this matter of self-definition back to the challenge of designing quantification surveys. Even "the best survey," with the most carefully crafted and evidence-based experiential or identitarian measures, might miss some experiences of violence. She elaborated that this was particularly concerning for those whose experiences diverged from dominant scripts, such as survivors of same-sex rape.

Researchers in prevention were comparatively less invested in precise or standard definitions, as their work sought to reduce sexual violence more broadly. Jenna, a public health scholar, shared the following: "Before, I was trying to define each [form of sexual violence] individually, give specifics for each of them, and I still do sometimes. But for the most part, I'm address-ing sexual violence overall. You know, whether that means harassment, whether that means touching, whether that means penetration. . . . It doesn't really change what I'm trying to do." Scholars who specialized in bystander prevention, many of whom were in public health, social work, and psychol-ogy, echoed Jenna's point. These researchers were invested in building a culture of prevention in which individuals recognized and intervened in attitudes and behaviors that constituted or otherwise contributed to sexual violence. It wasn't essential that people thought of themselves as specifically preventing rape, sexual assault, coercion, or harassment so long as they sought to recognize and intervene in aggressive or otherwise oppressive actions.

Definitions and measurement strategies were sometimes dictated by institutions or disciplinary conventions. Scholars who had collaborated with police or attorneys often found themselves compelled to work with legal discourses, even if they and their community partners found those dis-courses wanting. Diana, a public health scholar, described one such sce-nario: "We talk about every type of sexual violence in the context of 'what case made it to the DA's office' or 'which case then made it to [police].' . . . So we're always keeping in mind that there are all these different types of sexual violence, and we're definitely seeing them, but we know also that we're limited so much by what we can do because of those criminal justice definitions." Even though she and the criminal justice professionals with whom she collaborated wanted to address and document a substantial range of aggression and victimization, they felt constrained given their larger goals of improving reporting, police and prosecutorial processing, and court outcomes for sexual assault cases.

Funding agencies and disciplinary differences also exerted pressure on scholars' articulations of rape. Even while discussing her dislike for the term "sexual violence," Stacey noted that she might well (have to) use this language if she ever pursued Centers for Disease Control funding. Rebecca, a public health scholar, elaborated on this issue: "In order for us to be competitive and responsive to federal grants coming from the CDC or DOJ, we have a certain set of language that we use when we apply to those places. CDC, we're going to use the term 'sexual violence.' We're going to talk about survivors and perpetrators. If we're applying to the DOJ, we're going to talk about 'rape and sexual assault' and we're going to talk about victims and perps." These language shifts also entailed definitional shifts. Public health understandings of sexual violence constitute a broader range of actions than criminal justice understandings of rape and sexual assault. Humanities and social science definitions might be broader still, or further separated from state discourses. Rebecca commented that she often ran into conflicts with scholars from women's and gender studies programs who preferred the language of "gender-based violence." In these moments, she found herself torn between improving her chances of funding and maintaining mutual and effective scholarly collaborations. Further complicating matters, Miranda, an anthropologist, commented that different projects—and scholars affiliated with different disciplines and institutions—might tend toward fundamentally different conceptualizations of rape and other forms of sexual violence, and that this might impact definitions and overall study designs. Someone approaching rape as a "therapeutic object" might focus on people who self-identify as victims/survivors, as is common in projects that sample through victim support services. Alternatively, someone approaching rape as a "legal object" might prioritize people whose experiences of victimization or perpetration align with criminal statutes.[7]

Gender came up again and again in conversations about sexual violence definitions. More often than not, this occurred without immediate or direct prompting from me. While participants shared a range of personal approaches to this matter, many believed that the field was shifting toward an increasingly gender-neutral approach. Stacey mentioned that although she sometimes "still see[s] people writing things like, 'women can't perpetrate rape against men because it's only the penetration that defines it as rape, and defines it as that level of trauma,'" she also believed that scholars "usually now try to make [measures of sexual violence] gender-neutral." Tanya, a criminologist, spoke positively of "new gender-neutral statutes" and "definitions that incorporate the fact that sexual assault can be committed by and against men and women, boys and girls. And that it is not simply penile-vaginal intercourse."

Across these discussions, one particular tension stood out to me. Several participants expressed support for what they termed "gender-neutral" definitions, while also sharing concerns that neutrality might obscure the reality of pervasive gendered patterns in sexual violence. Similar concerns arose around queer and transgender inclusion. Rebecca commented:

> We have, I think, a little bit of a double-edged sword with intersectionality. In that sexual violence prevention and response has to be intersectional, right? Our women's movement was largely White educated women saying "here's what's what." And women of color have been ignored. LGBTQ folks have been ignored. And I think that we have to be intentionally intersectional with our work. The other side of that, I think, is that when we try very hard to be inclusive in a lot of ways, we also lose sight of the fact that most victims of sexual violence are cisgender straight women and most perpetrators of sexual violence are cisgender straight men.

In a similar vein, Leigh, a psychologist, remarked, "While I would argue rape is very much gendered, the hetero model of 'man rapes woman with penis in vagina' is obviously [problematic]. . . . The FBI changed their definition. So that's good, right, we're getting somewhere, but we have a long way to go to capture people's experiences." It is critical to note here that both Rebecca and Leigh—and other participants who expressed similar perspectives—were invested in documenting, preventing, and responding to all incidents of sexual violence regardless of who the perpetrators and victims were. The challenge was finding a way to do this without sacrificing a gendered analysis altogether.

The concept of gender inclusivity may be of value here. Whereas gender neutrality is essentially incompatible with a gendered analysis—provided that gender neutrality is equated with the assumption that gender is irrelevant—inclusivity offers a more nuanced intervention. Rather than precast individuals and communities in gender-specific trajectories, an inclusive approach would allow scholars and activists to retain emphases on patriarchy and violence against women while simultaneously acknowledging that people of any gender might enact the status of aggressor/perpetrator or victim/survivor. Patriarchal accounts of rape comprised and continue to comprise a profound feminist intervention in scientific and other social discourses (Brownmiller 1975; Lonsway and Fitzgerald 1994; Russell 1975; Yodanis 2004). Some opposition to Koss and others' projects is undoubtedly due to their association with feminism (Gavey [2005] 2018; Jhally 1994; Rutherford 2017). Male domination remains a powerful force within rape culture. Female empowerment remains a central and valuable component for many rape prevention and response initiatives (Senn 2011). I believe that gender-inclusive accounts, particularly those that incorporate but do not restrict themselves to patriarchal forces, will comprise a further feminist intervention into scientific knowledges of sexual violence.

COUNTING WITH ACCOUNTABILITY

The question "how common is rape?" is not inconsequential. Scientists' approaches to defining rape, developing sampling frames, designing and administering surveys, and interpreting findings serve to locate the problem in different populations and spaces. Once scientists have published their work, other actors may determine the impact of their efforts. Colleagues effectively shape the lifespan of publications and the scientific facts therein through opting or declining to cite them (Latour 1987). Journalists, state officials, activists, and other consumers of scientific knowledge may influence the trajectory of those facts outside of the academy. Given the credibility and overall significance awarded scientific knowledge in the United States, particularly statistical data (Epstein 1996; Jasanoff 2005; Shapin 1995; Waidzunas 2012; Woodward 1999), scientists who study rape have the potential to shape institutional policy, data collection practices, resource distribution, targeted prevention efforts, and the availability of services for people who have experienced and/or committed acts of sexual violence. The very perceptibility of violence, of survivors and assailants, is at stake (Cardi and Pruvost 2015; Murphy 2006; Proctor 2008).

In this chapter, content analyses of abstracts revealed substantive differences between the overall field of research on rape and the subfield of quantification. Whereas the broader field has consistently favored research with college students, quantifiers have favored the general population. Those counting rape have been more inclined to target smaller and/or marginalized populations, particularly in the past two decades. It seems that populations prioritized for quantification may receive comparatively limited attention from researchers who investigate individual and collective risk factors; social, health, and behavioral outcomes; and the impact/efficacy of policy and interventions. Moreover, scientists who study rape have consistently emphasized victimization over perpetration, and this pattern is particularly pronounced among quantification studies. This limits the capacity of prevalence research to inform perpetration prevention.

Close readings of individual studies served to illuminate the scope of decision-making required for quantification, and the capacity of these processes to shape conceptualizations of rape. In Koss, Gidycz, and Wisniewski's "The Scope of Rape" (1987) and the 2011 *NISVS*, definitions ensured the documentation of (men's) sexual violence against women and reduced or foreclosed the documentation of other gendered patterns. Wolff and colleagues reaffirmed Koss, Gidycz, and Wisniewski's finding that question wording affects estimates, in that general or identitarian measures (e.g., "Have you ever been raped?," "Do you consider yourself a rape victim or survivor?") produce lower counts than experience-based measures (e.g., "Have you ever been forced to have oral sex?," "Has anyone ever had sex with you against your will?").

Study authors revealed different perspectives regarding which variables to address and how to interpret (non)significance. Only one of the four studies assessed here directly addressed sexual orientation (Rothman, Exner, and Baughman 2011), and only one addressed religion (Koss, Gidycz, and Wisniewski 1987). While all four empirical studies addressed race/ethnicity, operationalizations varied. This was likely due to a range of factors including study population and sample size concerns (e.g., smaller proportions of Asian American and Native American inmates relative to the general population), varying consultations of Census forms and other state projects (which are themselves subject to change), and disciplinary conventions. When scientists found significant variation by race/ethnicity, they provided different interpretations. Koss and colleagues and Breiding and colleagues both documented elevated rates of victimization among Native American women (Breiding et al. 2014; Koss, Gidycz, and Wisniewski 1987). In the former study, researchers noted this briefly in the results section, and proceeded to concentrate on gender and heterosexual dynamics when interpreting data. In the latter case, researchers emphasized racial variation, and advocated that Native American women be considered a priority population for targeted interventions.

Such decision-making in science produces different answers to the question "how common is rape," and related questions such as "who can rape," "who can be raped," and "where does rape happen." Is rape fundamentally a matter of violence against women? Of men's violence against women? And if so, which women are most in need of social support and scholarly attention? Are women capable of raping anyone? Is it sufficient to consider patriarchy and sexism as causal forces? Do other forces of oppression such as colonialism and homophobia bear consideration? Would care services be more effective if they targeted particular regions, institutions, or demographic populations? These are empirical questions, surely. Yet it would be a mistake to presume that any of them have a single True (or even Truest) empirical answer. Answers will vary along with scientists' approaches to study design and data interpretation, which are themselves subject to influence by peers, institutional pressures, resource constraints, disciplinary conventions, gatekeeping in publishing, social movements, historical events, and (perceptions of) public opinion (Bourdieu 1975; Epstein 1996; Epstein 2006; Jasanoff 2004; Latour 1987; Shapin 1995; Shapin and Schaffer [1985] 2011; Waidzunas 2012).

Analyses of reception reaffirmed prior scholarship on the gravity awarded statistical knowledge (Jasanoff 2005; Porter 1995). However, simply utilizing "the language of numbers" was insufficient (Jasanoff 2005, 265). Figures that lent themselves toward compelling headlines and calls to alarm were more impactful. "The Scope of Rape" was widely praised and critiqued for documenting that "one in four women" had experienced completed or attempted rape, whereas the perpetration finding of "one in twelve men" was largely overlooked. Coverage of the *NISVS* frequently emphasized "one in five women" without dwelling on "one in fifty-nine men." Yet headline-worthiness, too, seems insufficient to explain variation in academic and other reception. Some studies garnered minimal attention despite high estimates. Rothman, Exner, and Baughman (2011) reported that up to 85% of queer women and 54% of queer men report lifetime sexual violence. Nonetheless, "four in five queer women" and "one in two queer men" have yet to attain anything close to the status of "one in four women." Whereas the Human Rights Watch's (2001) *No Escape* received immense attention from state officials and journalists, and was a driving force behind the *Prison Rape Elimination Act*, Wolff and colleagues' (2006) prevalence study has had far less of an impact in popular contexts. Dominant conceptualizations of prison rape continue to locate this problem in men's facilities. Dominant conceptualizations of rape more broadly, particularly outside of such institutions, continue to locate this problem in heterosexual encounters with cisgender men as aggressors and cisgender women as victims.

While I hesitate to draw overly firm or sweeping conclusions from such a limited inquiry, I suspect that quantification studies attract attention to the extent that they (a) produce noteworthy figures, such as "one in four women" *and* (b) otherwise do not disrupt dominant conceptualizations of rape. More specifically, based on my broader content analysis and in-depth review of these four studies, I argue that incidence/prevalence estimates receive more coverage to the extent that they do not disrupt the patriarchy model of rape (sometimes referred to as the "classic feminist model" or "feminist hypothesis"; see Eschholz and Vieraitis 2004). This model attributes the problem of rape wholly or predominantly to patriarchy, and envisions individual cisgender men's acts of sexual aggression toward cisgender women as an interpersonal manifestation of societal male dominance and female subordination (see also Fassin 2007; Haag 1996). Some scholars have expanded this to incorporate other dimensions of oppression, such as race and class (e.g., Eschholz and Vieraitis 2004). Nonetheless, and more importantly for this project, the patriarchy model understands rape as a subset of men's violence toward women. Of the four studies selected here for close analysis, those most widely cited within and beyond academia were those that most supported the patriarchy model.

Implicit reliance on patriarchal explanations may further account for the failure of rape among incarcerated women to achieve the social recognition awarded rape among incarcerated men. Indeed, multiple studies of inmate-on-inmate sexual violence in men's facilities have highlighted assailants' heterosexual identities and lives on the outside. Scholars investigating sexual violence in men's facilities may presume that inmates would target women, were any available, and commit same-sex rape merely as an adaptation to prison conditions. Victimized men are thereby (re)envisioned as surrogate women whose suffering may be accounted for by patriarchy (Brownmiller 1975; Collins 2004).[8] To consider that "the rage that motivates violence and the desire to dominant [sic] that motivates rape [may be] traversing the gender divide," to envision women as capable of perpetrating sexual violence, would represent a far greater challenge to dominant perspectives (Cardi and Pruvost 2015; Wolff et al. 2006, 844).

Interview participants further illuminated the complexities of quantification. For the sake of consistency and comparability, it can be valuable to standardize experiential measures for predefined types of sexual violence. Yet discursive variation can make it difficult to standardize across disciplines and (grant-providing) institutions. There are also political dimensions to these differences. Terms such as rape, sexual assault, sexual violence, unwanted sexual contact, nonconsensual sex, and gender-based violence carry different connotations and are apt to affect producers and consumers of scientific knowledge differently. The definition of rape is particularly high-stakes (Spohn and Horney 1992). Moreover, although experiential measures are widely considered to produce "better" estimates—and are necessary to ensure that individuals whom some scholars might classify as "hidden" or "unacknowledged" victims are counted—such approaches may run counter to study participants' perceptions, and deprive individuals of the capacity to define their experiences for themselves. Even some individuals who do "acknowledge" their experiences as rape or sexual assault may go uncounted if experiential measures exclude them. Related, several participants expressed a strong investment in building approaches that were inclusive of all genders and sexualities, but also worried that gender-neutral measures might mitigate efforts to combat patriarchy and to align anti-rape efforts with feminist efforts to end violence against women.

For all the concerns raised here, locating the problem of rape is not inherently problematic. This may be an unavoidable consequence of quantification, which remains central to raising awareness and developing effective prevention and response measures. The analyses here do not so much support a rejection of prevalence research as a move towards more critical scholarship. Scientists should continue to count rape. They/we must also pursue accountability. This means embracing reflexive approaches, and acknowledging our own partial perspective(s) as well as those of study participants and others who produce and consume knowledge about rape. It means striving for transparency in presentations and publications. Perhaps most importantly, it means recognizing our capacity to produce knowledge and ignorance, to draw attention toward some forms of violence while rendering others imperceptible. Accountable scholarship demands openness to diverse perspectives, including a willingness to reassess and sometimes revise our own definitions and assumptions. These aims align with a feminist successor science that regards objectivity as situated knowledge; recognizes intra-active connections among scientific observers, surveys and other instruments of measurement, and objects of study in the generation of scientific knowledge; and favors responsibility and justice over appeals to detached or innocent truths (Barad 2007; Flax 1992; Haraway 1988; Haraway 1997; Harding 1995; Harding 1986). Rather than shy away from quantification, or obscure the limited generalizability of particular findings, scientists might consider and transparently address the social influences, ethical concerns, and theoretical and methodological decision-making processes behind our efforts to count incidents of rape.

CHAPTER 3

Accounting for Rape

The only way [biologists] fit into the conversations was
that we were completely in agreement with the people
who had thought and written about rape, social scientists
and feminists, completely in agreement that we wanted to
end rape.   —Adam, biologist

Presumably, if we're talking about how complicated
consent is, one might say we're implying—and probably,
in some cases, we are implying—that sexual assault can
occur due to communication. And that's a potentially
controversial statement.   —Stacey, psychologist

CAUSAL INQUIRIES CONCERN the conditions/objects that pro-
mote and deter rape and other forms of sexual violence. Some seek to account
for the existence of such violence. Others prioritize strategies for prevention,
which may involve intervening in social circumstances, cultural practices,
ideologies, institutional policies, and other matters that might otherwise facilitate sexual aggression or victimization. From an agential realist perspective,
causality is a rather amorphous concept. The same is true of effects, which
feature in the next chapter (Barad 2007). Sexual violence may be conceived
as a distinct and quantifiable object (or event or outcome), as an object with
distinct and identifiable causes, or as a causal force that accounts for other
objects. Yet cause-effect relations are, themselves, entangled within phenomena. Scientists must enact particular agential cuts to distinguish an object from
its causes or effects or both. Even within "the same" study conducted by "the
same" scientist(s), agential cuts may vary in accordance with shifting research
questions or professional pressures or even dispositions and curiosities.

   The complexity of distinguishing causation may be made clearer with
an example. It is common in quantitative research to justify causal claims
with chronology. If event A occurs before event B, then event A might rea-
sonably be proposed as a cause (e.g., healthcare access and use during high
school might be proposed as causal predictors of general health during college, given that the former ends before the latter begins). Alternatively, one

might justify causal claims with claims about relative fixity or "stickiness." In this case, researchers expect that the more fixed a particular object or event or characteristic is, the more likely it is to serve a causal function (e.g., the status of having or not having a diagnosed chronic illness might be proposed as a causal predictor of how healthy one feels, given that diagnoses do not change as rapidly or readily as feelings of wellness). As a statistics professor, I have often instructed my students to think along these lines. But how easy is it to distinguish chronology or fixity? To determine when event A ends and event B begins, or which is stickier? How many approaches might scientists employ?

For a pertinent example, consider the relationship between rape myths and incidents of rape (Edwards et al. 2011; Lonsway and Fitzgerald 1994; Muehlenhard 2011; Ryan 2011). If Mitchell, a cisgender and heterosexual man, believes that "women who say 'no' are playing hard to get" and that "it's the man's job to initiate sex" and that "sexier men are more aggressive" and that "silence means 'yes,'" might these beliefs inform his own engagement in sexual aggression? Might he misinterpret a woman as consenting if she says "no" or says nothing? Might he commit an act of rape while simultaneously believing that he is simply having sex? Imagine that Gillian, a transgender and heterosexual woman, shares these beliefs to an extent. If Mitchell behaves aggressively with her, might she feel reluctant or even unable to stop him or to even conceive of him as problematically aggressive? Might she feel pressured to "let him be a man" or to downplay his violation of her own boundaries? Might she face additional pressures as a transgender woman to embrace stereotypically feminine sexual behaviors, or feel somehow "grateful" for Mitchell's attention? If Mitchell knows that Gillian is transgender, and that some of his (transphobic) friends might mock him for pursuing her, might he feel pressured to be particularly "manly" or "dominant" in the encounter?

If any of this is possible, how might a scientist account for an incident in which Mitchell rapes Gillian? To what extent might a variable such as "endorsement of rape myths" or "patriarchal attitudes" or "transphobic attitudes" cause that rape, and to what extent might these forces be part of it? Does the rape begin if/when Mitchell breaks the law? When he first interprets refusal as consent? When Gillian first feels violated? Perhaps shortly before their encounter, when Mitchell fantasizes about aggressively pursuing Gillian? Or when he makes sexist or sexual comments about her in front of friends, who then reward him by joining in or punish him by making transphobic jokes? Or perhaps well before that, when Mitchell and Gillian are both socialized to recognize and (at least to some extent) endorse strict gender roles in (hetero)sexual encounters? Might sexual aggression and endorsement of rape myths come to have a circular or reciprocal causal relationship, such that belief in rape myths facilitates sexual aggression which in turn increases investment in rape myths (particularly if Mitchell is accused of rape, and defends himself by appealing to problematic and sexist/transphobic beliefs about rape and seduction)? Cause and effect, like the beginning and end of events, cannot be disentangled within sexually violent and other phenomena. Nonetheless, scientific inquiries require the enactment of agential cuts that render various objects and relationships perceptible.

For the purposes of this project, I conceptualize "the causes of sexual violence" broadly, and often defer to scholars' own depictions of their scientific aims. Causal works may explore individual-level risk factors for aggression and victimization, including but not limited to knowledge and attitudes about sexual violence, engagement in what scientists understand as "risk behaviors," mental and physical health, and—somewhat circuitously— prior history of violence and traumatic experiences. On a more interpersonal level, causal works might explore the social dynamics that facilitate or prohibit intervention in dangerous circumstances, or the communication of sexual consent and refusal. Individual and peer group beliefs, such as the endorsement of what are broadly conceived as rape myths, are also frequently proposed as causal factors due to the (empirically supported) assumption that people who adhere to rape-supportive attitudes are more apt to engage in or downplay others' acts of sexual aggression.

On a more systemic level, causal inquiries might explore the capacity for social institutions to promote or justify rape. This might include school curricula, film and television programs, or religious practices that implicitly or explicitly convey patriarchal and other oppressive ideals. I have also included institutional prevention efforts in this chapter. This is consistent with the logic of the field. Bystander intervention curricula, for example, instruct people to identify social conditions that may promote or deter aggression and victimization. Program participants are not instructed to seek out and intervene in assaults in progress, but rather to intervene in the conditions that facilitate rape. Many programs further incorporate (hetero) sexual assumptions regarding who perpetrates and experiences victimization. The targets of such interventions are many. They include potential bystanders, who ultimately serve as preventive agents in the effort to end sexual violence; potential sexual aggressors, whose aims are meant to be thwarted by those agents; potential victims, whose safety is meant to be an active priority among those agents; and a considerable breadth of social practices ranging from sexist jokes to overt acts of aggression, all of which might arguably contribute to the complex phenomenon of rape culture. Again, I have largely deferred to scientists' own descriptions of their research as seeking to account (or not) for the existence of sexual violence.

Causal inquiries have not been without controversy. Two particularly contested lines of work concern evolutionary explanations, such as the work of Randy Thornhill and Craig Palmer (2000); and (mis)communication models that rely on scripted expectations of "token resistance" and complex understandings of consent, as introduced by Charlene Muehlenhard and her colleagues (Muehlenhard and Hollabaugh 1988; Muehlenhard and McCoy 1991; Muehlenhard and Rodgers 1998; Peterson and Muehlenhard 2007). These scholars and projects diverge in many respects. Thornhill and Palmer are experts in biology who draw sharp distinctions between scientific research and what they refer to as "social science" work driven by "feminist ideology" (Palmer and R. Thornhill 2003; R. Thornhill and Palmer 2000). Muehlenhard, by contrast, is a psychologist who openly aligns herself with feminist scholarship (2011). Evolutionary models have been subjected to immense public scrutiny (Dreger 2015; Gavey [2005] 2018), whereas conflict over token resistance models has been relatively contained within activist and scholarly domains (Muehlenhard 2011). Thornhill and Palmer approached their book with the assumption that human rape was connected with human evolution, though the precise mechanisms remained unknown (2000). When she began studying sexual (mis)communication, Muehlenhard seemed to consider the very existence of women's token resistance behaviors open to question (2011; Muehlenhard and Hollabaugh 1988).

For all their differences, there are important connections between evolutionary and communication-based accounts. Their audiences (if not necessarily their adherents) overlap, as noted by publication in common outlets such as the *Journal of Sex Research* (e.g., Palmer and R. Thornhill 2003; Peterson and Muehlenhard 2007). Furthermore, both approaches have drawn criticism through their refutation of dominant assumptions. More specifically, these scholars have faced credibility challenges for questioning closely guarded matters of scientific fact about rape. This is not to say that all criticisms faced by Thornhill and Palmer, on one hand, and Muehlenhard and colleagues, on the other, are attributable to this. Nonetheless, the fact that these scholars faced pushback for challenging presumably settled notions in rape research is valuable for understanding social processes within this scientific field.

In this chapter, I present a brief discussion of these two controversies and their overlapping challenges to established discourses in sexual violence research. Afterwards, I review my own findings regarding historical trends in causal literature via quantitative content analysis of abstracts, as well as dominant themes over time via close readings of the ten most highly cited causal works in each decade from 1975 to 2015 (forty studies total). I then present insights into causal research from interview participants. Throughout these analyses, I argue that causal research has been historically dominated by psychological and psychiatric inquiries, and that the most widely cited works seek to account specifically for cisgender men's violence toward cisgender women in heterosexual contexts. There is a rich literature on individual-level predictors for this particular gendered pattern in sexual violence. Considerable gaps remain regarding interpersonal and systemic causes as well as any and all factors that might promote or deter cisgender women's aggression, cisgender men's victimization, same-sex violence, and incidents involving transgender individuals (including transgender women, transgender men, and persons with nonbinary gender identifications). I further argue that fears of misuse comprise a central mechanism within causal research, influencing many scientists' approaches to accounting for rape as well as their reception and career trajectories within and beyond academia.

EVOLUTIONARY BIOLOGY AND THE CONTROVERSY OVER ULTIMATE CAUSATION

In *A Natural History of Rape*, Thornhill and Palmer (2000) offered a harsh critique of scholars and activists who approached sexual violence as nonbiological. More specifically, they rejected patriarchal theories that depicted rape as a cultural product of male domination, driven by efforts to humiliate and subordinate females and wholly unconnected to human evolution and sexual desire. Thornhill and Palmer did not suggest that sexist ideals and social practices were irrelevant to the problem of rape, but rather that such factors were only conceivable as *proximate* or immediate causes. They further argued that scientists, advocates, and other human actors would be unable to meaningfully understand and reduce sexual violence without inquiring into its *ultimate* or evolutionary causes.

By the time they published together, both scholars were already well established in biological research on sexual violence. Working with Nancy Thornhill, Randy Thornhill had previously published "completely testable" evolutionary hypotheses of men's sexual violence toward women, including variation in victims' and aggressors' age and social class (R. Thornhill and N. W. Thornhill 1983, 168); and a four-part series exploring biological explanations for women's psychological pain following rape (N. W. Thornhill and R. Thornhill 1990a; 1990b; 1990c; 1991). Two proposals in *A Natural History of Rape*—namely, that rape might be (1) an adaptation among humans or (2) a byproduct of the evolutionary development of male and female sexuality—were previously suggested by Palmer in a 1991 essay. He had also published multiple works challenging the patriarchy-only model of rape (Palmer 1988; Palmer, DiBari, and Wright 1999).

As per their own accounts (Palmer and R. Thornhill 2003), as well as a discussion of their experiences in a recent work on scientific controversies

(Dreger 2015), evolutionary models were well received among (biological) scientists. It was expansion to general audiences that drew controversy. Such controversy arose notwithstanding the fact that Thornhill and Palmer anticipated an audience familiar with dominant cultural and patriarchal explanations of rape, but unfamiliar with biological science. Given this, they took pains to introduce core principles in evolutionary theory, including numerous overviews of ultimate and proximate causation. They cautioned against the naturalistic fallacy, which occurs when "the natural" is inappropriately equated with "the morally correct." This point was reinforced through repeated insistences that understanding the ultimate causes of rape was essential for reducing the incidence of sexual violence and providing support for victims and other affected persons. In other words, they portrayed rape as simultaneously natural and morally reprehensible. In the introduction and conclusion chapters, they spoke of a friend and rape victim who had long been frustrated by widespread claims that "rape is about power, not sex," and who had found validation in their model's connection of human rape with human sexuality. They argued that scientists and others who ignored ultimate causation—that is, whose agential cuts precluded the perception of evolutionary forces—constrained their own capacity to understand and end rape.

From the moment of publication, *A Natural History of Rape* was subjected to immense criticism. Both authors received numerous hate letters and death threats (Dreger 2015). Many academic critics argued that the book provided justification for men's sexual violence toward women, questioned the authors' rejection of feminist (often described in the text as "ideological") causal models, and portrayed the authors' engagement with evolutionary data as incomplete or unconvincing (Dunbar 2000; Gavey [2005] 2018; Lloyd 2001; Seto 2000; Tang-Martinez and Mechanic 2001; Travis 2003; Wolfthal 2001).

In 2003, Thornhill and Palmer published a response in the *Journal of Sex Research*. They argued that many opponents uncritically disparaged the use of evolutionary models to account for human rape. They further criticized actors in scholarly and other domains for offering simplistic and misguided interpretations of their argument, rather than offering meaningful challenges to their specific theoretical and empirical analyses. Reiterating the potential for ultimate explanations to inform prevention work, they condemned what they perceived as others' perpetuation of the naturalistic fallacy and stated that "the question of whether traits such as human rape are adaptations or by-products cannot be answered unless hypotheses about adaptation are proposed" (255). Moreover, they noted that reception to their ideas within and outside of biology had not been strictly negative (see also Dunbar 2000).

In her review of the controversy surrounding *A Natural History of Rape*, Alice Dreger[1] (2015) further commented that hate mail and scholarly critiques came in alongside numerous letters from rape victims/survivors who found validation and comfort in Thornhill and Palmer's work.

Seduction Scripts, Token Resistance, and the Potential for Date Rape

Charlene Muehlenhard became interested in the notion of token resistance, or incidents in which individuals "say no to sex when they mean yes," through two personal encounters (as described in Muehlenhard 2011, 677). She was studying acceptance of the traditional sexual script at the time, and drafting a measurement tool to assess survey participants' belief that women engaged in token resistance. When discussing this project with the secretary of her psychology department, Muehlenhard was surprised when "she commented that she sometimes said no to sex when she meant yes." Muehlenhard quickly became "interested because I did not know that this actually happened" (677). Shortly afterwards, a student disclosed having previously engaged in token resistance behaviors with an ex-boyfriend. Later, when another partner declined to take this student's genuine refusals seriously (he happened to be a friend of this same ex-boyfriend), she reported having stopped engaging in token resistance altogether.

These experiences inspired what would prove to be decades of research in sexual communication, including real and perceived engagement in token resistance and the complexities of consent more broadly. The first of these studies assessed women's engagement in token resistance via the following prompt: "You were with a guy who wanted to engage in sexual intercourse and you wanted to also, but for some reason you indicated that you didn't want to, although *you had every intention to and were willing to engage in sexual intercourse*. In other words, you indicated 'no' and you meant 'yes'" (Muehlenhard and Hollabaugh 1988, 874, italics in original). Nearly 40% of women reported doing so at least once. Shortly afterwards, Muehlenhard and McCoy (1991) explored variation in women's reports of engaging in token resistance (described as "scripted refusal" in this text, as per the editors' request—see Muehlenhard 2011) as well as open acknowledgment behaviors, in which they both indicated and meant yes. Approximately 14% of women reported exclusive engagement in token resistance, whereas 24% reported both token resistance and open acknowledgment. Women in this latter group seemed to base their actions in part on their partners' perceived values and desires.

Other scholars soon joined this line of research, working to refine operationalizations of token resistance and incorporate a broader range of populations (Shotland and Hunter 1995; Sprecher et al. 1994). Muehlenhard continued to refine her methods and explore complexities in sexual communication.

In 1998, she coauthored a study of men's and women's engagement in token resistance (Muehlenhard and Rodgers 1998). In addition to its gender inclusivity, this study was innovative in that participants were asked to consider various contexts (e.g., heterosexual encounters with new partners vs. heterosexual encounters within ongoing relationships), and that participants who reported token resistance were asked to provide open-ended, qualitative accounts of their experiences. These narratives revealed tremendous complexity within sexual encounters, and further cast doubt on previous prevalence work: it seemed that many participants who indicated engagement in token resistance had genuinely meant "no" at the precise moment they indicated "no." A "yes" to the close-ended question above might pair with a narrative about shifting desires, conflicts between what individuals wanted and what they consented to, or ambivalence regarding a sexual encounter.

That Muehlenhard expected pushback—and may well have received some during peer-review processes—is evident from her publications. She seems to have anticipated that readers would perceive her work as reinforcing the cultural stereotype that "women mean yes when they say no," and providing justification for heterosexual men who declined to respect heterosexual women's refusals. Muehlenhard and her colleagues made repeated efforts to name and condemn rape, and to demand that women's (and eventually, also men's) refusals be taken seriously even if they might sometimes constitute token resistance or scripted refusal. The concluding paragraph to her first piece on token resistance in 1988 noted that most participants did not report engaging in this behavior, that most who had done so reported a small number of incidents, and therefore that, "when a woman says no, chances are she means it" and "regardless of the incidence of token resistance, if the woman means no and the man persists, it is rape" (Muehlenhard and Hollabaugh 1988, 878). Another piece concluded with a section entitled, "A Final Caution," noting that "we do not want to perpetuate the traditional sexual script by suggesting that women are not to be believed when they say no to sex. . . . Even if a man is certain that a woman's no really means yes, if she does mean no and he has sex with her, *it is rape*" (Muehlenhard and McCoy 1991, 460, italics in original). The 1998 piece, including qualitative narratives, ended with an insistence that "all refusals should be taken seriously. Engaging in sex with someone who does not consent is rape" (Muehlenhard and Rodgers 1998, 462).

Notwithstanding these efforts, Muehlenhard and others' work on token resistance, sometimes referred to as "miscommunication theory," received considerable pushback. Much of this concerned potential misuse. Critics worried that communication-based theories obscured systemic power inequalities, shifted blame away from sexually aggressive men, and reinforced harmful

stereotypes about men's and women's sexuality in ways that ultimately contributed to rape culture (Crawford 1995; Ehrlich 2001; Frith 2009; Frith
and Kitzinger 1997). In 2011, editors of the *Psychology of Women Quarterly*
invited authors of some highly cited pieces to write reflective commentaries
for their thirty-fifth anniversary special edition. Muehlenhard was invited
to reflect on her 1991 study, originally published with then-student Marcia
McCoy. She recalled a particularly dramatic experience in which a discus-
sant whom she had invited to a symposium "criticized our research in front
of the entire room of attendees, comparing it to the atomic bomb because
of its potential to be misused" (681). Noting that such misuses had not been
documented,[2] Muehlenhard reaffirmed the importance of asking difficult
questions about sexual communication and violence: "Indeed, it would be
ideal if no one accepted the sexual double standard, if everyone could convey their feelings clearly to potential partners without being judged unfairly,
and if no one ever felt ambivalent about sex. That's not the world we live in,
however" (681). Consistent with her own previous work, Muehlenhard further advocated that scholars who study controversial topics be critical about
their own and potential readers' assumptions, give participants opportunities
to speak for themselves, and strive to anticipate and circumvent potential
misuse.

Causation and Scientific Controversy

What can be learned from these distinct controversies? Their similarities and differences are both instructive. In their view, Thornhill and Palmer
received pushback for challenging dominant understandings of rape, developed through "ideological" and "feminist" (read: nonscientific) social science scholarship and activism (Palmer and R. Thornhill 2003; R. Thornhill
and Palmer 2000). In addition to weak understandings of evolutionary theory and endorsement of the naturalistic fallacy, they argued that their critics
were unable to tolerate challenges to the notion that "rape is about power
and not about sex." Connecting human rape with human sexuality, and
merely suggesting (recognizing?) that human beings were biological beings,
were thereby rendered dangerous and condemnable.

When discussing her years researching token resistance, Muehlenhard
reflected that "some people have found this entire line of research to be
objectionable" (2011, 681). In her case, it seems likely that the mere decision
to study token resistance challenged many scholars' assumption that such
behaviors did not exist. Indeed, literature on rape myths has sometimes
approached stereotypes pertaining to miscommunication and (women's)
dishonesty as blatantly false and problematic (Burt 1980; Edwards et al. 2011;
Lonsway and Fitzgerald 1994; Lonsway and Fitzgerald 1995; Payne, Lonsway, and Fitzgerald 1999). There are strong reasons for this. Individuals

who assume that "no sometimes means yes" might feel entitled to cross partners' boundaries to the point of committing sexual violence, and might also prove unwilling to believe victims/survivors whose accounts do not fit their perceptions of rape. Victims/survivors might struggle with self-blame if they internalize these same stereotypes. If approaching sexual communication as complex and ambiguous seems detrimental to such work, it is logical that the whole project of studying token resistance might seem problematic. Much like some critics of evolutionary explanations, critics of (mis)communication models may worry that such approaches shift responsibility away from aggressors and onto victims.

While all of these scholars faced resistance for challenging widely held assumptions in research (and activism), they also embraced strikingly different approaches in accounting for rape. One might argue that they were engaged with different phenomena, even as they strove to account for "the same" social problem. Thornhill and Palmer drew on evolutionary biology. When anticipating and receiving criticism, they endorsed strict boundaries around what they perceived as legitimate science. They argued that "the choice between the social science explanation's answers and the evolutionarily informed answers provided in this book is essentially a choice between ideology and knowledge" (2000, 189). Feminist ideals were particularly suspect, to the point that "feminist biologists" were depicted as less credible than scholars who were simply "biologists." The problem of rape was anchored in millennia of human and nonhuman development, and its solutions were presumed to lie (at least in part) therein. In contrast, Muehlenhard was trained in psychology and openly aligned herself with feminist ideals. She focused solely on what Thornhill and Palmer would have classified as proximate causes. When anticipating and facing criticism, she aligned herself with the aims of feminist social science rather than seeking to dismiss or discredit opponents. Simply put, Thornhill and Palmer perceived themselves as scientists facing critiques from nonscientists, whereas Muehlenhard perceived herself as facing critiques from peers. For her, the problem of rape was social and cultural, and its solutions lay (at least in part) in transforming the sexual double standard and problematic assumptions and communication practices surrounding sexual consent and refusal.

In light of these controversies and the empirical analyses below, it does not seem that controversy in causal research on rape is contained within any particular discipline, theoretical orientation, value system, or methodology. More likely, the decision to challenge widely held assumptions—to subject hitherto unquestioned matters of fact to empirical scrutiny—is what unites these scholars. Two additional commonalities are worth pointing out. Both evolutionary approaches and communication-based approaches presume that sexuality is relevant to the problem of sexual violence. Anyone who

adheres to the belief that "rape is about power, not sex," whether approaching this as a theoretical assumption or empirically grounded and scientific
matter of fact, will likely reject both causal frameworks. In addition, these
disparate models were both presumed dangerous due to perceptions of potential misuse.[3] Thornhill, Palmer, and Muehlenhard have all been accused of
providing ammunition for (female/women) victim-blaming and the absolving of (male/men) aggressors. The truth of this potential misuse may well
be irrelevant; such perceptions are sufficient to foster pushback within scientific and public communities.

EMPIRICAL FINDINGS FROM THE PRESENT STUDY

Much like the controversy over "one in four women" in the preceding chapter, scientific and public debates surrounding evolutionary and communication-
based models are valuable for understanding the ethical, ontological, and
epistemological politics—in Barad's terms, the ethico-onto-epistemologies—
surrounding scientific inquiries on rape. Yet these controversies do not, in
themselves, demonstrate dominant trends in scientific literature or reveal
much regarding changes in conceptualizations over time. Similarly, published
works rarely reveal the social processes "behind" them or "following" them.
Have scholars shied away from evolutionary or communication-approaches?
Why or why not? Are other causal accounts equally or more prominent among
rape researchers, but insufficiently controversial to garner much attention
beyond scientific circles? The following sections address these concerns. I
begin with quantitative findings from content analysis of forty years' worth
of publications, comparing the subfield of causality to the broader field of
sexual violence research; qualitative themes that emerged from in-depth
assessment of the most cited works from each decade within this subfield;
and insights on causal models and related scientific research from interview
participants.

CONTENT ANALYSIS: FORTY YEARS
OF CAUSAL RESEARCH

Causal research ranked first among all study aims from 1975 to 2004
and was slightly outpaced by research on the aftermath of rape in the following decade. More than half of the studies analyzed here incorporated
causal inquiries (669 studies, or 51% of the total pool of 1,313); this is equal to
the combined total of works addressing quantification, evaluation, and theoretical and methodological strategies for studying sexual violence. Figures 3.1–
3.4 present some of the general characteristics of causal works, stratified by
decade. Frequencies, percentages, and data from significance testing appear
in table 3.1; along with data from the overall field of sexual violence research
for comparison. Rather than repeat content from chapter 2, which focused

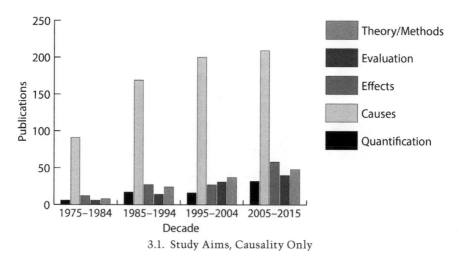

3.1. Study Aims, Causality Only

on the overall field of sexual violence research and the subfield of quantification in equal measure (and included visual representations of both), I focus primarily on the causality-only findings and comparisons between this subfield and the larger body of scientific research on rape.

Generally speaking, it is common for scientists to embrace multiple aims within a single project. When seeking to calculate prevalence estimates, for example, researchers might pair questions about prior victimization with questions about current mental well-being. This would combine quantification with inquiry into the aftermath of rape. As shown in figure 3.1, studies with multiple aims are less common in the subfield of causal research. Although causal studies have increasingly incorporated questions of prevalence, effects, and policy and program evaluation, most are more singular in focus. Researchers tend to focus their efforts solely on exploring rape-supportive attitudes, risk behaviors, or other predictors of aggression, victimization, and prevention/intervention.

Scientists who study sexual violence have consistently prioritized victims/victimization over other areas of focus. Figure 3.2 demonstrates that these trends have intensified over the past four decades, evidenced by significantly increased attention toward victimization and declining attention toward perpetration and bystanders/general publics. Causal research has been more varied. Scientists seeking to determine "why rape happens" have asked "why are particular individuals and populations victimized," "why do particular individuals and populations commit rape," and "how do bystanders contribute to and/or prevent the occurrence of sexual violence" in more comparable proportions. Admittedly, these patterns were shaped somewhat by coding strategies. Working with the assumption that rape culture is approached

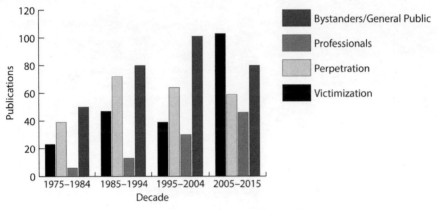

3.2. Areas of Focus, Causality Only

as causal, in that rape-supportive attitudes promote and justify sexual violence, I classified related investigations—works on rape myth acceptance, approaches to distinguishing consensual from nonconsensual contact in response to vignettes—in this category. This is consistent with previous literature, in that concepts such as rape myth acceptance and attitudes toward heterosexual relationships are frequently approached as predictors of aggression and willingness to intervene in potentially violent situations (Loh et al. 2005; McMahon 2010). Relatively few causal studies focused on professionals, such as therapists or police officers (particularly in earlier decades). This indicates that such actors are not often approached as causal or preventive agents.

Like the broader field, causal inquiries have favored violence perpetrated by men or against women over other gendered patterns. However, as shown in figure 3.3, this subfield demonstrates proportionally greater attention to (men's) perpetration, particularly in earlier years. This is likely due to an overall stronger emphasis on assailants/perpetration across efforts to determine the causes of sexual violence. These general patterns persist in spite of significantly increased attention toward violence perpetrated by women and/or against men over time, as well as significant declines in causal assessments of men's sexual aggression. Across all four decades, approximately one quarter of causal inquiries demonstrated the sort of precasting assessed in content analysis, engaging gender nonspecific language in abstracts to describe gender-specific projects (e.g., describing a study of exclusively female rape victims as a study of "rape victims"; not shown in a graph, but noted in table 3.1).

As evident in figure 3.4, causal inquiries rely heavily on college populations, with general population and community samples ranking a distant second. In other words, the bulk of scientific knowledge regarding the causes/deterrents of rape has been produced with (if not ostensibly for) student

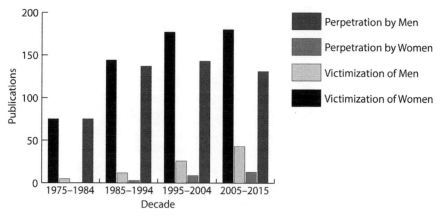

3.3. Gendered Patterns, Causality Only

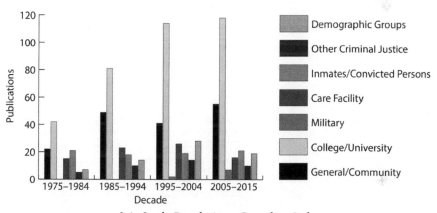

3.4. Study Populations, Causality Only

populations. A majority of investigations into such diverse areas as rape myth acceptance, substance use, sexist attitudes, rape proclivity, and sexual (mis)communication—and empirical associations between these phenomena and sexual victimization, aggression, bystander intervention, and the cultural promotion and justification of sexual violence (i.e., rape culture)—have been conducted by college faculty with samples of college students who were often drawn from researchers' home institutions. While the proportion of causal studies with military populations has increased significantly over time, this is largely a reflection of the utter lack of military-specific research prior to 2004. Causal research with incarcerated populations has declined over time, notwithstanding public and institutional outcry over prison rape in the early 2000s (Human Rights Watch 2001; Wolff et al. 2006).

TABLE 3.1
Descriptive Statistics for All Publications and Causality Pieces, by Decade

	All Publications				Causality Pieces			
	1975–1984	1985–1994	1995–2004	2005–2015	1975–1984	1985–1994	1995–2004	2005–2015
Precasting[ac]	53 (30%)	91 (30%)	102 (26%)	90 (21%)	23 (25%)	47 (28%)	55 (28%)	53 (25%)
Study Aims:								
Quantification	11 (6%)	32 (10%)	33 (8%)	49 (11%)	6 (7%)	17 (10%)	16 (8%)	32 (15%)
Causes of Rape[b]	91 (52%)	169 (55%)	200 (50%)	209 (49%)	–	–	–	–
Effects of Rape[b]	78 (44%)	113 (37%)	177 (44%)	221 (51%)	12 (13%)	27 (16%)	27 (14%)	58 (28%)
Evaluation	41 (23%)	76 (25%)	108 (27%)	115 (27%)	6 (7%)	14 (8%)	31 (16%)	40 (19%)
Theory/Methods[b]	16 (9%)	42 (14%)	63 (16%)	83 (19%)	8 (9%)	24 (14%)	37 (19%)	48 (23%)
Overall Focus:								
Victimization[b]	82 (47%)	140 (46%)	221 (55%)	283 (66%)	23 (25%)	47 (28%)	39 (77%)	103 (49%)
Perpetration[bc]	43 (24%)	77 (25%)	69 (17%)	68 (16%)	39 (43%)	72 (43%)	64 (32%)	59 (28%)
Professionals	49 (28%)	88 (29%)	118 (30%)	134 (31%)	6 (7%)	13 (8%)	30 (15%)	46 (22%)
Bystanders/General Public[bc]	59 (34%)	88 (29%)	118 (30%)	93 (22%)	50 (55%)	80 (47%)	101 (51%)	80 (38%)
Gendered Patterns:								
Victimization of Women	154 (88%)	275 (89%)	367 (92%)	387 (90%)	75 (82%)	144 (85%)	177 (89%)	180 (86%)
Victimization of Men[b]	12 (7%)	37 (12%)	60 (15%)	90 (21%)	5 (5%)	12 (7%)	26 (13%)	48 (23%)

TABLE 3.1 (continued)

	All Publications				Causality Pieces			
	1975–1984	1985–1994	1995–2004	2005–2015	1975–1984	1985–1994	1995–2004	2005–2015
Perpetration by Women	3 (2%)	8 (3%)	14 (4%)	21 (5%)	0 (0%)	3 (2%)	9 (5%)	13 (6%)
Perpetration by Men[bd]	115 (65%)	196 (64%)	202 (51%)	172 (40%)	75 (82%)	137 (81%)	143 (72%)	131 (63%)
Study Population:								
General/Community	42 (24%)	91 (30%)	107 (27%)	142 (33%)	22 (24%)	49 (29%)	41 (21%)	55 (26%)
College/University	51 (29%)	106 (34%)	157 (39%)	165 (38%)	42 (46%)	81 (48%)	114 (57%)	118 (57%)
Military[b]	0 (0%)	0 (0%)	10 (3%)	21 (5%)	0 (0%)	0 (0%)	2 (1%)	7 (3%)
Care Facility[bd]	62 (35%)	73 (24%)	107 (27%)	95 (22%)	15 (16%)	23 (14%)	26 (13%)	16 (8%)
Inmates/Convicted Persons[b]	23 (13%)	33 (11%)	22 (6%)	27 (6%)	21 (23%)	18 (31%)	19 (10%)	21 (10%)
Other Criminal Justice	25 (14%)	52 (17%)	55 (14%)	43 (10%)	5 (5%)	10 (6%)	14 (7%)	10 (5%)
Demographic Groups	10 (6%)	22 (7%)	40 (10%)	45 (11%)	7 (7%)	14 (8%)	28 (14%)	19 (9%)

[a]$p<.05$, [b]$p<.01$ for full sample of publications in chi-square analysis; [c]$p<.05$, [d]$p<.01$ for quantification pieces

NOTE: Categories for study aims, overall focus, gendered patterns, and study population are not mutually exclusive. For example, a study may address both victimization of women and victimization of men.

Close Readings: Dominant Voices
in Causal Research

After reviewing forty years' worth of abstracts, I selected the ten most-cited causal works from each decade for qualitative analysis. Table 3.2 provides basic information about these forty publications. Close readings helped me to identify several patterns and shifts in dominant priorities and perspectives. Scientists have engaged different sexual scripts and different strategies for identifying sexually violent encounters over the past forty years. Earlier emphases on "forcible" rape, characterized by overt physical violence by assailants and sometimes active resistance by victims, gave way to emphases on (non)consent and alcohol-facilitated rape. Other aspects of research remained more consistent. Top-cited studies have consistently favored quantitative approaches, and further precast men and women as perpetrators and victims, respectively. There were also notable trends regarding the representation of specific authors and disciplines over time, with individual-focused fields (e.g., psychiatry and psychology) better represented than fields that favor institutional and systemic inquiries (e.g., sociology and anthropology).

Decade One: 1975–1984

Dominant works in this decade comprised two major lines of inquiry. The first sought to account for some individuals' tendency toward sexual aggression, in some cases with an emphasis on sexual responsiveness to the concept of rape (Abel et al. 1977; Groth, Burgess, and Holstrom 1977; Malamuth 1981; Malamuth, Haber, and Feshbach 1980; Scully and Marolla 1984; R. Thornhill and N. W. Thornhill 1983). Such responsiveness was often categorized as "sexual deviance" or "deviant arousal," and measured through penile plethysmography. The second line of inquiry explored cultural causes of sexual violence through assessments of rape myth acceptance and reactions to rape depictions (Burt 1980; Calhoun, Selby, and Warring 1976; Check and Malamuth 1983; Feild 1978). These works often considered participants' relative tendency to blame assailants and victims, as well as differential responses to stranger and acquaintance rape.

In both lines of research, scientists drew on rape scripts featuring the overt use of force by cisgender male assailants, along with demonstrable resistance—and in some cases, signs of physical anguish—by cisgender female victims. Calhoun, Selby, and Warring provided the following prompt to participants in a study of victim-blaming attitudes (1976, 20):

Background. Laura S. is a 24-year-old student at a middle-sized university. She was raised in an average-size family, is married, and has no children.

Incident. One night, while crossing the campus on her way from the library, she was accosted and raped. A passerby heard her screams and called the police, who arrived and apprehended the man a few minutes after he had completed his sexual assault.

Students were then provided with anywhere from zero to all three of the following statements:

a. Police records show that seven other women had been raped on the campus in the past 6 months before Laura S. was raped.
b. She was raped once before about 1 year prior to this recent assault.
c. She had been in class with the rapist the previous semester.

Even the acquaintance rape scenario in this study applied many aspects of "real rape" stereotypes in U.S. and Canadian culture (Estrich 1987; Ryan 2011): the assault occurred at night, outdoors and in a public location, and the victim screamed loudly enough for passersby to hear. Moreover, police were sufficiently convinced by the victim and bystanders' reports that they pursued and immediately apprehended the assailant. Other dominant works in this decade depicted force and resistance even more explicitly, sometimes including assailants' use of weapons (Abel et al. 1977; Malamuth, Haber, and Feshbach 1980) and physical struggle between assailants and victims (Check and Malamuth 1983).

Burt's (1980) "Cultural Myths and Supports for Rape" was the top-cited piece across all four decades and all areas of focus, and provided somewhat of an alternative perspective. Although she did not provide vignettes depicting (or producing/constituting) "typical" scenarios, she incorporated notions such as voluntary intoxication and misinterpretation of (non)sexual cues into her Rape Myth Acceptance Scale (RMAS), and heavily emphasized acquaintance encounters. She further connected acceptance of rape myths with more general attitudes toward gender roles, (hetero)sexuality, and interpersonal violence. The RMAS also comprised an early effort at standardization within sexual violence research (Porter 1995; Timmermans and Epstein 2010) and remains influential to this day, even if other instruments have surpassed it as the go-to assessment for measuring rape myth acceptance.

Two pieces provided causal models that diverged from these patterns. Drawing on reports from victims and assailants, Groth and colleagues (1977) advanced a power and control model for rape over explanations that relied on (deviant) sexual desire. Thornhill and Thornhill (1983) provided a combined evolutionary and cultural account of rape, with the latter subordinate to the former. Their model addressed both perpetration and victimization, due to emphasis on reproductive competition that ensued as particular (relatively unfit or undesired) males pursued particular (relatively fit or desired) females.

Throughout this decade in causal research, there were notable patterns regarding top-cited authors, disciplines, and scientific publications. Psychiatry and psychology were particularly well represented. Most of the works reviewed above appeared in discipline journals such as the *Journal of Personality and Social Psychology* (three of the ten top-cited pieces), *Journal of Research in Personality, American Journal of Psychiatry,* and the *Archives of General Psychiatry.* Other works appeared in interdisciplinary social science journals such as *Social Problems* and the *Journal of Social Issues.* Professionals in psychology and psychiatry—whether by training and/or departmental affiliation— contributed to nine of the ten most cited causal works (all except for Scully and Marolla 1984). Among authors, Malamuth appears to have been most dominant in causal research in this period. He was sole author on one piece (Malamuth 1981), first on another (Malamuth, Haber, and Feshbach 1980), and second on another (Check and Malamuth 1983). His work emphasized rape proclivity among incarcerated and so-called normal college men, based on associations among diverse measures including self-reported likelihood of committing rape, acceptance of rape myths, and penile tumescence measures in phallometric tests. He also investigated college men and women's overall reactions to rape vignettes, and self-reported likelihood of enjoying such an experience (as aggressor for men, and as victim for women).

Decade Two: 1985–1994

Whereas the previous decade emphasized accounts of aggression and featured overtly violent assaults, these years gave rise to a marked departure in priorities and strategies in scientific explanations for rape. Six of the ten top-cited works addressed victimization, and four of these focused solely on victimization (Gidycz et al. 1993; Koss 1985; Koss, Dinero, and Seibel 1988; Wyatt 1992). Causal explanations for victimization included a range of individual, interpersonal, and cultural factors including rape myth acceptance, attitudes toward heterosexuality, approaches to dating, sexual history, sexual communication, alcohol and other substance use, engagement in physical and other forms of resistance, victim/assailant relationship, and prior experiences of victimization. Wyatt's piece on sexual violence toward African American and White women (1992), the first study with a demographic focus to make the top ten, engaged a historical analysis through connecting the sexual victimization of African American women with slavery and broader histories of racial and sexual oppression. As in the first decade, causal works with a bystander or general public focus emphasized rape myths and associated perspectives on gender and sexuality (Lonsway and Fitzgerald 1994;

Martin and Hummer 1989). Warr's (1985) piece introduced a new element to such scholarly conversations through attention toward fear of rape.

While accounting for sexual aggression remained a priority, causal models expanded. Scientists incorporated more institutional and interpersonal factors than represented in the previous decade. Martin and Hummer (1989) investigated fraternity culture, including practices that facilitated sexual violence toward women (e.g., use of alcohol as a weapon) and protected the fraternity brothers who perpetrated such violence (e.g., valuing secrecy within the house). These authors further addressed universities' complicity through support for fraternities and lenience toward assailants involved with them. Bachman, Paternoster, and Ward (1992) investigated relationships between rape proclivity and personal morality, perceived likelihood of social sanctions, and perceived likelihood of university or criminal justice sanctions among university men. Muehlenhard and Linton (1987) explored interpersonal dynamics and communication within heterosexual dating. Mosher and Anderson theorized sexual arousal to rape depictions as a major predictor, which was more consistent with research in the first decade (1986); however, they did not use penile plethysmography technology but rather inquired after men's self-assessments of arousal and genital sensations.

Relative to those who came before them, scientists in this decade drew on—and perhaps also produced—a broader range of cultural scenarios when conceptualizing "typical" rapes. Acquaintance rape scripts, characterized less by overt violence and more by (cisgender male) aggressors' refusal to acknowledge (cisgender female) victims' nonconsent, grew increasingly prominent. Voluntary intoxication was more likely than involuntary intoxication to feature in such scenarios. Muehlenhard and Linton defined rape as "sexual intercourse against the woman's will" (1987, 189). They did not specify a need for physical force or demonstrable barriers to consent, nor did they set expectations regarding "the woman's" resistance or lack thereof. Bachman, Paternoster, and Ward (1992) approached physical violence as a variable. In their assessment of rape proclivity, they provided stranger and acquaintance rape vignettes featuring varying degrees of force and asked participants to assess assailants' behavior, probable interpersonal and institutional consequences, and self-likelihood of committing a similar act. Wyatt defined rape as "the involuntary penetration of the vagina or anus by the penis or another object" (1992, 82). In all three studies, nonconsensual sexual intercourse might constitute rape even in the absence of physical force, threats of force, intoxication (voluntary or otherwise), or incapacitation.

Dominant voices shifted considerably between the periods of 1975–1984 and 1985–1994. Malamuth authored no pieces in the top ten during this second decade, though one publication relied heavily on his work (Mosher and

Anderson 1986). Koss and her colleagues' research drew the most attention. In the broader field of sexual violence research, this decade also saw the publication of "The Scope of Rape," with its groundbreaking and controversial finding that one in four college women had experienced completed or attempted rape (Koss, Gidycz, and Wisniewski 1987). Among causal inquiries, Koss had one sole-authored and one first-authored piece (Koss 1985; Koss, Dinero, and Seibel 1988). Gidycz, second author on "The Scope of Rape," published an additional first-authored piece (Gidycz et al. 1993). All three works focused on women's victimization, with further emphases on repeat sexual assault, victim-offender relationship, and women's experiences and self-identification (or nonidentification) as rape victims. These changes in dominant voices did not, however, constitute a shift in dominant disciplines. Seven of the ten top-cited works included psychologists and/or psychiatrists among the authors. Six of those works appeared in psychology and psychiatry journals, including *Psychology of Women Quarterly* (four studies total), *Journal of Research in Personality,* and the *Journal of Counseling Psychology;* the seventh was published in the *Journal of Social Issues.* However, social scientists in other fields—particularly sociology—entered the dominant causal literature in greater numbers. Sociologists Patricia Yancey Martin, Ronet Bachman, and Mark Warr were each first author on one piece in this sample; their works appeared in *Gender and Society, Law & Society Review,* and *Social Problems*, respectively.

Decade Three: 1995–2004

Scientists continued to broaden conceptualizations of the causes of rape in this decade, including social and psychological conditions that might promote or deter sexual violence. Top-cited works featured increasingly complex and multifaceted models. Alcohol and substance use emerged as major/priority predictors that functioned alongside factors such as (mis)communication and endorsement of rape myths. Studies of repeat sexual assault, in which prior incidents were understood as risk factors for subsequent incidents, began to gain traction. Theoretical and methodological critiques began to appear, evaluating the merits of various approaches to accounting for rape.

Alcohol and other substance use was conceptualized as an important predictor for both (cisgender female) victimization and (cisgender male) aggression. Regarding the former, Abbey and colleagues (1996) suggested that a complex combination of alcohol consumption by women and men, men's misperception of women's sexual intentions, and dating experiences contributed to victimization risk among college women, with interactions occurring among some of these factors. Consumption by women might activate seduction scripts for men, and the physical and cognitive impairments associated with intoxication might inhibit women's capacity to resist. In a subsequent study, Abbey, McAuslan, and Ross (1998) explored relationships between alcohol consumption and sexual aggression among college men. Once again, they offered a multifaceted causal model: rape-supportive beliefs, expectations about dating and sexual encounters, expectations regarding alcohol and sexuality, misperception of sexual intent (particularly likely when drinking), and self-reported rape proclivity (i.e., likelihood of committing sexual violence if there would be no punishment) were all associated with risk of perpetration. Mohler-Kuo and colleagues (2004, with Koss among the coauthors) investigated the prevalence of rape while intoxicated among college women, as well as institutional-level and individual-level correlates of sexual violence in general and intoxicated sexual violence in particular. On the institutional level, high prevalence rates of heavy drinking were associated with higher rates of sexual violence among students. On the individual level, heavy drinking prior to college, other substance use, and age (underage women at greater risk) contributed to victimization risk.

The concept of revictimization emerged as a strong theme in this decade. Follette and colleagues (1996) explored the notion of cumulative trauma, which accrues over multiple victimizations and may exacerbate the risk of further assault. Humphrey and White (2000) approached prior victimization as a predictor of (re)victimization. Working with a sample of undergraduate women, they documented an increased risk of adolescent sexual assault for survivors of child sexual assault, an increased risk of freshman year college sexual assault for survivors of adolescent sexual assault, and an increased risk of later college sexual assault for survivors of freshman year sexual assault. In addition, they noted that women who reported more "severe" victimization histories before college (i.e., completed or attempted rape) were more likely to experience more severe assaults in college. Gidycz, Hanson, and Layman (1995) documented similar patterns, though their longitudinal study also explored additional individual and interpersonal factors including family adjustment, psychological adjustment, sexual behavior, interpersonal functioning, and alcohol use. Of the two pieces focused on perpetration, one focused on recidivism among convicted sex offenders (Rice and Harris 1997). Investigators determined that interactions between psychopathy and "sexual deviance," as measured through arousal to rape depictions and other "deviant" stimuli in phallometric testing, were effective for predicting sexual recidivism.

The rise of theory/methods literature speaks to the establishment of sexual violence studies as a scientific field and the development of a rich literature in causality. By the mid-1990s, sufficient work had been published for scholars to conduct critical systematic reviews; debate theoretical models to account for victimization, aggression, and rape culture more broadly; and provide comparative analyses of standardized assessment tools and evidence-based calls for new standardized measures. After publishing a thorough critique of rape myth literature at the end of decade two (1994), Lonsway and Fitzgerald confronted ongoing theoretical issues (e.g., conflation of "adversarial sexual experiences" with "hostility toward women" in previous studies, when the latter was a better predictor of rape myth acceptance) and developed the now widely used *Illinois Rape Myth Acceptance Scale* in two subsequent publications (Lonsway and Fitzgerald 1995; Payne, Lonsway, and Fitzgerald 1999). Rice and Harris's piece on the *Violence Risk Appraisal Guide* also fit well within this theme (1997).

The only exception to these three dominant themes was Goodman's (1997) piece on the prevalence, correlates, and outcomes of sexual violence among women with serious mental illness (particularly schizophrenia). While much of this piece focused on prevalence rates and health outcomes, Goodman also wrote about serious mental illness as a risk factor for victimization, given the prevalence estimates documented in prior studies. Goodman further drew attention to vulnerabilities associated with impairments in cognitive processing, which might make seriously mentally ill women more "desirable targets" for assailants.

The discipline of psychology was more dominant between 1995 and 2004 than in either of the previous decades. Several scholars appeared on multiple top-cited causal works, and all of them were trained or working in the field of psychology. These included Antonia Abbey and her coauthors Lisa Thomson Ross and Pam McAusalan, whose work focused on alcohol and risk; and Kimberly Lonsway and Louise Fitzgerald, who continued their previous work on rape myth acceptance. Also continuing previous trends, Christine Gidycz and Mary Koss each contributed to top-cited causal works in this decade (as first and third author, different publications). Most of these pieces were published in discipline journals including *Psychology of Women Quarterly* (two of the ten top-cited studies), *Journal of Social and Clinical Psychology*, *Journal of Traumatic Stress*, *Schizophrenia Bulletin*, *Journal of Personality and Social Psychology*, and the *Journal of Research in Personality*. Other works appeared in more interdisciplinary journals including *Law and Human Behavior*, *Journal of Adolescent Health*, and the *Journal of Studies on Alcohol*.

Decade Four: 2005–2015

Alcohol and other substance use (Abbey 2011; Armstrong, Hamilton, and Sweeney 2006; Krebs et al. 2009; McMahon 2010), repeat sexual assault (Loh et al. 2005), and theoretical and methodological refinement (McMahon and Banyard 2012; Suarez and Gadalla 2010) continued to feature in top-cited works. Cultural and behavioral expectations received more attention than in previous decades. In a drastic departure from prior emphases on overt acts of violence and stranger assaults, dominant rape scripts advanced in this decade emphasized parties and other social gatherings involving alcohol consumption by victims and assailants. While notions of physical force were not entirely absent from these pieces, they were far less prevalent than in previous years. Explanatory models that relied on evolution, psychopathology, and sexual arousal (particularly as measured through plethysmography) were entirely absent.

Another notable trend in this decade was the emergence of bystander approaches (Coker et al. 2011; McMahon 2010; McMahon and Banyard 2012). This perspective conceptualizes sexual violence prevention as a community issue. Rather than focus on perpetrators and victims, bystander analyses and programs seek to engage all members of a community—most often college students—as agents in primary, secondary, and tertiary prevention. Some bystander assessment tools also incorporated perpetration prevention measures, such as stated likelihood of ceasing advances when a partner says "no," as well as more bystander-specific behaviors, such as challenging a sexist comment, or intervening when a man attempts to bring an intoxicated woman to his room. McMahon and Banyard were key figures in this area of research; although Banyard had only one publication among the top ten causal works analyzed here, others drew repeatedly on her publications and intervention approaches.

Whereas psychology scholars and journals were remarkably dominant in decade three, top-cited causal literature in decade four demonstrated unprecedented multidisciplinarity. Lead authors included psychologists and sociologists as well as professionals in more practice-focused fields such as public health, obstetrics and gynecology, and social work. The two most dominant scholars were psychologist Antonia Abbey and social work scholar Sarah McMahon; each published two works in this sample (for a total of four between them), including one sole-author and one first-author piece. Most top-cited causal works were published in interdisciplinary journals including the *Journal of Interpersonal Violence* (two of the ten top-cited studies), *Violence against Women* (two), *Journal of American College Health* (two), *Social Problems*, and *Trauma, Violence, and Abuse*.

Forty Years of Precasting in Causal Research

The most consistent practice across these studies may well have been gendered precasting. All studies of sexual aggression were conducted with men, all studies of sexual victimization were conducted with women, and all vignettes and bystander scenarios reflected this pattern. Such gendered dynamics were implicitly or explicitly incorporated as baseline assumptions, rather than empirical questions that might be tested and subsequently inform study design. When discussing their decision to restrict a study on rape

TABLE 3.2
Ten Top-Cited Causal Works from Each Decade, as of February 2016

Lead Author	Title	Journal	Year	Citations
Burt, Martha R.	Cultural Myths and Supports for Rape	Journal of Personality and Social Psychology	1980	1,142
Malamuth, Neil M.	Rape Proclivity among Males	Journal of Social Issues	1981	238
Check, James V. P.	Sex Role Stereotyping and Reactions to Depictions of Stranger versus Acquaintance Rape	Journal of Personality and Social Psychology	1983	219
Feild, Hubert S.	Attitudes toward Rape: Comparative Analysis of Police, Rapists, Crisis Counselors, and Citizens	Journal of Personality and Social Psychology	1978	207
Scully, Diana	Convicted Rapists' Vocabulary of Motive: Excuses and Justifications	Social Problems	1984	199
Abel, Gene G.	The Components of Rapists' Sexual Arousal	Archives of General Psychiatry	1977	171
Groth, A. Nicholas	Rape: Power, Anger, and Sexuality	American Journal of Psychiatry	1977	152
Thornhill, Randy	Human Rape: An Evolutionary Analysis	Ethology and Sociobiology	1983	147
Malamuth, Neil M.	Testing Hypotheses Regarding Rape: Exposure to Sexual Violence, Sex Differences, and the "Normality" of Rapists	Journal of Research in Personality	1980	129
Calhoun, Lawrence G.	Social Perception of the Victim's Causal Role in Rape: An Exploratory Examination of Four Factors	Human Relations	1976	128
Muehlenhard, Charlene L.	Date Rape and Sexual Aggression in Dating Situations: Incidence and Risk Factors	Journal of Counseling Psychology	1987	412
Lonsway, Kimberly A.	Rape Myths: In Review	Psychology of Women Quarterly	1994	310

TABLE 3.2 *(continued)*

Lead Author	Title	Journal	Year	Citations
Koss, Mary P.	Stranger and Acquaintance Rape: Are There Differences in the Victim's Experience?	Psychology of Women Quarterly	1988	249
Koss, Mary P.	The Hidden Rape Victim: Personality, Attitudinal, and Situational Characteristics	Psychology of Women Quarterly	1985	216
Gidycz, Christine A.	Sexual Assault Experience in Adulthood and Prior Victimization Experiences	Psychology of Women Quarterly	1993	208
Wyatt, Gail Elizabeth	The Sociocultural Context of African American and White American Women's Rape	Journal of Social Issues	1992	156
Warr, Mark	Fear of Rape among Urban Women	Social Problems	1985	145
Martin, Patricia Yancey	Fraternities and Rape on Campus	Gender and Society	1989	135
Bachman, Ronet	The Rationality of Sexual Offending: Testing a Deterrence/Rational Choice Conception of Sexual Assault	Law and Society Review	1992	127
Mosher, Donald L.	Macho Personality, Sexual Aggression, and Reactions to Guided Imagery of Realistic Rape	Journal of Research in Personality	1986	122
Follette, Victoria M.	Cumulative Trauma: The Impact of Child Sexual Abuse, Adult Sexual Assault, and Spouse Abuse	Journal of Traumatic Stress	1996	215
Goodman, Lisa A.	Physical and Sexual Assault History in Women with Serious Mental Illness: Prevalence, Correlates, Treatment, and Future Research Directions	Schizophrenia Bulletin	1997	187
Abbey, Antonia	Alcohol and Dating Risk Factors for Sexual Assault among College Women	Psychology of Women Quarterly	1996	183

(continued)

TABLE 3.2 *(continued)*

Lead Author	Title	Journal	Year	Citations
Payne, Diana L.	Rape Myth Acceptance: Exploration of Its Structure and Its Measurement Using the Illinois Rape Myth Acceptance Scale	Journal of Research in Personality	1999	180
Lonsway, Kimberly A.	Attitudinal Antecedents of Rape Myth Acceptance: A Theoretical and Empirical Reexamination	Journal of Personality and Social Psychology	1995	179
Gidycz, Christine A.	A Prospective Analysis of the Relationships among Sexual Assault Experiences	Psychology of Women Quarterly	1995	179
Rice, Marnie E.	Cross-Validation and Extension of the Violence Risk Appraisal Guide for Child Molesters and Rapists	Law and Human Behavior	1997	170
Humphrey, John A.	Women's Vulnerability to Sexual Assault from Adolescence to Young Adulthood	Journal of Adolescent Health	2000	151
Abbey, Antonia	Sexual Assault Perpetration by College Men: The Role of Alcohol, Misperception of Sexual Intent, and Sexual Beliefs and Experiences	Journal of Social and Clinical Psychology	1998	145
Mohler-Kuo, Meichun	Correlates of Rape while Intoxicated in a National Sample of College Women	Journal of Studies on Alcohol	2004	141
Armstrong, Elizabeth A.	Sexual Assault on Campus: A Multilevel, Integrative Approach to Party Rape	Social Problems	2006	81
Martin, Sandra L.	Physical and Sexual Assault of Women with Disabilities	Violence against Women	2006	62

TABLE 3.2 (*continued*)

Lead Author	Title	Journal	Year	Citations
Krebs, Christopher P.	College Women's Experiences with Physically Forced, Alcohol- or Other Drug-Enabled, and Drug-Facilitated Sexual Assault before and since Entering College	Journal of American College Health	2009	59
Abbey, Antonia	Cross-Sectional Predictors of Sexual Assault Perpetration in a Community Sample of Single African American and Caucasian Men	Aggressive Behavior	2006	58
Loh, Catherine	A Prospective Analysis of Sexual Assault Perpetration	Journal of Interpersonal Violence	2005	56
Suarez, Eliana	Stop Blaming the Victim: A Meta-analysis on Rape Myths	Journal of Interpersonal Violence	2010	70
Coker, Ann L.	Evaluation of Green Dot: An Active Bystander Intervention to Reduce Sexual Violence on College Campuses	Violence against Women	2011	40
McMahon, Sarah	Rape Myth Beliefs and Bystander Attitudes among Incoming College Students	Journal of American College Health	2010	36
McMahon, Sarah	When Can I Help? A Conceptual Framework for the Prevention of Sexual Violence through Bystander Intervention	Trauma, Violence, and Abuse	2012	33
Abbey, Antonia	Alcohol's Role in Sexual Violence Perpetration: Theoretical Explanations, Existing Evidence, and Future Directions	Drug and Alcohol Review	2011	33

NOTE: Articles are organized first by decade, and then in descending order by number of citations.

proclivity to men, Bachman, Paternoster, and Ward asserted that "since we were interested in those factors that may constrain would-be offenders from committing an act of sexual assault, we restricted the study to males only because females are unlikely to commit sexual assault. Females' contemplation of the offense after reading the scenarios would, therefore, be highly contrived" (1992, 350–351). Lonsway and Fitzgerald defined rape myths as "attitudes and beliefs that are generally false but are widely and persistently held, and that serve to deny and justify male sexual aggression against women" (1994, 134), and utilized this definition in subsequent works (Lonsway and Fitzgerald 1995; Payne, Lonsway, and Fitzgerald 1999). Consequently, rape myths such as "men can't be raped," "women are never sexually aggressive," and "rape never happens in queer communities" were omitted from consideration. In their work on recidivism, Rice and Harris worked with exclusively cisgender male participants and further asserted that "sex offenders whose victims come from all categories (adult women, male and female children) are the most dangerous of all" (1997, 239)—as though these were truly all categories of potential victims.

Gendered precasting shifted in form during the fourth decade, in that researchers began to explicitly reference the possibility of multiple gendered patterns in violence; however, neither same-sex violence, women's aggression, men's victimization, nor incidents involving individuals with nonbinary gender identities made it into the ten top-cited pieces. Abbey stated that "although men can be victims and women can be perpetrators, the vast majority of sexual assaults involve male perpetrators and female victims who know each other, in relationships that vary from casual acquaintances to marital partners" (2011, 482). Analyses were then restricted to perpetration by men. Suarez and Gadalla (2010) noted an increase in reports of sexual violence toward men, and then clarified that their analysis of rape myth acceptance literature was restricted to myths concerning men's violence toward women.

INSIGHTS FROM THE (SUB)FIELD

Participants expressed support for a variety of causal models. However, there were notable patterns regarding which models received unqualified endorsement—that is, support without any explicit justification or seeming expectation of opposition—and which received more qualified or tentative endorsement. More generally, many participants called for more systematic and intersectional approaches to accounting for rape. In addition, several called for shifts in prevention strategies, primarily through an expansion or comprehensive assessment of bystander approaches and investment in sex education.

Qualified and Unqualified Accounts

The extent to which scholars provide qualified descriptions of a scientific idea or fact does not reveal its quality or truthfulness. Such patterns rather indicate consensus and controversy among scientists, and the relative capacity of varying discourses to influence thought within and beyond scientific spheres (Epstein 1996).[4] Researchers advancing widely accepted positions may feel little if any need to justify those positions, or even to describe them in detail. Researchers advancing marginal or contested positions may feel compelled to provide more extensive accounts, and may seek to predict and preempt various criticisms.

In this project, scientists who adhered closely to the patriarchy model of rape and/or who argued that aggressors were "made" rather than "born" seemed to anticipate that these views were noncontroversial. Susan, a sociologist, questioned "the reasons why we even produce people who would assault someone in the first place. You know, something's going on. They're not born that way." Echoing this sentiment, Stephanie, a psychologist, approached gender socialization as a straightforward causal force in sexual aggression: "Men are not violent because they're men, necessarily. But society defines maleness and masculinity in terms of violence, therefore, a biological male that wants to be seen as male or masculine may resort to violent behavior, sexually assaultive behavior, as a way of conforming to societal expectations. Rather than being driven by testosterone or something like that." Note that Stephanie both endorsed a cultural and socialization-based account and rejected biological explanations. While their positions were not universal in scholarship on sexual violence, Susan and Stephanie did not seem to expect pushback from me or from fellow researchers. They rather seemed to expect comprehension and agreement.

Scientists who advanced a power and control model that distinguished all sexual violence from sexual desire tended to provide unqualified endorsements of this perspective.[5] These individuals approached sexual violence as inherently violent, but not inherently (and for some scientists, not ever) sexual. Madeline, a sociologist, explicitly defined rape as a "bodily violation of a sexual nature . . . not about sex, but about power." Karen, a criminal justice scholar, commented that sexual violence in prisons was "usually driven by something other than just sexual desire, because we know that sexual assault is not about sexual desire." There was no need to elaborate or argue further; the irrelevance of sexual desire was simply something "we" knew.

In contrast, participants who embraced evolutionary explanations, who emphasized sexual communication and complex notions of consent, and who perceived of sexual violence as both violent and sexual seemed to anticipate pushback. They were more apt to provide qualified descriptions of their positions. They were more apt to provide justifications or evidence without my prompting. Such practices relate to credibility struggles that may arise when scholars challenge dominant ideas and established colleagues within their fields (Bourdieu 1975; Epstein 1996; Latour 1987; Shapin 1995). In striking contrast from Karen and Madeline, Amy, a legal scholar, insisted that sexuality was very much relevant to the phenomenon of rape: "People sort of don't want to admit that sexual violence is about sex, right? There's that whole weird erasure in thinking about sexual violence, like rape is about violence, not sex. Well, no, it's sexual violence. It's actually sexual violence . . . and you know, we can deal with the sex, or we can deal with the violence, but we can't deal with them together." Amy demonstrated a keen awareness that her stance was controversial. She incorporated criticism of other scholars(hip) directly into her position, rather than simply state that "sexual violence is about both sex and violence" and move on.

Researchers who studied sexual communication and consent were often delicate in advancing these as causal forces in rape. Audrey, a public health scholar, expressed concern about college students' capacity to communicate sexual consent and refusal, but presented this as a plausible or likely issue rather than a settled matter: "I think a lot about the college students, because a lot of them are relatively young. These are often in their first few sexual relationships. So talking about things openly may not be, they might not yet have that skill set to say 'oral sex is ok, but anal sex is off the table' or something." Audrey shared concerns that students "might not" be capable of clearly communicating sexual consent and refusal. She implied that this might exacerbate risks of violence without directly linking students' ability to "talk about things openly" with the problem of rape. Scientists were still more cautious when explicitly considering potential connections between sexual communication and incidents of violence. Wendy, a social work scholar, shared ongoing struggles with research and programming in this area:

Men will say, "But she wanted it. I didn't realize that's what I was doing. I was drunk." Whatever. Even if they did realize, they're not going to say that. And there's a disconnect. Because the guys are saying, "I didn't know that's what I was doing" and the women are like, "You violated me, and now I'm having traumatic symptoms." So there's a disconnect, and it's not like these—I don't imagine these guys, these college guys being these evil—there are some predators on campus, but most sexual assaults, I don't imagine these evil guys. I imagine these drunk sloppy guys that aren't paying attention to cues. Right? This is not to justify it, and it's still sexual violence because they need to be paying attention to that shit, but how do we give them the space to understand that, and not do it? Some people have been focusing more on hookup culture, how to raise guys to not think they have to score. Maybe that's part of it, but, I don't know.

Whereas scholars who believe that sexual violence is entirely about power and not about sex might protest that the men described above were enacting masculine power and knowingly (or at least carelessly) violating women, Wendy offered a more complicated and ambivalent analysis. She incorporated masculine socialization, alcohol, and hookup culture as important variables to account for men's sexual aggression. She evoked a "disconnect" between the perceptions of sexually aggressive men and sexually victimized women, and suggested that the former may not always be "evil" or conscious predators. Even while offering this nuanced commentary, even within a broader conversation in which she repeatedly expressed investment in supporting survivors, she took a moment to explicitly state that "this is not to justify it, and it's still sexual violence." She seemed prepared for the sort of criticism that Charlene Muehlenhard and others have faced in their work, but not so concerned that she shied away from advancing this position.

Adam, a biologist, was the only participant in this study who had incorporated evolutionary theory into his research on rape. Like Wendy, he seemed to anticipate and preemptively respond to criticism for his position:

All features of life, all features of living things are products of some kind of evolutionary process. That's just a statement of fact. And then from that, you know, rape is a feature of life, and therefore it is caused ultimately by some kind of evolutionary process. . . . And then you can go more and more detailed there, like what kind of evolutionary process? Sexual coercion is a mode of sexual selection, so that's the body of evolutionary processes. And then, sexual selection is the basic area of evolutionary process that made the psychology and behavior by which men rape. And what I've said is not controversial in biology.

Here, Adam prefaced a contested argument—an evolutionary account of rape—by pointing out that the relevance of evolution to "all features of life" was "just a statement of fact." The "in biology" point here is also crucial. Research that draws harsh opposition in fields such as psychology, sociology, social work, or public health might nonetheless be noncontroversial within biology.

Researchers who endorsed controversial positions shared a range of approaches for handling colleagues' opposition. These included careful selection of journals for publication and agencies for grant support. Even when submitting work to those prescreened institutions, many anticipated and answered critiques directly within manuscripts. Stacey, quoted at the beginning of this chapter, recalled being accused of reinforcing the very rape myths that she was actively working to dismantle. She had taken to reviewing the editor lists of journals before submission, in case anyone might be particularly likely to misinterpret or politically oppose her work. She had also developed a habit of including statements such as "these findings are in direct opposition to the widespread rape myth that . . ." into her writing.

Several participants seemed almost to shrug off opposition to their points of view, refusing to restrict expertise to particular scientists or reviewers. While this approach did not necessarily improve their odds of publication, or their odds of securing tenure or tenure-track positions, it did lessen the impact that harsh critiques might have. When I asked about his experiences embracing controversial positions, Adam responded by endorsing strict boundaries around science. He insisted that his ideas were entirely noncontroversial among legitimate scientists, and that opponents of evolutionary work on rape were driven by political rather than scientific concerns. When I asked Amy the same question, she expressed a willingness to leave academia if "intellectual policing" prevented her from engaging in meaningful and explicitly feminist work.

Calls for Systematic and Intersectional Causal Inquiries

As discussed in the preceding close readings of well-cited texts, psychology and psychiatry have historically and consistently dominated causal inquiries in sexual violence research. Yet scholars from a range of fields have long been involved in the work. In this project, scientists across disciplines valued the contribution of psychological and psychiatric investigations of individual predictors of aggression, victimization, and bystander behaviors. Nonetheless, many—including some who were, themselves, trained in these disciplines—described a pressing need for more interdisciplinary and systemic investigations. These concerns often dovetailed with a call for more intersectional approaches in causal research. This is not to suggest that psychological research and intersectional research are inherently at odds— neither I nor study participants make such claims here—but rather that the complexity and nuance facilitated by multilevel and interdisciplinary work complement the aims and politics of intersectional approaches.

Participants frequently expressed support for multilevel causal models and study designs. Denise, a psychologist, had moved increasingly in this direction throughout her career:

> Over time, I take more and more and more of a community point of view. . . . I always knew that was important, but I think for a long time I was very much a product of my training, which was as a psychologist. Which is being focused on not only the individual, but what's

happening in their head. And now, I spend enough time collaborating with sociologists and people in social work and people in community psychology that I think it's more of a habit of thinking to really take in that broader perspective. And not just to give it lip service.

Julia, a social work scholar, suggested that multilevel and systemic approaches were necessary for building effective prevention efforts:

> We need to be looking not only at the individual, but we need to be figuring out what kinds of peer level and community level and beyond interventions work. . . . How do things like sense of community, how does a campus—in terms of their administration, and the way that they convey their attitudes about sexual violence—how does all of that affect whether or not sexual violence is happening, and the sort of climate that students find themselves in? Moving beyond the individual to look at the other ecological issues, I think, is a really important issue.

As researchers discussed gender socialization, interpersonal communication, campus climate, the social distribution of power, and other cultural and systemic causal forces, they consistently expressed investment in scholarship and prevention efforts that engage those forces. Notably, such systemic efforts were broadly conceived as compatible with individual-level inquiries. The aim was to extend, rather than replace, more established lines of inquiry. Gretchen, a psychologist, recalled a project on peer violence in schools that combined individual attitudinal and behavioral assessments with ethnographic environmental scans to observe shifts in social norms. Her more systemic analysis did not supersede so much as complement her more conventional psychological assessments.

These calls for systemic and interdisciplinary inquiries often emerged alongside calls for intersectional research. Systemic models approached rape as a complex and multifaceted issue, which allowed for the recognition that various causal forces and prevention strategies had varying impacts across individuals and communities. After expressing support for ecological approaches, Julia, quoted above, went on to note that "we need a lot more research to figure out what works, and for whom it works. So just because a bystander intervention program works for one part of a population on one campus doesn't mean it will for others." Questions such as "is this program effective?" or "does this policy prevent rape?" were rarely approached as yes/no matters. Julia and others encouraged scholars to consider that shifting cultural norms might not meaningfully affect all individuals' risk of aggression and victimization, just as preventing some potential assailants from doing harm would not automatically eradicate sexist and other oppressive attitudes and practices on campus.

Many participants expressed concerns that causal research focused too much on the experiences of White, middle class, heterosexual, cisgender, nondisabled college students. In some cases, this came down to sampling and analytical strategies (i.e., which variables were incorporated and emphasized). The historical dominance of micro-level projects might be further limiting here, in that forces such as the systemic feminization and racialization of poverty are difficult to discern in individual-level analyses. Researchers' demographic and experiential backgrounds were also important. Wendy connected such concerns with my own project when she speculated that, "I don't know what the demographics are of the people you've been interviewing, but my assumption is that many of them are White women" (she was correct, and I said as much). Miranda, an anthropologist, suggested that researchers' discomfort might also play a role in obscuring intersectional realities: "I'm also really interested in thinking about precarities and vulnerabilities. And broader issues of inequality. Because sexual violence is—I think people get uncomfortable thinking about it—I mean, it's not equally distributed across all demographics, right? . . . So the distribution of vulnerability is something that I've more lately tried to be thoughtful about." This speaks again to the importance of distinguishing between neutral and inclusive scholarship. A disability-neutral project on sexual violence against women, for example, might approach disability as wholly irrelevant. A disability-inclusive project would provide avenues for recognizing that, while a substantial majority of victims/survivors might be nondisabled women, disabled women experience sexual violence at disproportionately high rates (Goodman et al. 1997; Martin et al. 2006).

As noted in the preceding quantitative and qualitative content analyses, causal research has overwhelmingly prioritized cisgender men's violence toward cisgender women in heterosexual contexts. Participants were divided regarding whether this was appropriate or concerning. This divide seemed to center on two basic questions: (1) Given the pervasiveness of this gendered pattern in sexual violence, is it justifiable to focus time and energy elsewhere? and (2) Do the causes of sexual violence vary by gender and sexuality? The first question overlaps considerably with the discussion of precasting and definitions in chapter 2; consequently, I will not devote space to it here. The second question is of more direct relevance to the subfield of causal research, and warrants further consideration.

If the causes of sexual violence are identical across genders and sexualities, there is no empirical reason to move toward gender-inclusive scholarship (though there might be philosophical or political reasons to call for it nonetheless). If the causes vary, all or in part, then present scientific practices are inadequate for understanding same-sex violence, sexual violence involving transgender people, victimization of cisgender men, and aggression by cisgender women. Gretchen shared several participants' frustration with polarization among scholars around this issue: "It's like you have people who are just on these opposite ends. Like, women can never be violent—I think most people wouldn't say that. But [there are] people who say there's absolutely no parallel. And then other people that say it's 100 percent the same. To me, we're supposed to be academics and thinking about things in more nuanced, complex ways. And both of those seem overly simplistic."

Participants who had studied gendered patterns in sexual violence were somewhat divided on the presence/scope of variation. Max, a criminologist, recalled projects on sexual offending in which "the models for women generally explain less than half of the variance of the models for men." She was staunchly critical of precasting in causal studies: "I think it's that, for so long, we've fixated on males' violence, sexual and psychological and physical, or all three. We really haven't done enough to study women's violence alone to get a sense of what the heck's going on. . . . There are sort of those crisscrosses that take place, and yes, we've myopically focused on women as victims, so we're probably better at predicting women's victimization than men's."

Clara, a psychologist, also expressed support for gender-inclusive approaches. However, unlike Max, she was skeptical that people of different genders required different causal models or should be assessed separately: "Certainly, you know, women are far more likely to be sexually assaulted and raped than are men. However, you know, there are a lot of boys and men who are sexually assaulted and raped. And they are completely ignored. And so it seems to me that you almost have to include both just to see what's going on, because both get negated, you know? So what's happening? And [to suggest that] here's this theory for girls and here's one for boys—I don't buy it."

Such questions can only be settled through gender-inclusive, empirical research. Of course, this would require researchers (and perhaps also grant-providing institutions) to believe that there are questions to settle, and that diverse gendered patterns in sexual violence merit investigation notwithstanding the pervasiveness of cisgender men's violence toward cisgender women.

Prevention Strategies: Bystander Approaches and Sex Education

Many scholars who study the causes of sexual violence engage in prevention work. For the past several years, bystander programs have dominated such work in the United States. These programs aim to produce active bystanders through raising awareness of sexual violence, training people to recognize risky situations, and to develop individuals' skills for actively intervening. The concept of "risky situations" is often broadly conceived, encompassing imminent and in-progress acts of sexual violence as well as more subtle behaviors, such as telling sexist jokes or expressing victim-blaming attitudes when discussing a high profile sexual harassment case. Bystander trainees are often provided with a range of tools for intervening in such situations, such as verbally challenging the use of sexist language, checking in with people who seem uncomfortable, and distracting potential assailants and/or victims in higher risk situations. Freshman orientation programs in colleges and universities frequently incorporate sexual violence prevention units with an emphasis on bystander intervention.

Several participants in this study had worked on bystander programming before, or collaborated with scholars and providers in this area. While they expressed enthusiasm for the logic of bystander efforts—particularly the notion that rape is a community issue—some shared concerns about the pace with which such programs had become the national standard. It seemed that large-scale adoption of bystander prevention by state and higher education officials had preceded rigorous evaluation and refinement. Wendy commented that "campus climate surveys, bystander intervention, consent trainings are all over in college campuses—but we don't have a good handle on whether they're effective or helpful." Stacey echoed and expanded on this sentiment, embracing the community accountability aspect of bystander programming but questioning the impact on actual rates of violence:

> I think the cultural climate piece is really good. Sort of this idea that we're all responsible for changing the environment around us . . . [but] there's not good data to support that this is actually reducing sexual assaults at all. That doesn't necessarily mean it's pointless—like, it still might be worthwhile to change how we all talk, and how we all behave—but it's not clear that's changing behavior. . . . It's not clear that if someone intervenes and stops someone from taking a drunk woman up to the room, that this person doesn't go find another drunk woman to take up to the room. . . . It's not that I'm opposed to it, and I think it could be really useful. But I think it needs more testing, and I think we've all kind of latched onto it before we have the data.

Audrey was a bit more pessimistic:

> I think the evidence shows that we're not doing a great job with our current efforts, in terms of actually preventing violence. I think a lot of the trainings that we've done—I actually don't have great confidence that even the bystander stuff is going to do it. Because I think so much of this happens in places where there isn't a third person. And/or the people who are around are not in a position where they could actually bystand. And I say as someone who believes, I don't think they hurt things, but I don't believe they're the solution. They're not likely to lead to the population level change that we need.

Scholars who shared these concerns were not arguing that bystander prevention was wholly ineffective or counterproductive, but rather that the evidence was too incomplete to justify the present scope of investment in these programs (at least within the United States). They called for further evaluation research, continued efforts to adapt existing interventions to address logistical barriers to effective bystanding, such as intoxication and peer pressure against intervening, and investment in tailoring programs to meet the needs of diverse communities.

A single intervention program could never mitigate or eliminate all factors identified in the literature as promoting or justifying rape. Bystander behaviors are largely distinct from issues with sexual communication, for example, such as capacities for conveying and interpreting sexual consent and refusal, that many scholars and activists have written about. Consequently, even participants who were enthusiastic about bystander intervention expressed a need to supplement these programs with additional efforts. Rebecca, a public health scholar, posed an intriguing question in this vein: "does rape prevention have to look like rape prevention?" And if not, what else might it look like? She elaborated:

> Let's talk about sex education, and if we can teach people how to have—not just healthy and consensual sex, but also fulfilling orgasmic sex. Like, will we still see rape? Why don't we go to an assets-based approach instead of a deficits-based approach? And why don't we also consider the fact that even comprehensive sex education is values-based in a lot of ways? A lot of it is very heteronormative. And a lot of it also is based on this idea of healthy relationships, and there are many young people—whether they're in middle school, high school, college—that don't necessarily want to have a relationship, but they still want to have sexual interactions.

Significantly, Rebecca proposed an emphasis on pleasure and personal fulfillment, and for recognizing and valuing diversity in sexual desires and behaviors. She argued that this might comprise a powerful approach to reducing sexual violence.

While many curricula prioritize abstinence or, in the case of what is often called "comprehensive" sex education, understanding and avoiding sexual risk, sex education programs can and sometimes do encourage critical and reflective engagement with concepts such as sexual consent and sexual autonomy. Jeff, a philosopher with a background in sexuality research, commented, "Through all those sex education programs, I've always found something missing. And the thing that I think is missing is broadly construed as some sort of character building, or certain techniques of the self where people have to realize what they want and what they desire. Instead of following the same sort of sexual or relationship script." When I asked him to envision a more ideal program, he elaborated:

> I think having a very robust picture of consent would be great. They could go through philosophical case studies, and then just bring up whether this is an instance of consent or there's something problematic with it. Because I think a lot of students don't recognize how complicated consent can be. And I think just bringing up various scenarios would help. I also think that they can bring in a gender dynamic . . . especially [for] young men who think consent is, "well, I heard a 'yes' and I got a 'yes,' so now it's ok," without recognizing that there's a whole context about why, usually, the woman said yes. Is it because she genuinely wanted to? Or because that was the least option available? Or she was pressured, or she was afraid of the alternatives? And I think bringing those out into the classroom, the framework helps students recognize that consent is much more complicated. And hopefully gets them to thinking about how they, themselves, would exercise consent when that time comes.

This approach to sex education might work for children, adolescents, or young adults, provided that content and language were tailored appropriately.

Participants with backgrounds in sex education and sexual violence research consistently portrayed these fields as complementary. Marion, a public health scholar, recalled that her experiences in sex education provided "the perspective of knowing what people don't know . . . and the interests people have around healthy relationships and communication styles." Stacey advocated strongly for sex education as a means of preventing sexual assault: "How do people talk about consent when they don't even have terms for sexual acts? So many of these college students, really the first formal sex education they get is like this online rape prevention program, which seems like not the place to be starting." Echoing Rebecca's comments about whether rape prevention needs to look like rape prevention, Stacey further suggested "framing it as kind of sex communication and pleasure training. But with a sort of hidden agenda that we think this is also helpful in terms of better consent communication and other things."

Of course, these approaches would require the same sort of rigorous development, refinement, tailoring, and evaluation that Stacey and others advocated for bystander interventions. Although there has been some progress in this direction, specifically regarding the development and evaluation of rape prevention programming for women that is attentive to matters of sexual communication, consent, and desire (e.g., Senn 2011), such efforts lag considerably behind in comparison with work on bystanding.

COMPLEX AND CONTENTIOUS ACCOUNTINGS

Causal inquiries comprise a rich and vibrant subfield within rape research. In as little as four decades, scientists have moved through a range of research priorities and theoretical and methodological frameworks to account for sexual violence. Whereas research emphasizing sexual arousal and using penile plethysmography to predict men's aggression was dominant in the late 1970s and early 1980s (Malamuth 1981; Malamuth, Haber, and Feshbach 1980); investigations emphasizing bystander intervention reached farthest in recent years (McMahon 2010; McMahon and Banyard 2012). Accounts that rely on sexual (mis)communication or evolution remain controversial, largely due to (empirically unexamined) fears of misuse—yet the former remains relatively prominent in sexual violence research, whereas the latter seems to have declined. At the same time, the most widely cited research has consistently situated rape within—or rather, engaged cultural scenarios that presume—heterosexual encounters with cisgender individuals, informed by men's capacity for aggression and women's vulnerability to assault. The historical, though presently declining, dominance of psychological research has produced an immense body of knowledge on individual-level predictors of aggression, victimization, and bystanding. Causal studies have also consistently prioritized (or at least relied on) college students, even more than the broader field of sexual violence research.

Collectively, these historical trends indicate that scientists are well-poised to account for sexual aggression by individual heterosexual and cisgender undergraduate men, sexual victimization of individual heterosexual and cisgender college women, and bystander attitudes and behaviors in both groups. If the forces that promote and deter violence within undergraduate communities also apply in other contexts, the emphasis on campus research is not necessarily a problem. If this is not the case, there are scientific reasons to expand causal inquiries to encompass a broader range of populations and spaces. Likewise, if the forces that promote and deter violence do not vary by gender and sexuality, there may be little cause for more gender inclusive scholarship. If this is not the case, scientists should work to broaden dominant conceptualizations regarding who may enact the roles of aggressor and victim/survivor.

Interview participants offered several promising directions for causal research that are worth reiterating here. Many scientists and other scholars called for more interdisciplinary scholarship, as well as overall greater involvement among scholars in disciplines such as sociology and anthropology who are trained to consider institutional, cultural, and other systemic dimensions of social problems. This suggestion was accompanied by calls for more intersectional research. Even if the individual and systemic causes of sexual aggression and victimization do not vary by gender and sexuality, the populations of "cisgender heterosexual men" and "cisgender heterosexual women" are hardly monolithic. Their members vary by race, ethnicity, skin color, disability status, education, class background, immigration background, citizenship status, place of origin, place of residence, political orientation, religious affiliation or nonaffiliation, spiritual beliefs, alignment with or divergence from normative beauty standards, and more. These and other factors may affect what Miranda referred to as "the distribution of vulnerability" (see also Alcoff 2018).

In the realm of prevention, many participants expressed support for bystander intervention while also calling for critical and rigorous evaluation of such approaches' impact on rates of aggression and victimization. Several also pointed to sex education as a promising avenue for social change. Programs labeled as "sex education" might be more effective than those labeled "rape prevention" for promoting critical engagement with sexual consent. Moreover, some participants suggested that prioritizing the development of sexual subjectivity and fulfillment—and recognizing and valuing a substantial range of sexual desires, behaviors, and discourses—might ultimately serve to promote agentic sexuality and reduce violence.

CHAPTER 4

Investigating the Aftermath

For sexual violence generally, I mean there are things we know. We know the criminal justice system is shitty. So do we need to spend more [grant] dollars learning that?
—Wendy, social work scholar

The assumptions made about forensic evidence and rape kits have been problematic. These are not "black-boxed" neutral tools or facts—they are socially constructed in their production and use, and, as such, are infused with the cultural biases inherent in a society that is imbued with rape myths and a fundamental distrust (and often disdain) of and for women. . . . I am also surprised that there is so little critical questioning of forensic evidence and such trust (and "magic") placed in it by the general population, and also by many criminal justice system professionals.
—Madeline, sociologist

THIS CHAPTER CONCERNS scientific efforts to address the aftermath of sexual violence. In scientific discourse, this often entails a search for "effects" of which rape is a "cause." I conceptualize "the effects of sexual violence" broadly. This includes individual-level outcomes for aggressors and victims/survivors, such as changes in mental and physical health; as well as broader impacts for these individuals, such as shifts within interpersonal relationships, changes in educational and professional trajectories, and the acquisition/expansion (or not) of criminal records. Effects also include the impact of disclosures and publicized incidents on aggressors' and victims' social and professional networks, larger social communities, and institutions. As Linda Alcoff (2018) has argued, the interests and welfare of these various actors may be at odds. Scholars and activists have often critiqued the "willfully inadequate" response to sexual violence that may emerge when "other concerns trump the concern for the harm to victims" (16).

Aftermath research sometimes addresses the labeling of experiences. When a sexually violent incident occurs, the victim/survivor, assailant, personal acquaintances of these individuals, local community members, jurors, journalists, and other actors may disagree about what happened. Each of these individuals, themselves, may vary in what language they use to describe the incident. This question of whether something counts as rape may have considerable and diverse consequences. High-profile cases often center around whether an incident constituted rape or (criminal) sexual violence. Such matters are hotly contested in senate confirmation hearings, criminal courts, campus adjudication proceedings, and the "court of public opinion." On a more individual level, survivors who label their own experiences as rape may be more likely to pursue rape care services and to report their experiences to criminal justice institutions. Survivors whose experiences are labeled as rape by others may receive more social support, whereas those who are doubted or whose experience of violence is (re)cast as consensual or fictional may face distrust, violence, and harassment. Assailants who believe themselves to have committed rape may seek to change their behavior or perhaps agree to restorative justice conferencing; those who do not believe that they have committed rape may push back against and seek to discredit survivors.

Effects research may also address help-seeking behaviors by victims/ survivors and their significant others, as well as institutional responses in domains such as police departments, courts, prisons, schools, rape crisis centers, workplaces, colleges and universities, hospitals and clinics, and legislatures. As a counterpart to evaluations of bystander interventions in chapter 3 on causal research, I have included evaluations of clinical and criminal justice processes in this chapter. Such works often concern a range of aftermath events, more so than may be immediately apparent. A study on the treatment of PTSD among rape survivors, for example, may address mental health outcomes (the development or not of PTSD), support-seeking behaviors (pursuit of mental health resources, potentially including those that require a waiting period), persistence in therapeutic programs (particularly through the measurement and analysis of attrition before and during treatment), and the ultimate impact of various therapies on post-rape diagnosis or symptomology. Some scholars in this subfield also consider the capacity for sexual violence to influence the social distribution of power and other resources. Rather than conceive of patriarchy solely as a causal factor, they might consider the extent to which men's violence against women perpetuates gender inequality and the cultural devaluing of women.

Much like causal inquiries, effects research appears somewhat murky or amorphous through an agential realist lens. Such work requires scientists to distinguish the object of sexual violence from its aftermath. Assessing institutional responses to sexual violence, a common theme in this research (not to mention a categorization that I, myself made when describing scientists' various roles in this field in chapter 1), requires enacting agential cuts between those institutions' actions and the events/practices/objects that came "before." But when, truly, does sexual violence end? When does the institutional response begin, and how well can this be distinguished from individual and interpersonal responses?

Sexual assault forensic examinations (SAFEs), commonly known as "rape kits," are instructive here. These exams are quite involved and can feel as much if not more invasive and traumatizing as the violence that precedes them (Mulla 2014). Completing a SAFE requires telling and retelling one's experience of sexual victimization. Victims/survivors who pursue care in the immediate "aftermath" are advised not to bathe or change their clothes, and to neither consume anything nor relieve themselves before the exam lest they lose evidence. They are routinely asked to surrender their clothing. If assailants committed oral, anal, or vaginal penetration—with fingers, penises, tongues, or other body parts or objects—victims will be asked to submit to medical penetration (e.g., with a speculum or swab). In some states and municipalities, survivors are expected or even required to speak with law enforcement in order to access medical care. Advocates may or may not be available.

If these experiences feel like a "second rape" for some survivors (Campbell et al. 2001; Madigan and Gamble 1991; Mulla 2014), is it necessarily accurate to locate SAFEs solely within the aftermath? To describe forensic examinations solely as a response to, rather than a furtherance or enactment of, sexual violence? Can the same object/event/practice be both a continuance of and an institutional response to sexual violence? As in previous chapters, I have largely deferred to scientists' own characterization of their work in determining what counted as an effect or aftermath event. I conceive of these characterizations as enacting agential cuts within the phenomena of (scientific research on) sexual violence.

Throughout data collection and broader literature searches, I could not find a public or scientific controversy in aftermath research comparable to those around communication-based models, evolutionary accounts, or the "one in four women" statistic discussed in previous chapters. Given this, I was surprised when participants shared more frustrations with this subfield than any other. Some criticism concerned a perceived tendency toward needless replication. Wendy, quoted above, was joined by several others in worrying that scholars repeatedly looked to confirm "things that we know" rather than pursuing new or hitherto neglected lines of inquiry. Participants who had studied legal responses were often disappointed with scholarship that seemed to uncritically endorse forensic examinations and criminal prosecution as inherently positive and necessary. Several participants also shared Madeline's concern, shown above, that criminal justice professionals and the general public were misguided in approaching forensic evidence as providing "magic" access to the truth or automatically improving the odds of prosecution and conviction. Finally, consistent with the previous chapter on casual research, participants called for more systemic and intersectional approaches in scientific work.

In this chapter, I argue that the subfield of effects or aftermath research has been dominated by psychological investigations that precast cisgender men as aggressors and cisgender women as victims. Consequently, systemic outcomes, as well as the outcomes of other gendered manifestations of sexual violence, have been relatively neglected. Aftermath research has also emphasized victimization and neglected aggression. Whereas there is a substantial literature on assault survivors' potential to develop post-traumatic stress disorder (PTSD) and demonstrate other mental health outcomes such as anxiety and depressive symptoms, the psychological effects of perpetrating sexual violence remain largely unknown. Finally, more so than other subfields, I argue that effects research has been characterized by a tendency to endorse and reform existing institutional resources, such as criminal investigation and prosecution, with minimal attention toward alternatives such as restorative justice. To justify these arguments, I review statistical trends in effects research and provide close assessments of the ten most-cited works from each decade. I then turn to participants' insights on this subfield, and consider their criticisms alongside the quantitative and qualitative trends in my own analysis.

FORTY YEARS OF EFFECTS RESEARCH

Effects research ranked second among all study aims from 1975 to 2004, and barely surpassed causal inquiries in the following decade. Approximately 45% of studies analyzed here investigated the effects of sexual violence (589 out of 1,313). Figures 4.1–4.4 present some of the general characteristics of effects pieces, stratified by decade. Frequencies appear in table 4.1, along with data for the whole field of sexual violence research for comparison. As quantitative trends for the broader field have been reviewed previously in chapter 2, I do not discuss them here except to make comparisons with the subfield of effects research.

Effects pieces incorporated other study aims infrequently, as noted in figure 4.1. When they did, causality and evaluation were most likely to be included. The former might occur when investigators classified victims and nonvictims by demographic characteristics and pre-assault behaviors (often conceptualized as risk and protective factors). Mental health was sometimes proposed as both cause and consequence within individual studies. Various symptoms and diagnoses might mitigate or exacerbate risks of violence, and they might also manifest or change following victimization. Effects

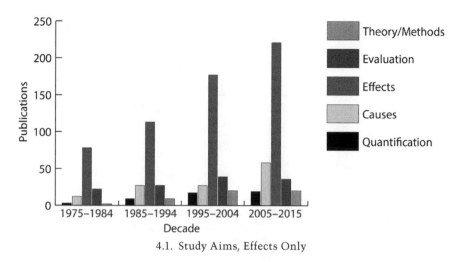

4.1. Study Aims, Effects Only

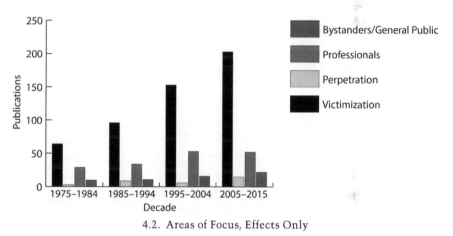

4.2. Areas of Focus, Effects Only

inquiries paired with evaluation in studies concerning different approaches to therapy, criminal justice reporting and processing, and other institutional engagement with individuals who had experienced or perpetrated sexual violence.

Aftermath inquiries have prioritized outcomes for survivors of violence. These include the impact of sexual victimization on such diverse matters as personal relationships, medical and mental health, sexual functioning, and broader perceptions of consensual and nonconsensual sexual scripts. Professionals consistently ranked a distant second, as demonstrated in figure 4.2. Such studies investigated the impact of sexual violence on therapists, crisis counselors, and other professionals who serve victims and/or aggressors. Perpetrators and bystanders have received minimal attention in this subfield. This suggests that the impacts of committing sexual aggression, and of

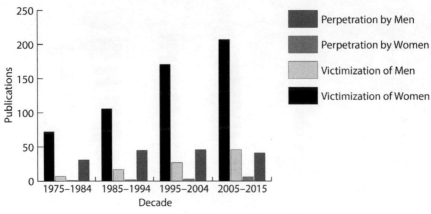

4.3. Gendered Patterns, Effects Only

directly or indirectly witnessing sexual violence, constitute relatively low priorities. These patterns have not varied significantly over time.

Much like the broader field, effects inquiries have consistently and substantially prioritized the victimization of women. This trend appears in figure 4.3. Perpetration by men, victimization of men, and perpetration by women ranked second, third, and fourth, respectively, in the first three decades considered here; work on men's victimization slightly outpaced work on men's perpetration in effects research between 2005 and 2015. The only significant shift in gendered patterns concerned a decline in studies with direct references to men's aggression, which peaked at 40% for the effects inquiries from 1975 to 1994, dropped to 26% in the following decade, and fell further to 19% of publications from 2005 to 2015. The sort of precasting incorporated into quantitative analysis, in which researchers employed gender-neutral language in abstracts to describe gender-restricted projects, was less pronounced in effects research than in the larger field. There were significant declines in this writing practice over time, dropping from 28% in 1975–1984 to 13% in 2005–2015.

Whereas most studies of sexual violence have focused on college/university students across all four decades, with general population and community samples coming in second, figure 4.4 demonstrates that this pattern was reversed in the effects subfield. Undergraduates received consistently less attention than the general population; care recipients, such as survivors who contacted rape crisis centers or pursued forensic exams, received the most attention for several decades. Whereas research with inmates and convicted persons consistently outpaced research with military personnel in the broader field from 1995 to 2015 (no military studies met inclusion criteria in earlier years), this pattern was also reversed in outcomes research. Several

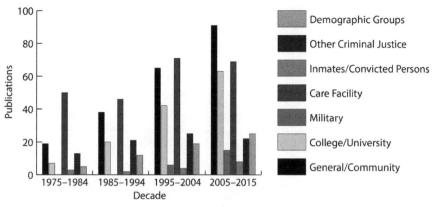

4.4. Study Populations, Effects Only

shifts in target population were statistically significant. These included effects researchers' increasing attention to college and university students, even if they remained a lower priority than care recipients and general populations (inconsistent with the broader field); an increase in military studies over time (consistent with the broader field); and a decline in studies with care facility populations (more pronounced than but otherwise consistent with the broader field).

CLOSE READINGS: DOMINANT VOICES IN AFTERMATH RESEARCH

Close readings of the ten most-cited effects studies from each decade (forty studies total) revealed a range of steady and shifting patterns in dominant priorities and perspectives. Whereas victims/victimization received consistent attention, professionals such as jurors and medical providers received more intermittent attention. None of the pieces analyzed here explored the impact of perpetrating sexual violence on aggressors or their interpersonal networks. Consistent with causal research, scholars embraced increasingly social and multifaceted models over time. Other trends were more unique to this subfield. Sexual violence committed against men or by women was addressed with some regularity in the earlier years, although rape was largely and increasingly conceptualized as a matter of cisgender men's violence against cisgender women ("woman" and "female" were treated as synonymous terms in this literature across all four decades, and this is reflected in the overviews below). Scholars studying the aftermath of rape also seemed less likely to recruit participants or assess their experiences through the use of explicit definitions; instead, sampling frames such as "women who have sought services at rape crisis centers" served to identify victims.[1] Finally, and perhaps most interesting for this project, top-cited effects works did not always emphasize

TABLE 4.1

Descriptive Statistics for All Publications and Effects Pieces, by Decade

	All Publications				Effects Pieces			
	1975–1984	1985–1994	1995–2004	2005–2015	1975–1984	1985–1994	1995–2004	2005–2015
Precasting[ac]	53 (30%)	91 (30%)	102 (26%)	90 (21%)	22 (28%)	24 (21%)	37 (21%)	28 (13%)
Study Aims:								
Quantification	11 (6%)	32 (10%)	33 (8%)	49 (11%)	3 (4%)	9 (8%)	17 (10%)	19 (9%)
Causes of Rape	91 (52%)	169 (55%)	200 (50%)	209 (49%)	12 (15%)	27 (24%)	27 (15%)	58 (26%)
Effects of Rape[b]	78 (44%)	113 (37%)	177 (44%)	221 (51%)	–	–	–	–
Evaluation	41 (23%)	76 (25%)	108 (27%)	115 (27%)	22 (28%)	27 (24%)	39 (22%)	36 (16%)
Theory/Methods[b]	16 (9%)	42 (14%)	63 (16%)	83 (19%)	2 (3%)	9 (8%)	20 (11%)	20 (9%)
Overall Focus:								
Victimization[b]	82 (47%)	140 (46%)	221 (55%)	283 (66%)	64 (82%)	96 (85%)	153 (86%)	203 (92%)
Perpetration[bc]	43 (24%)	77 (25%)	69 (17%)	68 (16%)	3 (4%)	9 (8%)	6 (3%)	15 (7%)
Professionals	49 (28%)	88 (29%)	118 (30%)	134 (31%)	29 (37%)	34 (30%)	53 (30%)	52 (24%)
Bystanders/General Public[bc]	59 (34%)	88 (29%)	118 (30%)	93 (22%)	10 (13%)	11 (10%)	16 (9%)	22 (10%)
Gendered Patterns:								
Victimization of Women	154 (88%)	275 (89%)	367 (92%)	387 (90%)	72 (92%)	106 (93%)	171 (97%)	207 (94%)
Victimization of Men[b]	12 (7%)	37 (12%)	60 (15%)	90 (21%)	7 (9%)	17 (15%)	27 (15%)	46 (21%)

TABLE 4.1 (continued)

	All Publications				Effects Pieces			
	1975–1984	1985–1994	1995–2004	2005–2015	1975–1984	1985–1994	1995–2004	2005–2015
Perpetration by Women	3 (2%)	8 (3%)	14 (4%)	21 (5%)	1 (1%)	2 (2%)	3 (2%)	6 (3%)
Perpetration by Men[bd]	115 (65%)	196 (64%)	202 (51%)	172 (40%)	31 (40%)	45 (40%)	46 (26%)	41 (19%)
Study Population:								
General/Community	42 (24%)	91 (30%)	107 (27%)	142 (33%)	19 (24%)	38 (34%)	65 (37%)	91 (41%)
College/University	51 (29%)	106 (34%)	157 (39%)	165 (38%)	7 (9%)	20 (18%)	42 (24%)	63 (29%)
Military[b]	0 (0%)	0 (0%)	10 (3%)	21 (5%)	0 (0%)	0 (0%)	6 (3%)	15 (7%)
Care Facility[bd]	62 (35%)	73 (24%)	107 (27%)	95 (22%)	50 (64%)	46 (41%)	71 (40%)	69 (31%)
Inmates/Convicted Persons[b]	23 (13%)	33 (11%)	22 (6%)	27 (6%)	3 (4%)	2 (3%)	4 (2%)	8 (4%)
Other Criminal Justice	25 (14%)	52 (17%)	55 (14%)	43 (10%)	13 (17%)	21 (19%)	25 (14%)	22 (10%)
Demographic Groups	10 (6%)	22 (7%)	40 (10%)	45 (11%)	5 (6%)	12 (11%)	19 (11%)	25 (11%)

[a]p<.05, [b]p<.01 for full sample of publications in chi-square analysis; [c]p<.05, [d]p<.01 for quantification pieces

NOTE: Categories for study aims, overall focus, gendered patterns, and study population are not mutually exclusive. For example, a study may address both victimization of women and victimization of men.

sexual violence as a key issue in itself. Several studies (or rather, several scientists) approached rape victims/survivors as an ideal population for advancing certain forms of scientific knowledge. Illuminating the complexities of PTSD or promising therapeutic techniques might be prioritized as major contributions over and above—or perhaps even without direct mention—of refining responses to sexual violence. Table 4.2 provides basic information about all forty publications.

Decade One: 1975–1984

Broadly speaking, dominant effects inquiries prioritized two areas in these years: (a) health outcomes for victims of sexual violence such as depression and substance use (Atkeson et al. 1982; Burgess and Holmstrom 1979; Groth and Burgess 1980; Janoff-Bulman 1979; Kaufman et al. 1980; Kilpatrick, Resick, and Veronen 1981; Kilpatrick, Veronen, and Resick 1979), and (b) empirical or speculative criminal justice outcomes such as reporting, conviction, and sentencing (Deitz et al. 1982; Olsen 1984 provided a feminist critique of legislation that touched on these matters; Williams 1984). Among health outcomes studies, one approached rape victims as an ideal population for understanding different forms of self-blame (Janoff-Bulman 1979); others established depression as a psychological outcome of rape, setting the stage for subsequent studies that would rely on (cisgender female) rape victims as an ideal population for investigating major depression and PTSD (e.g., Kilpatrick, Resick, and Veronen 1981).[2]

As noted above, gendered patterns across these works diverged somewhat from their causal counterparts. Two pieces focused on sexual violence toward men; both were published in the *American Journal of Psychiatry* in 1980 (volume 137, issues 2 and 7). These studies explicitly mentioned "male rape" in the titles; while this read (to me) like a qualified version of "rape," it nonetheless established the possibility of male victimization in the literature (Groth and Burgess 1980; Kaufman et al. 1980). The remaining works conceived of rape primarily or completely as a subset of men's violence against women. Some employed language that rendered "rape" indistinguishable from "the rape of women" and "rape victim" indistinguishable from "female rape victim"—for example, the abstract for Kilpatrick, Resick, and Veronen's (1981) longitudinal assessment on the psychological impact of rape specifies twenty "adult victims" who are not revealed to be exclusively female until the methods section (see also Atkeson et al. 1982).

Sampling frames in this decade and subfield stood out relative to causal research, prevalence studies, and the larger field of sexual violence research. College students were minimally represented. Scientists often recruited victims/survivors through care facilities such as rape crisis centers and hospitals (Atkeson et al. 1982; Kilpatrick, Resick, and Veronen 1981; Kilpatrick,

Veronen, and Resick 1979). This strategy allowed researchers to bypass the challenge of defining rape or other forms of sexual violence; individuals (women) who sought rape crisis services or sexual assault forensic examinations were presumed eligible. These same researchers routinely recruited "nonvictim" comparison samples from the general population or agencies that were not directly associated with violence prevention such as the YWCA. As far as I could surmise, these "nonvictim" samples were not asked about their victimization histories. This practice reveals an assumption that women who experience rape (all three pieces had exclusively women participants) will seek treatment, and further demonstrates that these studies predate the (re)conceptualization of rape as a common occurrence.

A majority of these studies featured psychologists and/or psychiatrists among the authors. Moreover, seven of the top-cited works were published in psychology and psychiatry journals, including the *American Journal of Psychiatry* (three of the ten top-cited studies), *Journal of Personality and Social Psychology* (two), *American Journal of Orthopsychiatry*, and the *Journal of Consulting and Clinical Psychology*. A team of researchers led by Dean Kilpatrick was particularly well-cited; he was lead author on two studies (1981; 1979); his coauthor, psychiatrist Patricia Resick was coauthor for both of these as well as a third piece led by psychologist Beverly Atkeson (1982). Nursing scholar Ann Burgess was lead author on one piece (Burgess and Holmstrom 1979) and second author on another (Groth and Burgess 1980), both published in the *American Journal of Psychiatry*.

Decade Two: 1985–1994

Whereas top-cited works in the previous decade were somewhat split between health and criminal justice outcomes, all ten pieces in this decade prioritized victim health outcomes. These included various indicators of mental well-being (Burnam et al. 1988; Foa, Feske, et al. 1991; Foa, Rothbaum, et al. 1991; Gidycz et al. 1993; Kimerling and Calhoun 1994; Koss 1985; Koss, Dinero, and Seibel 1988; Resick and Schnicke 1992; Rothbaum et al. 1992) and physical well-being (Golding 1994; Kimerling and Calhoun 1994). One piece approached treatment seeking as an additional major outcome, with social support as a mediating factor (Kimerling and Calhoun 1994).

Several studies here relied on treatment-seeking victims for recruitment, consistent with the previous decade (Kimerling and Calhoun 1994; Resick and Schnicke 1992; Rothbaum et al. 1992). However, there were notable expansions in recruitment strategies for victim and nonvictim samples. The Los Angeles Epidemiologic Catchment Area study, a population-based investigation of public health with a special section on sexual violence in Latino and non-Latino communities, produced two top-ten effects pieces in this decade (Burnam et al. 1988; Golding 1994). A study of PTSD treatment recruited female rape victims from victim-serving community agencies and through advertisements in local newspapers, suggesting an assumption that sexual violence victims do not necessarily seek treatment (Foa, Rothbaum, et al. 1991). Mary Koss and her colleagues published two top-cited effects pieces with college populations (Koss 1985; Koss, Dinero, and Seibel 1988). Kimerling and Calhoun (1994) recruited female rape victims through a hospital rape crisis center and recruited a comparison sample from social service agencies and public housing projects; however, all women in the latter group were surveyed for victimization histories and excluded from the comparison sample if they reported prior adult or child sexual assault. This reflects an increasing tendency to approach sexual violence as a widespread problem, likely informed by the work of Mary Koss and her colleagues (both pieces cited above, as well as Koss, Gidycz, and Wisniewski 1987, which featured the "one in four women" statistic).

Definitions of rape and other forms of sexual violence appeared in approximately half of the top-cited effects pieces. Studies that relied on treatment-seeking samples were again able to bypass definitions, as individuals who sought sexual assault forensic exams or pursued therapy for sexual victimization were simply presumed to be victims. Kimerling and Calhoun screened comparison participants for victimization histories, but did not provide explicit definitions or survey items employed in this process (1994). The studies that directly confronted the matter of what "counts" were those connected with quantification projects (i.e., Koss's individual and collaborative work, and the Los Angeles public health study). These research teams took quite different approaches—Koss and colleagues relied on the Sexual Experiences Survey (Koss and Oros 1982), with questions adapted from Ohio criminal statutes and FBI definitions, designed to assess men's aggression toward women and women's victimization by men (Koss 1985; Koss, Dinero, and Seibel 1988; see chapter 1). The Los Angeles researchers conceptualized sexual assault as "forced or pressured sexual contact," documented via the following gender-inclusive survey question: "In your lifetime, has anyone ever tried to pressure or force you to have sexual contact? By sexual contact I mean their touching your sexual parts, your touching their sexual parts, or sexual intercourse?" (Burnam et al. 1988, 845; Golding 1994).

In the first decade assessed here, two of the ten top-cited effects pieces focused on sexual violence against men. In this second decade, top-cited effects pieces were overwhelmingly focused on sexual violence against women. The original Sexual Experiences Survey, utilized in two publications, only documented heterosexual incidents with men as aggressors and women as victims (Koss 1985; Koss, Dinero, and Seibel 1988). While the

Los Angeles study posed victimization questions to men and women—who reported lifetime sexual assault rates of 9.4% and 16.7%, respectively (Burnam et al. 1988)—men were excluded from analyses in one of the two studies assessed here (Golding 1994). Consistent with the first decade, some scholars rendered "rape victim" synonymous with "female rape victim" by utilizing gender-nonspecific language in abstracts to describe samples that were later revealed to be exclusively female (Foa, Feske, et al. 1991; Foa, Rothbaum, et al. 1991; Resick and Schnicke 1992).

Finally, there were notable patterns in top-cited authors, disciplines, and surveys. Koss and her colleagues emerged as major figures in effects research; she was lead author on two top-cited pieces (Koss 1985; Koss, Dinero, and Seibel 1988), and Christine Gidycz (coauthor on the "The Scope of Rape") was lead author on another (Gidycz et al. 1993). Notably, all three of those works were also among the top-cited causal pieces in this decade. Collectively, and given the immediate attention given to "one in four women" in the same period, this suggests that scholars whose work focused on the prevalence, causes, and consequences of rape were all likely to engage with Koss's work. Jacqueline Golding was sole author on one piece and third author on another (Burnam et al. 1988; Golding 1994). A research team led by Edna Foa and Barbara Rothbaum published three works on mental health and cognitive outcomes of sexual violence, with particular attention toward strategies for diagnosis and treatment (Foa, Feske, et al. 1991; Foa, Rothbaum, et al. 1991; Rothbaum et al. 1992). Regarding discipline, all ten pieces featured psychologists or psychiatrists—or at the very least, scholars working in psychology and/or psychiatry departments—among the authors. All were published in journals specific to these disciplines, including the *Journal of Consulting and Clinical Psychology* (four of the ten top-cited studies), *Psychology of Women Quarterly* (three studies), *Journal of Abnormal Psychology*, *Health Psychology*, and the *Journal of Traumatic Stress*. Finally, the Sexual Experiences Survey and the Los Angeles Epidemiologic Catchment Area study (and its associated assessment tools) were each utilized in two publications.

Decade Three: 1995–2004

These works revealed a remarkable expansion in scientific understandings of the effects of rape. After a decade of overwhelming emphasis on victim health outcomes, the top-cited effects studies broadened to encompass more social and institutional impacts. Moreover, top-cited scholars expanded the scope of what might constitute an outcome of sexual violence. Rebecca Campbell and colleagues (2001) explored the "second rape," or experiences of victim-blaming and other marginalization that many survivors experience when engaging with institutions. They further noted that such experiences varied across arenas; criminal justice and medical services

were particularly lacking, whereas rape crisis centers, mental health services, and religious communities were perceived as more supportive. Sarah
Ullman investigated social reactions to disclosures of victimization, and
connected these reactions with more established individual outcomes such
as PTSD symptoms (Ullman 1996; Ullman and Filipas 2001). In an investigation of vicarious trauma, Laura Schauben and Patricia Frazier (1995)
demonstrated that incidents of sexual violence do not merely affect victims
and their significant others, but also counselors and other professionals.

Investigations of mental health outcomes and therapeutic practices
continued to feature within the top-cited effects literature, and sexual violence victims continued to feature as an ideal population for exploring particular mental health issues such as PTSD. However, this area of research
demonstrated several noteworthy changes. Scholars explored novel indicators of recovery, such as the length and composition of survivors' victimization narratives (Foa, Molnar, and Cashman 1995) and the presence of
chronic nightmares among survivors with PTSD (Krakow et al. 2001). Resick
and colleagues (2002) built on much of the work described above (particularly studies involving Foa, Resick, and Rothbaum) to compare treatment
strategies—cognitive processing therapy and prolonged exposure—that
had already proven effective. In other words, the dominant research question shifted from "what is effective" to "which effective treatment is most
promising."

Other investigations of individual health outcomes complicated the
research questions and findings in previous top-cited work. Victoria Follette and colleagues (1996) introduced the notion of cumulative trauma.
Lisa Goodman and colleagues (1997) complemented this research through
an exploration of reciprocal associations between sexual violence and health
outcomes among women with serious mental illness. The possibility of post-
traumatic growth, that positive changes might occur after or even alongside
the negative outcomes typically prioritized in sexual violence research, was
highlighted in a study by Patricia Frazier, Amy Conlon, and Theresa Glaser
(2001).

Top-cited effects works in this decade were overwhelmingly focused
on women's victimization. All samples were entirely female (most likely all
cisgender women), though some studies employed gender-inclusive language
in abstracts to describe them (e.g., referencing "rape victims" rather than
"female rape victims"). Schauben and Frazier's piece on vicarious trauma
was somewhat of an exception, in that they focused on professionals who
serve victims rather than on the victims, themselves. Their study also indirectly acknowledged male victimization, as psychologists and sexual assault
counselors reported that 87% and 94.5% of their sexually victimized clients
were female, respectively. Study authors further noted that four male

counselors had completed and returned questionnaires, but that their responses "were excluded because there were so few" (Schauben and Frazier 1995, 52). The authors did not clarify the significance of counselors' sex assignment, or otherwise explain why male and female counselors' reports merited separate consideration.

Notwithstanding an expansion to more social and institutional outcomes, psychology and psychiatry continued to dominate. All ten pieces included at least one author from these disciplines. With the exception of Campbell and colleagues' piece (2001), which was published in the interdisciplinary *Journal of Interpersonal Violence*, the top-cited effects pieces were published in the *Journal of Traumatic Stress* (three studies), *Journal of Consulting and Clinical Psychology* (two studies), *Psychology of Women Quarterly* (two studies), *Schizophrenia Bulletin*, and the *Journal of the American Medical Association*. As for individual scholars, Sarah Ullman was the only person who was first or sole author on multiple pieces in this sample; Patricia Frazier was first on one piece and second on another. Three scholars who were already well established in this subfield—Edna Foa, Patricia Resick, and Mary Koss—also contributed to the top-cited works from 1995 to 2004. Trends in causal and aftermath research aligned again, with two studies making the top ten in both subfields (Follette et al. 1996; Goodman et al. 1997).

Decade Four: 2005–2015

Consistent with the three previous decades, several studies explored health outcomes of sexual victimization. These works collectively served to complicate and refine scientific knowledge on PTSD, including the delineation of Complex PTSD (Miller and Resick 2007), relationships between PTSD and other individual and interpersonal factors such as substance use and social support/reactions (Ullman et al. 2005; Ullman et al. 2007), and evidence-based practices for therapeutic intervention (Resick et al. 2012; Rothbaum, Astin, and Marsteller 2005). Outcomes more typical of public health and medical research also entered the top-cited effects literature in this decade, sometimes alongside investigations of mental health outcomes such as PTSD. These included pregnancy, sexually transmitted infections, support-seeking behaviors (McFarlane et al. 2005), and HIV risk behaviors (Stockman, Campbell, and Celentano 2010).

For the first time since decade one, criminal justice outcomes emerged as a priority in top-cited aftermath research. Daly and Bouhours (2010) studied attrition within the legal process for rape survivors in five English-speaking countries, including the United States and Canada (both had increases in reporting rape to the police from the 1970s to 1990s, and declines in the first decade of the 2000s). Wolitzky-Taylor and colleagues replicated the National Women's Study from the 1990s to assess changes in U.S. women's reporting of rape (few changes were documented). It's important to situate these differences in the broader historical context. Studies in the late 1970s and early 1980s predated or occurred alongside widespread rape law reform, whereas these more recent works were produced post-reform and also came on the heels of a considerable surge in academic research and state attention to sexual violence (at least in the United States).

Campbell, once again, was lead author on a project that emphasized professional accountability and posed potential challenges to the broader field of rape research (Campbell et al. 2010). This study utilized feminist interviewing techniques to explore the impact of participating in research on rape survivors. Many participants reported that taking part in research had been positive, and that they felt supported and heard by the researchers.

As mentioned above, effects researchers are often able to bypass matters of definition. Studies of treatment outcomes might utilize a sampling frame of treatment seekers and assume that all people seeking counseling for sexual violence have in fact experienced it. The same goes for studies of criminal justice and medical treatment outcomes to an extent, although in the former case statutory definitions are implicit. Nonetheless, I observed an increasing tendency in this decade to explicitly define one or more forms of sexual violence. Such definitions often read as heteronormative. These definitional trends were compounded by the fact that all empirical studies of victimization were conducted with entirely female samples, often with explicit or implicit restrictions to incidents with male aggressors. Stockman, Campbell, and Celentano (2010), for example, restricted analyses to penile-vaginal contact. Using the Sexual Assault Subscale of the Severity of Abuse against Women assessment tool, McFarlane and colleagues (2005) asked women if their partners had done any of the following: "Make you have sexual intercourse against your will? Physically force you to have sex? Make you have oral sex against your will? Make you have anal sex against your will? Use an object on you in a sexual way?" (100). Note that object sexual penetration is rendered synonymous with sexual violence here; in contrast, the instrument assumes that penile-vaginal intercourse, oral sex, and anal sex might all occur in both consensual and nonconsensual contexts. Wolitzky-Taylor and colleagues treated men and women as potential assailants, but only in some contexts. For example, when asking about forcible sexual violence, they asked women whether "anyone, male or female, ever made you have oral sex by force or threatening to harm you" and inquired separately about penile-vaginal and penile-anal assaults with male aggressors (2011, 828). However, when asking about alcohol and drug-facilitated assaults, they only documented those committed by "a man or boy" (828–829).

Previous trends regarding authorship and discipline carried into this decade. Resick was first author on one piece and second on another, and Ullman was first author on two pieces. Psychology and psychiatry were well represented, although these fields were less dominant than in previous years. As far as I could surmise, seven of these ten studies featured psychologists or psychiatrists among the authors. Interdisciplinary journals, including *Violence against Women* and the *Journal of Interpersonal Violence*; and public health and medical journals including *Obstetrics and Gynecology*, *Journal of Acquired Immune Deficiency Syndrome*, and *Journal of Studies on Alcohol*; joined psychology publications such as the *Journal of Consulting and Clinical Psychology*, *Psychology of Women Quarterly*, and the *Journal of Traumatic Stress* as producers of top-cited research on the aftermath of rape.

INSIGHTS FROM THE (SUB)FIELD

When considering the subfield of effects research, many participants called for more systemic and intersectional scholarship. Some of this criticism was linked with a perceived dominance of psychological and other individual-level inquiries. As with causal research, participants across disciplines appreciated the value of individual-level investigations, but cautioned against treating such work as comprehensive or exhaustive. In addition, some scholars were critical of what they perceived as unnecessary replication in this subfield. Participants who had studied legal responses to sexual violence called for specific shifts in this arena, many of which included seeking alternatives to criminal investigation and prosecution.

Calls for Systemic and Intersectional Effects Inquiries

Psychology and psychiatry have historically and consistently dominated this subfield, even more so than causal research. Participants across disciplines appreciated the substantial literature on individual outcomes (of victimization), including health and wellness as well as individual experiences with navigating criminal justice and care systems. This appreciation was often paired with calls for more interdisciplinary and systemic investigations, along with greater emphasis on intersectional analyses.

The sociologists and anthropologists in this study called for more attention toward sexual violence within their own disciplines. Virginia described sexual violence as "kind of invisible" in sociological research on "poverty, eviction, labor market processes, lots of processes of inequality." When scholars in these fields encountered stories of victimization among poor and working-class women, sexual violence was analytically "glossed over instead of being [treated as] a core process in the reproduction of poverty." Even pervasive accounts might be "glossed over" as an afterthought rather than

TABLE 4.2
Ten Top-Cited Effects Works from Each Decade, as of February 2016

Lead Author	Title	Journal	Year	Citations
Janoff-Bulman, Ronnie	Characterological versus Behavioral Self-Blame: Inquiries into Depression and Rape	Journal of Personality and Social Psychology	1979	566
Atkeson, Beverly M.	Victims of Rape: Repeated Assessment of Depressive Symptoms	Journal of Consulting and Clinical Psychology	1982	161
Olsen, Frances	Statutory Rape: A Feminist Critique of Rights Analysis	Texas Law Review	1984	120
Kilpatrick, Dean G.	The Aftermath of Rape: Recent Empirical Findings	American Journal of Orthopsychiatry	1979	116
Kilpatrick, Dean G.	Effects of a Rape Experience: A Longitudinal Study	Journal of Social Issues	1981	110
Williams, Linda S.	The Classic Rape: When do Victims Report?	Social Problems	1984	106
Kaufman, Arthur	Male Rape Victims: Noninstitutionalized Assault	American Journal of Psychiatry	1980	100
Deitz, Sheila R.	Measurement of Empathy toward Rape Victims and Rapists	Journal of Personality and Social Psychology	1982	96
Groth, A. Nicholas	Male Rape: Offenders and Victims	American Journal of Psychiatry	1980	94
Burgess, Ann Wolbert	Adaptive Strategies and Recovery from Rape	American Journal of Psychiatry	1979	86
Foa, Edna B.	Treatment of Posttraumatic Stress Disorder in Rape Victims: A Comparison between Cognitive–Behavioral Procedures and Counseling	Journal of Consulting and Clinical Psychology	1991	655
Rothbaum, Barbara Olasov	A Prospective Examination of Post-traumatic Stress Disorder in Rape Victims	Journal of Traumatic Stress	1992	487

TABLE 4.2 (*continued*)

Lead Author	Title	Journal	Year	Citations
Resick, Patricia A.	Cognitive Processing Therapy for Sexual Assault Victims	Journal of Consulting and Clinical Psychology	1992	470
Burnam, M. Audrey	Sexual Assault and Mental Disorders in a Community Population	Journal of Consulting and Clinical Psychology	1988	361
Foa, Edna B.	Processing of Threat-Related Information in Rape Victims	Journal of Abnormal Psychology	1991	254
Koss, Mary P.	Stranger and Acquaintance Rape: Are There Differences in the Victim's Experience?	Psychology of Women Quarterly	1988	249
Koss, Mary P.	The Hidden Rape Victim: Personality, Attitudinal, and Situational Characteristics	Psychology of Women Quarterly	1985	216
Gidycz, Christine A.	Sexual Assault Experience in Adulthood and Prior Victimization Experiences	Psychology of Women Quarterly	1993	208
Kimerling, Rachel	Somatic Symptoms, Social Support, and Treatment Seeking among Sexual Assault Victims	Journal of Consulting and Clinical Psychology	1994	197
Golding, Jacqueline M.	Sexual Assault History and Physical Health in Randomly Selected Los Angeles Women	Health Psychology	1994	182
Resick, Patricia A.	A Comparison of Cognitive-Processing Therapy with Prolonged Exposure and a Waiting Condition for the Treatment of Chronic Posttraumatic Stress Disorder in Female Rape Victims	Journal of Consulting and Clinical Psychology	2002	465

(*continued*)

TABLE 4.2 (*continued*)

Lead Author	Title	Journal	Year	Citations
Follette, Victoria M.	Cumulative Trauma: The Impact of Child Sexual Abuse, Adult Sexual Assault, and Spouse Abuse	Journal of Traumatic Stress	1996	215
Foa, Edna B.	Changes in Rape Narratives during Exposure Therapy for Posttraumatic Stress Disorder	Journal of Traumatic Stress	1995	211
Krakow, Barry	Imagery Rehearsal Therapy for Chronic Nightmares in Sexual Assault Survivors with Posttraumatic Stress Disorder: A Randomized Controlled Trial	Journal of the American Medical Association	2001	199
Frazier, Patricia	Positive and Negative Life Changes Following Sexual Assault	Journal of Consulting and Clinical Psychology	2001	192
Goodman, Lisa A.	Physical and Sexual Assault History in Women with Serious Mental Illness: Prevalence, Correlates, Treatment, and Future Research Directions	Schizophrenia Bulletin	1997	187
Schauben, Laura J.	Vicarious Trauma: The Effects on Female Counselors of Working with Sexual Violence Survivors	Psychology of Women Quarterly	1995	151
Ullman, Sarah E.	Predictors of PTSD Symptom Severity and Social Reactions in Sexual Assault Victims	Journal of Traumatic Stress	2001	144
Campbell, Rebecca	Preventing the "Second Rape": Rape Survivors' Experiences with Community Service Providers	Journal of Interpersonal Violence	2001	133
Ullman, Sarah E.	Social Reactions, Coping Strategies, and Self-Blame Attributions in Adjustment to Sexual Assault	Psychology of Women Quarterly	1996	128
Rothbaum, Barbara Olasov	Prolonged Exposure versus Eye Movement Desensitization and Reprocessing (EMDR) for PTSD Rape Victims	Journal of Traumatic Stress	2005	125
McFarlane, Judith	Intimate Partner Sexual Assault against Women: Frequency, Health Consequences, and Treatment Outcomes	Obstetrics and Gynecology	2005	100

TABLE 4.2 (*continued*)

Lead Author	Title	Journal	Year	Citations
Ullman, Sarah E.	Structural Models of the Relations of Assault Severity, Social Support, Avoidance Coping, Self-Blame, and PTSD among Sexual Assault Survivors	Psychology of Women Quarterly	2007	89
Ullman, Sarah E.	Trauma Exposure, Posttraumatic Stress Disorder, and Problem Drinking in Sexual Assault Survivors	Journal of Studies on Alcohol	2005	75
Miller, Mark W.	Internalizing and Externalizing Subtypes in Female Sexual Assault Survivors: Implications for the Understanding of Complex PTSD	Behavior Therapy	2007	75
Resick, Patricia A.	Long–Term Outcomes of Cognitive–Behavioral Treatments for Posttraumatic Stress Disorder among Female Rape Survivors	Journal of Consulting and Clinical Psychology	2012	51
Daly, Kathleen	Rape and Attrition in the Legal Process: A Comparative Analysis of Five Countries	Crime and Justice	2010	37
Campbell, Rebecca	"What Has It Been Like for You to Talk with Me Today?": The Impact of Participating in Interview Research on Rape Survivors	Violence against Women	2010	27
Wolitzky-Taylor, Kate B.	Is Reporting of Rape on the Rise? A Comparison of Women with Reported versus Unreported Rape Experiences in the National Women's Study – Replication	Journal of Interpersonal Violence	2011	27
Stockman, Jamila K.	Sexual Violence and HIV Risk Behaviors among a Nationally Representative Sample of Heterosexual American Women: The Importance of Sexual Coercion	Journal of Acquired Immune Deficiency Syndrome	2010	26

NOTE: Articles are organized first by decade, and then in descending order by number of citations.

highlighted as a scientifically or socially important finding. Virginia and other scholars were also critical of the extent to which researchers had emphasized individual-level outcomes and experiences. A study of individual women's victimization experiences might well control for income or education as a proxy for social class, but this would be insufficient to capture the capacity of rape to reproduce and (re)feminize poverty.

Cynthia, a psychologist, commented that research projects and normative assumptions about "what victims should do" were often based on the lives and experiences of White women in well-resourced communities. She recalled a project on sexual violence in Native American reservation communities that challenged her own "understanding [of] what it meant to be White" and led her to recognize "how all of these things I had seen as neutral or default . . . were just really ways of performing race and class and culture that I had not been previously aware of." When I asked her for an example, she elaborated:

> The majority of victims, [police involvement] doesn't make things better. But I think with particular regard to a lot of reservation communities, many of them are literally on the verge of extinction. And even compared to other communities of color in the United States or elsewhere, I mean you can talk about the injustices of the criminal justice system with respect to African Americans or Latinos, and there is certainly a lot to say about that. A lot of harms that get taken about the imprisonment of such a huge proportion of those communities. But when you're talking about [small tribal communities], and when you're looking at any particular generation of them, every individual guy that you take out of that community for whatever reason is literally a threat to the whole community in a way that I don't think White people can possibly understand. [Outsiders ask,] "Why don't you just call the police? Why don't you just leave?" And you know, they're trying to preserve their tribe, their culture and their whole way of life. You can't afford to write men off in the way that is such a common response in White culture.

In sharing these insights, Cynthia called for tailoring research and activist projects to specific populations and spaces, and involving in-group participants when possible. Many efforts that might seem promising in predominantly White communities, such as improving procedures for reporting an assault to the police, or even ensuring that victims/survivors have access to supportive advocates at trial, might have minimal impacts when community preservation takes priority over holding aggressors criminally accountable. Similar concerns might apply in other marginalized populations—other ethnic or racial minority communities, queer communities, transgender communities, religious minority communities—that are close-knit, fear losing members, or are wary of inadequate or harmful treatment by criminal justice professionals and institutions.

Geographic variation also emerged as an important dimension of the institutional aftermath. Max, a criminologist, suggested that "the same" resources often vary in impact among urban and rural spaces:

> We tend to think of crime as being an urban problem. But when we look at interpersonal crime, it's just as prevalent in rural areas . . . [if not] more prevalent in rural areas. And a large part of that is because the victim and offender relationship, you know, sexual assaults are more likely to occur among acquaintances. And in rural areas, the acquaintance density rates are much, much higher. Everybody knows everybody. And so consequently, when somebody's assaulted, they may not report to the police, but they're much more likely to go to a rape crisis center. You know? Even, maybe even precisely because everybody knows everybody. So if your car is parked at the cop shop, are they going to call your husband and say, "Hey, I saw your wife the other day at the cops'. What's going on?" So in other words, is it a safer avenue?

Max's insights reinforce Cynthia's point that, relative to other forms of help-seeking, contacting the police may seem too risky or even counterproductive in smaller communities. Such matters might easily be missed if professional researchers—many of whom are based in urban settings—prioritize local or single-site studies, or do not take sufficient account of social inequalities and demographic variation in sampling and/or data interpretation. It can be dangerous to assume that the criminal justice and other services most often pursued by White, heterosexual, middle class, nondisabled, and cisgender women in urban spaces may be generalized to sexual violence survivors of all identifications, locations, and backgrounds.

"Settled" and "Unsettled" Questions

In scientific research, it is common for multiple scholars to pursue similar projects and compare findings. "Replication" with similar populations and environments can reveal in-group consistencies and variation. Replication with different populations and environments can aid in identifying the sorts of intersectional issues addressed in the previous section. Ultimately, with enough consistency or consensus or other sufficiently compelling evidence, matters of scientific fact may become "settled" or "established." Scholars in science studies have criticized the practice of replication as circular and problematic, arguing that scientists may selectively engage disparate studies to confirm or dispute theoretical assumptions (Collins 1975; Godin and Gingras 2002; Shapin and Schaffer [1985] 2011). Imagine that a team of researchers produces study A, and are wary of challenges from peers. If study B reinforces their work, the authors of study A may count this as a successful replication and draw upon it to strengthen their (or their work's) credibility. If study C diverges, these same researchers may strategically point to variation in conditions rather than allowing for the possibility of problems in their original findings. Perhaps the sampling frames varied, and so participants gave different answers. Perhaps the survey questions were too dissimilar, and should not really be compared. In this hypothetical scenario, which many scholars believe reflects an established pattern within science, scientists reserve the term "replication" for studies that confirm initial findings (if they accept those findings) or challenge them (if they do not).

It is also important to note that the settling of scientific facts is a collective process. There is no universal measurement for determining when this occurs, nor is there generally a definitive moment of settling that closes lines of inquiry. An individual researcher or team may not authoritatively declare some matters decided and others undecided, but must seek to build something close to scientific consensus or at least provide forms of evidence that are considered too compelling to dispute (Epstein 1996; Jasanoff 2005; Shapin and Schaffer [1985] 2011).Yet once such consensus has been reached, scientists may draw criticism for pursuing presumably needless replication of prior inquiries. If a matter of fact seems settled, or a line of inquiry has been deemed unproductive, researchers may expect their peers to pursue other questions. Some aspects of this settling process appeared in the preceding qualitative content analyses, as dominant psychological and psychiatric literature moved from asking whether and to what extent female rape victims develop PTSD towards asking how best to treat female rape victims with post-traumatic symptoms. The former line of research approached survivors' development of PTSD as an open question; the latter treated PTSD outcomes as a given. In 2018, it might be difficult to publish work with a central finding that "people who experience sexual victimization may develop mental health issues," but there is likely still support for refining therapeutic services.

Several participants criticized what they perceived as stagnation or unnecessary repetition in aftermath research. I heard this criticism most often regarding criminal justice processes and individual responses to sexual victimization. Wendy, quoted at the beginning of this chapter, was frustrated with lines of research that seemed simply to confirm "things that we know," such as that "the criminal justice system is shitty." Kristen, a sociologist, offered a similar perspective:

> Based on systems and institutions that are failing us—I think we really
> need to think about how, and this is a conversation maybe with carceral

feminism, like how do we get away from that? What can we get into play that will empower people, and heal people, that we do not have to use these broken systems? I'm kind of frustrated with the reform, reform, reform. This goes in hand with some of the Title IX stuff happening. We need to have really important, ground-breaking discussions about transformation getting us outside of all that. . . . We need to get together and talk about this. Everyone wants it, but we don't know how to do it. And everyone's stuck. We're stuck. We've got to think of something.

It's notable that Kristen described more transformative scholarship as something "everyone wants, but we don't know how to do it." During their interviews, she and Wendy both expressed an interest in more collective engagement among researchers to generate new ideas and critical (re)assessments of rape scholarship.

In some instances, participants connected unproductive lines of research to broader issues within academia. The imperative to "publish or perish" might encourage scientists to pursue projects that seem easy to design and complete, or likely to produce (statistically) significant and thus publishable results, even if they do little to advance scientific knowledge or affect social change. Cynthia raised this concern when I asked what advice she might give a young scholar entering the field of sexual violence research:

So, probably what I would most like to say is that it is really important to "stay woke" not only to the things that violence researchers and others with a social justice bent rail against all the time, but also to the conventions and biases that are part of the academic world too. There are many, many institutional forces that can push people into mediocre, incremental, and even repetitive research. Some forty years after the phenomenon has been fully established, I still see so many papers on basic findings, such as "people don't like getting victimized." That's no more scientific than another carefully crafted study showing that the earth is round.

While such institutional forces are not restricted to the research on the aftermath of sexual violence, I rarely encountered such criticisms when discussing causal or quantification work with participants.

Legal Responses: Reconsidering Reliance on Forensics and Criminal Prosecution

A range of institutions respond to rape. Criminal justice looms particularly large here, and not merely in more obvious contexts such as police departments, prosecutorial agencies, courts, and prisons. Title IX sexual violence investigations and adjudication proceedings in higher education function as surrogate police and prosecutorial proceedings, albeit with different standards of proof and punitive capacities. Hospitals and clinics that provide sexual assault forensic examinations, commonly known as "rape kits," seek to care for survivors and build evidence for criminal investigations simultaneously (Mulla 2014). Rape crisis centers often provide referrals and basic information for navigating criminal justice processes, and participate in those processes directly through medical and court accompaniment.

Although interview participants touched upon a range of institutional responses to sexual violence, many reserved their harshest critiques and most comprehensive recommendations for law and (criminal) justice. These insights took two general forms. Some scholars criticized what they perceived as overreliance on and misplaced faith in sexual assault forensic examinations. Others called out what they perceived as uncritical endorsement of criminal prosecution and criminal justice notions of "success" in responding to rape, and advocated for more investment in providing alternatives such as restorative justice conferencing.

Some researchers regarded the prosecutorial value of sexual assault forensic evidence as an open question. The broader context of public scandal over untested rape kits (Reilly 2015) lent urgency to the matter. Tanya, a criminologist, commented: "I think the whole rape kit issue is one that needs additional work. We need to know why these kits aren't tested, and what would happen if more of them were. You know, would that enhance the odds of prosecution and conviction." Note that Tanya did not demand that all untested rape kits be thoroughly processed, but rather wanted to account for testing practices to date and to determine whether testing rape kits would substantively affect prosecution.

Across all interviews, no one offered an unqualified endorsement of forensic examinations. If the matter had been settled, it was settled in the negative. Pam, a criminologist, suggested that overreliance on forensics was not only unproductive but potentially harmful:

> We talk a lot about victims getting rape kits completed, but when you look at the research . . . most of the cases that involve sexual assault involve people known to the victim. And the rape kit doesn't have much value in the cases. And the argument that "we're doing it because maybe that person raped somebody else," it almost perpetuates the idea of a serial rapist. And the question is, is that correct? And is that right? And what's the implication for victims who are going through these rape kits, that are pretty intensive and personal and, you know, potentially traumatizing? Are we doing what's right for the victim, or are we doing what's right for what the system wants?

Researchers and advocates tend to consider sexual assault forensic exams invasive and potentially traumatizing (Mulla 2014). Pam suggested that this established harm to victims be considered alongside the impact of forensic evidence at trial. She was critical of arguments that justified widespread pursuit of rape kits as a means of identifying serial rapists, and worried that this deployment of forensic technology might produce the very scientific knowledge that justified its use.

If sexual assault forensic evidence has minimal impact at trial, why is there a controversy over untested rape kits? Many researchers' uncertainty or skepticism toward such exams does not extend to the general public, or the police and prosecutors tasked with addressing rape. Madeline, quoted at the beginning of this chapter, shared frustration with public (mis)trust in forensics. Miranda offered a similar critique of public perceptions, particularly regarding the varying credibility awarded to forensic evidence and individual—most often individual women's—narrative accounts:

MIRANDA: The public loves their forensics, right? And then people get very outraged about DNA backlogs, rape kit backlogs, for example. And for me, that is a manufactured crisis. Because you know, it is not important to process a rape kit if you know who the assailant is. . . . And then it is not important to insist that we have some kind of physical evidence, if you have credible testimony. And I think that pushing that narrative forward, that we have to have this forensic evidence—which is really inconclusive, often, and people just argue. Even in stranger assaults, what we've seen is that people argue that it was consensual, or it was transactional. . . . The number of times a defense attorney will say, "Oh, it was transactional sex." And the prosecutor will say, "Why is she arguing it was sexual assault?" and "Oh, he didn't pay her, so then it became rape." I mean, it's very ridiculous. But I think part of it is, we're continually demoting testimony, particularly the testimony of women, right? And that's been documented.
ETHAN: Right, but if the crisis is the backlog, then . . .
MIRANDA: Yeah, so if you just solve the backlog, then we would solve all the rapes. That's not going to happen. Because that's not what's happening.

When I asked what recommendations she had for future scholarship in this area, Miranda suggested "taking really good research and turning it over to a team of publicists" so that empirically-based doubts about the value of forensic evidence "can make their way into the public." She hoped for a shift in criminal and public perceptions of evidence, over and above "solv[ing] the backlog."

Many participants shared concerns regarding police and prosecutorial responses to sexual violence as well as scientific research on those responses. Amy, a legal scholar, noted that conceptualizations of "good outcomes" in criminal justice often favored institutional actors at the expense of victims/survivors: "So the victim witness comes in, and is raked over the coals during cross-examination, but nevertheless they get a conviction. And right, the prosecutor might see that as a success, the victim witness and the advocate might be like, not sure. Not sure about that. If that sends her back to therapy for two years, maybe that wasn't a success, right?" In this scenario, the interests of the victim seem to be at odds with those of the state. Consequently, it is difficult to conceive of an outcome that would be "good" or "successful" for the prosecutor, complainant, and antiviolence advocate simultaneously.

While there were certainly no calls for an end to criminal investigation and prosecution, several participants expressed a need for alternatives. Madeline noted that "conviction rates have never really increased and are dismally low," and cautioned that "I also don't really think increased incarceration in general is a great direction for any society." Lisa, a psychologist, called for alternatives when considering how she and her family might respond to sexual victimization:

> I'll tell you personally, if I were raped, if my daughter were raped, I would—we would go and report, and then we would go home. I would not go through this process. Our adversarial legal system is a killer. And I've watched enough rape trials that just, they just go after the victim. . . .
>
> That's why I really like that . . . restorative justice approach. If the victim and the offender can meet, or come to some common agreement, the victim wants to say, "This was not my fault, I was done wrong." And if somebody would say that with authority, that often is extremely helpful. And yet what family members and friends often say is, "Why were you there? What did you wear? What did you do to give him that impression? Why did you go out with him? Why did you get in that car?"

Restorative justice repeatedly emerged as an alternative. This approach involves meetings between victims/complainants and assailants/respondents, facilitated by a third party. The "justice" restored is not comprised of convictions or incarcerations but rather takes varied forms that are tailored to victims' and others' needs. For example, if a survivor simply wants to have their story heard, and to have the person who harmed them listen and openly admit to that harm, this may be achieved within restorative justice conferencing.

Rebecca, a public health scholar, commented that criminal justice processes tend to center solely on state conceptualizations of harm done by an individual defendant to an individual complainant. She believed that restorative justice offered a way to incorporate broader concerns:

There are many people who are victimized that want to be able to confront the person who harmed them in a place where there's a facilitated meeting to minimize chances of re-abuse. And be able to say, "This is the harm that you did to me, and here's the impact it had." And I think restorative justice is a promising way to do that.

And I think I like it because it also really looks at the ripple effect of harm. In restorative justice conferencing, you also can include people beyond the direct victim. So you can include the victim's family and friends, you can include the family and friends of the perpetrator. And they can also express how the harm affected them. You know, because it can be really jarring. Let's say we're dealing with a campus sexual misconduct. The person who is admitting that, "yeah, I harmed someone sexually on campus." I mean, their parents, what happens to them? There is an emotional toll that goes beyond the direct people involved. And then community harms. When we hear that a sexual assault happens on campus, it affects people's feelings on campus safety.

Victims and aggressors, as well as other individuals in their social networks who have been affected by an incident (or accusation) of violence, may all participate and have opportunities to share their perspectives.

STUDYING THE AFTERMATH

How can scientists determine the effects of rape? One strategy has been to approach numerous communities and spaces. Local, municipal, and larger communities; colleges and universities; and individuals pursuing services through rape crisis centers, hospitals and clinics, and criminal justice institutions are all well represented in this literature. In this sense, effects research is particularly well poised to consider variation in individual, interpersonal, institutional, and cultural dimensions of sexual violence, particularly if scholars heed the calls for intersectional and multilevel or systemic inquiries featured in this chapter. It is also important to note that such diversity in sampling diverges from other subfields. Generally speaking, scientists look to different populations to investigate the scope, causes, and consequences of sexual violence.

Even relative to the broader field, and the subfields of causal research and quantification, effects research has prioritized victimization and neglected perpetration. This was evident in quantitative content analysis of nearly six hundred studies from 1975 to 2015 as well as close readings of widely cited research. There are ample reasons to focus on survivor experiences, and to develop and refine resources and social responses to victimization. Such work should continue. Moving forward, it is also worth considering whether and how scholars could explore the aftermath of perpetration in greater detail. Hundreds of studies have asked whether and to what extent sexual violence "changes" victims via mental health outcomes, physical health outcomes, identification as a victim or survivor (or neither), and changing perceptions of consent and refusal. A smaller but considerable number of projects have explored the impact of sexual violence on victims' social relationships and reputations, often through vignettes or inquiries into social responses to disclosure. Might committing acts of sexual aggression "change" someone? Do experiences of perpetration have substantive effects on aggressors' mental and physical health, social relationships, reputation, or understandings of sexual consent and refusal? Are there social and institutional consequences beyond conviction and sentencing? How might personal acquaintances and institutional actors such as therapists and educators respond to disclosures of perpetration? Within the field of sexual violence research, are there particular ethico-onto-epistemological entanglements that foreclose such lines of inquiry? Are there practical or methodological or political barriers? If these questions have been explored in detail, this has not occurred in studies easily recognizable as pertaining to "rape," "sexual violence," "sexual assault," or "rapists" as sampled for this project. Yet these questions seem increasingly urgent. In the era of #MeToo, decades-old incidents of sexual violence and harassment have begun to surface with regularity. Some survivors feel empowered to come forward for the first time, and others feel obliged to share their stories (Pattani 2018). Providing support for these survivors is, of course, crucial. Also important is determining what, if anything, to do with or provide for aggressors. If committing an act of rape can change people in meaningful ways, then even isolated and decades-old acts of violence may matter for understanding someone's present-day character and capacity for (non)violence.

The historical—if somewhat declining—dominance of psychological and psychiatric research has produced a substantial body of knowledge on individual and, to a lesser extent, interpersonal outcomes of sexual victimization. Consistent with the previous chapter, participants in this study pointed to those trends to call for greater involvement among scholars in disciplines such as sociology who are trained to consider multilevel and systemic dimensions of social problems. This suggestion was again accompanied by support for more intersectional research. The outcomes of sexual violence, and the accessibility and value of institutional resources such as rape crisis centers and police departments, are difficult if not impossible to generalize. Conceptualizations of "positive" outcomes and "good" institutional resources merit (re)assessment (Alcoff 2018). Scientific projects and investigations might emphasize variation and flexibility rather than striving for universal "best practices" for addressing sexual violence across all geographic and identity-based communities.

Participants expressed some frustrations with aftermath research. These often concerned a seemingly uncritical endorsement of criminal justice processes, particularly sexual assault forensic examinations and prosecution. In the former case, several scholars argued that forensic science has been mischaracterized as an invaluable resource for investigating and prosecuting criminal sexual violence. Given that members of the public serve on juries, this public mischaracterization has real consequences at trial. Matters are complicated further by the reality that sexual assault forensic exams may be experienced as invasive and traumatizing. If forensic evidence is of limited value in sexual assault trials, and if its collection is harmful to victims—who may or may not pursue reporting and prosecution, even after submitting to an exam—scientists might need to work towards shifting public perceptions. Perhaps scandals over the backlog of untested rape kits will someday give way to scandals over the widespread practice of subjecting victims/survivors to unnecessary medical procedures. To be clear, participants in this study were not calling for an end to forensic science altogether or sexual assault forensic exams in particular, but rather for a critical reassessment of the impact and value of forensic evidence specifically in sexual assault cases.

Skeptical of prosecutorial notions of success, and wary of victims' often profoundly negative experiences in court, several scholars called for alternatives. Investment in noncriminal resources such as rape crisis centers might support individuals who were unable to pursue—or simply uninterested in pursuing—criminal justice. Restorative justice emerged as another promising approach. Restorative justice would not be a replacement for criminal prosecution, university adjudication, and other established processes. None of the participants in this project conveyed it as such. Restorative justice conferencing requires that the actors involved agree that harm has been caused, and are willing and able to meet and address that harm, which is neither desirable nor feasible for all people who have experienced sexual violence. What participants in this project have argued—and I agree with them—is that contemporary criminal justice processes in the United States and Canada are not adequate for responding the problem of rape. Efforts to reform those institutions can and should be accompanied by efforts to provide additional avenues for seeking justice and support.

PART TWO

Social Mechanisms

CHAPTER 5

Choosing to Study Rape

RAPE CRISIS COUNSELORS are often trained to anticipate tough questions. When we disclose that we have chosen to do "rape work" (Martin 2005), even to strangers or casual acquaintances, we learn to expect inquiries into our personal histories—"Have you ever been raped?" or "Was your mother or daughter raped? Maybe your best friend?"—and skepticism toward our volunteer or professional choices—"That sounds awful and depressing, why would anyone do that?" or perhaps, depending on how we are perceived, "Do you hate men?" or "Isn't that more of a women's issue?" We are also encouraged to prepare for sudden disclosures of others' encounters with violence. These might be brief and straightforward—"Oh, well, I was raped" or "My friend was accused of that once"—or they might be indepth and richly detailed. Such experiences intensify the already substantial emotional work of supporting and advocating for survivors and their significant others, or working to rehabilitate and resocialize assailants.

These same concerns apply to studying rape. Scholars who choose this work may encounter the same invasive questions, skepticism, and unsolicited disclosures that advocates face. Faculty who teach about sexual violence might become known as safe or supportive people to confide in, and receive disclosures from students on a regular basis. The research itself may involve substantial and direct contact with victims/survivors, aggressors, and their significant others, as well as detailed narratives of violence in such contexts as police reports and court transcripts. Psychologist Rebecca Campbell, who has been active and widely cited in this field for some time (see chapter 3 for a discussion of some of her contributions to effects research), wrote an entire book on the subject entitled *Emotionally Involved: The Impact of Researching Rape* (2002). Psychologist Sarah Ullman, who has also been active and widely cited in sexual violence research for decades (see chapter 3 for a discussion of some of her contributions to effects research), devoted an entire chapter of her book, *Talking about Sexual Assault: Society's Response to Survivors*, to the personal challenges of studying rape (2010). Yet the instruction in self-care routinely offered to rape crisis counselors, and the ongoing encouragement to be reflective and make adjustments or take breaks as needed, rarely occur in the domain of professional science.

This chapter explores personal and social mechanisms that encourage scientists to choose this work. I conceive of choosing as an ongoing rather than singular or momentary process. Therefore, I do not only consider factors that lead people to study rape, but also factors that sustain them in this often difficult work.

Participants described a variety of pathways into the field.[1] Although several were driven by prior investment in addressing sexual violence or political commitments to feminist and other social movements, some were drawn to this work by chance opportunities or intriguing scientific questions about human behavior. Mentoring and collective care work emerged as important social and professional mechanisms that facilitate continued engagement. These mechanisms are essential for the production of any scientific knowledge of rape, as this is an enterprise requiring continued human participation.

In addition to illuminating important social processes within rape research, understanding how scientists choose this work may advance the literature in science studies more broadly. This field occupies a contested status within science (discussed further in chapter 6), is highly feminized in terms of reputation and participation (in that many within and outside of science consider rape to be a women's issue, and in that the field is itself dominated by cisgender women), and requires participants to repeatedly confront emotionally heavy and politically controversial content. The overtly political nature of much rape scholarship further contributes to marginalization within science. Many scientists approach the study of rape as value-driven from the outset. Those motivated by commitment to feminist and other anti-oppressive ideals and social movements, or who develop feminist ideals through engagement in sexual violence research, often struggle or outright refuse to depoliticize their work. Yet dominant positivist models within science reserve legitimacy for detached and ostensibly apolitical ethico-onto-epistemologies. Social mechanisms informed by such conditions will be missed in a literature that prioritizes STEM and other masculine-coded fields. Indeed, although some of the processes identified here may apply to a substantial range of sciences, the heaviness and contested/devalued status of sexual violence research within the larger domain of science lends a particular urgency to mentoring and care work.

PATHWAYS INTO THE FIELD

Throughout this project, I strove for transparency and nonhierarchical interactions with participants (Campbell et al. 2010). When someone requested information about the project—in-depth summaries of my aims and methodology, Institutional Review Board (IRB) approval paperwork, interview guides, practices for ensuring confidentiality—I provided this. When participants asked that various parts of our conversations be modified in or omitted from transcripts, I did so. I welcomed any questions about my own experiences in rape research and advocacy, as well as my findings to date in the project.

Across all interviews, the question I heard most often concerned pathways into the field. Participants wanted to know what led their peers to study rape. I do not presume to know why this question was so popular, though I am confident that the motivations behind participants' inquiries differed sharply from those of the skeptical outsiders described above. Some simply seemed curious about their peers. Many were actively mentoring younger researchers or working to recruit new scholars or students. Some suspected that the most common pathway would entail years of antiviolence advocacy, or rather that practice would precede research. Some expected strong (feminist) political motivation. Given the emotional and professional demands of academic rape work (Campbell 2002; Martin 2005; Ullman 2010), it seemed unlikely to these scholars that anyone would enter the field—or at least manage to last for long—without such commitments.

What I found, and thus what I told these participants, was that pathways were variable and sometimes nonlinear. Any number of experiences and opportunities might lead someone to assist with a study of sexual violence, or to design and complete their own. Although antiviolence and/or feminist commitments were certainly important in some cases, much also seemed to depend on graduate work assignments and relationships among scientists. Contrary to my and several participants' expectations, I learned that it was quite possible to work in this field without particular investment in the issue of sexual violence. Individuals with and without such investment might enter the field and stay for years or even decades, enter and leave swiftly, or move back and forth throughout their careers.

In the following paragraphs, I review participants' narratives of choosing to study sexual violence. Given how specific educational and career trajectories can be, and concerns about revealing participants' identities, I incorporate minimal direct quotations in this section.

Life experiences often forced an awareness of sexual violence. Several participants recalled hearing disclosures of sexual victimization in their families and peer groups, often in high school and college. Some disclosed personal histories of victimization. These and other researchers often shared frustrations with institutional responses. Participants who had experienced sexual violence in college, or had provided support to other survivors in this context, were often critical of the support resources and adjudication procedures on campus. Inadequate resources or institutional responses might motivate activist as well as academic engagement.

A considerable number of participants had more meandering pathways. That is, they began by studying something else, only to find themselves investigating questions about rape. Scholars studying human reproduction or sexual health might repeatedly confront matters of sexual consent and refusal. Those studying poverty and other dimensions of social inequality might encounter pervasive narratives of violence in marginalized populations (see Virginia's comments in chapter 2). Clinical psychologists might hear disclosure after disclosure of sexual victimization or aggression from patients. In these instances, individuals might study sexual violence to further their initial career paths—psychologists and social workers with all specializations may serve (or research) clients (or study participants) with victimization histories, and thus may benefit from greater knowledge of its clinical implications. Alternatively, as some participants described, they might shift their focus entirely toward this issue.

Scientists who had served in the military before entering academia spoke of pervasive sexual violence in this context. This unfortunate reality was exacerbated by institutional practices that seemed to serve aggressors better than victims. Clara recalled an incident in which her commanding officer declined to punish a known sexual harasser for fear that it might "hurt his wife if we take away his money and his rank." Other participants had initially pursued careers in support services with a focus on interpersonal violence, and subsequently encountered challenges that motivated a shift toward academia. Frustrated that "the system, it's not set up to be victim friendly," Wendy had left professional social work for professional research in order to identify and address systemic barriers to supporting victims and rehabilitating offenders. Recalling her years of providing clinical services to survivors, Julia pointed to "a number of questions . . . that I wanted to answer through evaluation and research."

Across the previous examples, participants were committed to the work of ending—or at least improving responses to—sexual violence before they began to study it. In other cases, scholars seemed to fall into this line of work. Individuals with no background or prior investment in rape research might be recruited for a project for their expertise in quantitative analysis or grant writing, or simply through proximity or social connections to others already immersed in this field. Several participants recalled being assigned to a particular advisor or graduate assistant position. Those initial efforts sometimes inspired a strong commitment to addressing sexual violence. Even those who were not so personally moved might find their work in this field sufficiently publishable or well-received to be worth continuing.

Historical events and controversies were also sources of inspiration. Several participants described researchers as having an important capacity to test common assumptions about human behavior and culture. Those who had entered the field in the 1970s and 1980s often referenced widespread debates over the "true" causes of rape—particularly the relative contributions of human biology and evolution, patriarchal values and institutions, and pornography—as scientifically intriguing. The intellectual challenges of operationalizing and measuring "the impact of pornography on sexual aggression" and "the capacity for 'normal' men to commit acts of rape" drew many scholars' attention. Those working in the early 2000s, when the Human Right's Watch's (2001) *No Escape* report was published and the Prison Rape Elimination Act was passed, were sometimes curious about the empirical justification for and implications of state interventions in prison sexual violence. Criminal justice and legal scholars who were active in academia during or after rape law reform commented on researchers' capacity to provide empirical and critical analyses of the impact of reforms. More recently, a similar opportunity has arisen regarding sexual assault forensic examinations. The widespread adoption of such exams in the United States and Canada, and ongoing controversy over the backlog of untested kits (Reilly 2015), have led scholars with and without prior commitments to studying rape to question the medical and criminal justice implications of this technology.

MENTORING

Mentoring is crucial in many career fields. It can also be a source of inequality if, as often occurs in science and academia more broadly, support and networking resources are most available for the most privileged individuals. At the same time, mentoring may provide a countermeasure against such inequalities when employed to support people in marginalized communities or nontraditional career paths (Beaulieu et al. 2017; Mancl and Lee 2016; Primé et al. 2015). Given this, it was unsurprising that several participants emphasized mentorship. What stood out more, and merited a section in this chapter, was the urgency with which scientists approached mentoring specifically within rape scholarship. There seemed to be a sense that studying sexual violence was uniquely difficult, and was neither broadly appealing nor emotionally or intellectually feasible for many students and scholars. Public interest and institutional support were inconsistent, and a substantial range of obstacles within and beyond science might deter engagement. For these reasons, participants depicted mentoring as a vital professional mechanism in the scientific study of sexual violence.

Quite a few participants had faced criticism for choosing this work. Some were told outright that their research was unimportant. Others were told that their research was too biased or unscientific, or that no university or scientific organization would want to hire a "rape scholar" (such challenges will be analyzed in greater detail in chapter 6). Although such experiences

were discouraging, those who persisted often emerged with a keen awareness that others might face similar obstacles, and consequently invested in
building support among sexual violence researchers.

As a graduate student, Clara had often been told that sexual violence
was unworthy of academic study. She nonetheless managed to earn a PhD
in psychology, publish numerous articles, and obtain a university post without leaving the field. Some years into her academic career, Clara was
approached by a graduate student who was struggling a great deal in her
own program: "She started telling me how she was really interested in the
topic of rape myths, but somebody was trying to dissuade her from going
into it—some male faculty—because 'it's not important enough.' And I said
I'd heard that. And I just said it is really important." This encounter provided an opportunity to support an up-and-coming scholar who might
otherwise feel pressured to leave the field. In Clara's understanding, it also
featured an all-too-common gendered dynamic in scientific conflict—
"male faculty" devaluing the interests of female graduate students. During
our conversation, she elaborated that sexual violence researchers seemed to
face uniquely harsh discouragement relative to others in her field of psychology, that women who studied sexual violence often faced criticism
from men who did not, and that these trends were not attributable to disciplinary standards of rigor or significance. She felt particularly suspicious of
men in psychology who rejected the concept of studying rape:

CLARA: You've got to question his agenda, you know? They study all
    sorts of things. And some of it is really minute. They don't say "schizo-
    phrenia isn't important because of how rare it is." You can't say any-
    thing isn't important 'cause it's rare. I mean, [sexual violence] is something
    that happens to a good 20 percent of women and, what is it, 10 percent
    of men or something like that. That's huge.
ETHAN: Right, and that's just on the victim side. That's not considering
    how many aggressors there are.
CLARA: Right. Right. It's an enormous group of people. So we're going
    to focus on something that's in the 1 to 2 percent range of the popula-
    tion, that's important? And I'm not saying it's not, but anybody that says
    [sexual violence] isn't important, you've really got to question their
    agenda. And that's what I told her. And that really resonated with
    her. . . . I said, any time somebody tells me that, that tells me I'm on the
    right track. I've hit a nerve. I'm totally hitting a nerve with them. And
    that tells me there's work to be done.

Clara had come to approach opposition as fuel. Years of facing such challenges had nurtured an investment in mentoring younger scholars, and per-
sisting even (or especially) when she "hit a nerve."

Some participants shared similar stories about receiving mentorship. Jenna, a public health scholar, had considered leaving sexual violence research due to some discouraging feedback from professors:

> I was definitely having a hard time, because I was still new to this and feeling unsure, and getting a lot of backlash from people telling me that it wasn't important. . . . So once I felt supported and in a good place to do it, I feel like I've really just taken off. . . . I think that it's hard when you don't feel like you are supported, or you don't feel like you have people in your circle to help you through it. I think that having a mentor that can just give you some, not like validation, but just to let you know that what you're doing is important or help you along a little bit is helpful.

Early on, Jenna recalled feeling "like a lost sheep" in graduate school. Her advisors suggested on numerous occasions that sexual violence was not a priority in public health, and was thus a poor choice of focus. Once she connected with someone who specialized in the study of sexual violence, she found sufficient support and guidance to "take off" as a researcher. It's worth noting here that I was only able to connect with Jenna because she had remained in this field. Any scholars who took the advice that Jenna (and Clara and several other participants) initially received would not have been recruited. Given that, and the nonrandom sampling applied for this project, I cannot speculate on the rates at which such discouragement drives people from sexual violence research altogether.

Although many researchers conceptualize sexual violence as a persistent or even permanent social problem, participants in this study depicted sexual violence scholarship—or, rather, the community of scholars who choose this work—as more contingent or precarious. Several commented that the field seemed to have expanded and contracted at various points.[2] Others worried that academic pressures might stifle innovation (see Cynthia's comments in the previous chapter). In that case, sexual violence research might substantively decline, even if participation and publication in the field increased.

Concerns about maintaining a scholarly community often motivated active recruitment and mentoring. When I asked what advice she might give a young scholar who planned to study sexual violence, Gretchen commented:

> I do have students that come to me now that are like, "I'm so passionate about violence prevention" or "I'm so passionate about social justice." And so, first of all, totally validating that. Because it's so exciting. Those are the people—you know, I'm retiring one day. I'm going to be gone. We've got to make sure that all the people doing this work, and this is what my mentor said, we've got to find young, excited enthusiastic

people, because we're nowhere near ending this issue. So when I first hear a student say that, of course it's a lot of validation and praise and enthusiasm to really kind of reinforce that.

Even graduate students might feel pressure to keep the field going through ongoing recruitment and mentorship. While completing her doctorate in public health, Rebecca had "realized that my mentor is going to retire at some point" and began working to bolster institutional supports for students who might choose this field. She became proactive in supporting younger graduate and undergraduate colleagues. The perception that "we're nowhere near ending this issue" made Gretchen, Rebecca, and others feel obliged to take a communal and long-term view of rape scholarship.

COLLECTIVE CARE WORK

Scientific research is often intellectually challenging, and the professional demands to publish at high rates and/or carry heavy teaching loads are burdensome for scholars in diverse fields. Those who investigate controversial or heavy social matters may face additional emotional work. As mentioned toward the beginning of this chapter, researchers who study rape experience many of the challenges that victim advocates and batterer intervention providers face, including risks of burnout and vicarious trauma (Campbell 2002). Given these concerns, I argue that collective practices of care work comprise a central mechanism within the scientific study of rape. To further appreciate the value of this social mechanism within science, and the relative lack of attention to care work within science studies literature, it is worth a short detour through feminist research on gender and labor.

Feminist researchers have long been critical of supposedly nongendered notions of an abstract laborer that seem to represent and benefit cisgender men to the detriment of cisgender women. Acker (1990) challenged discourses that portrayed organizations as gender neutral and asexual. She argued that gendered logics drove the production and ranking of positions, as well as the workers who sought and filled them. Consequently, job descriptions and compensation were not characterized by detached objectivity, but rather by implicitly gendered logics whereby "advantage and disadvantage, exploitation and control, action and emotion, meaning and identity, are patterned through and in terms of a distinction between male and female, masculine and feminine" (146).

This was readily apparent in comparable worth evaluations. The skills required in male-dominated positions, such as managing money, were consistently recognized and highly valued. The so-called softer skills required for female-dominated positions, such as providing emotional support to supervisors and clients, were either devalued or overlooked altogether. Masculine-associated traits and experiences, such as competitiveness and military experience, were regarded as desirable. Feminine-associated traits and experiences, such as emotionality and childbearing, were grounds for exclusion from the upper ranks. Masculine-associated positions were granted more prestige and higher compensation, whereas feminine-associated positions were devalued (see Cech 2013 for a recent example within science and engineering professions). Furthermore, when managers envisioned the workers who would fill each position, they imagined persons whose primary obligations were professional. These abstract workers were implicitly free from the obligations associated with women's roles in heterosexual partnerships (Hochshild [1989] 2003; Legerski and Cornwall 2010); that is, they did not need to "balance" household and childcare responsibilities with professional ones.

Expanding these arguments, one might add that managers also envisioned laborers who were unburdened by discrimination and hostility in the workplace, and might thus focus their energy entirely on assigned tasks. In this case, any marginalized identification might detract from the archetypal abstract laborer. The work of navigating sexual harassment, queer and transgender (in)visibility, racism, ableism, and other oppressive forces might affect productivity and thus contribute to poor performance evaluations for marginalized laborers, rather than indicate a need for institutional and cultural change. Care work might be perceived as a distraction or personal indulgence, rather than a necessary practice for sustaining labor participation.

Professionals in science and higher education, like the managers in Acker's (1990) work, may envision themselves or the people they supervise as (masculine-coded) abstract workers. Those who view science as characterized by detached objectivity (Cech 2013) may further envision scientific labor as free from the burdens of more politicized fields. Yet, as many participants in this project demonstrated, the study of rape is rarely (if ever) detached. Such labor entails emotional and moral processes that render care work essential.

When I asked whether her career had involved any emotional labor (Hochschild [1983] 2012), Amy described sexual violence research as uniquely burdensome, even relative to other difficult subjects: "I think that is very clear to me. And you know, this may be my own lack of objectivity or intellectual distance from the subject—I have colleagues who study human rights, wartime violence, people who do really heavy stuff . . . but it doesn't seem to be quite the same kind of emotional labor. And again, I'm totally willing to own that might be my own minimal emotional resources and/or lack of objectivity. But no, I feel that that has been one of the defining aspects of the work as a researcher." Emotional labor was not a minor or secondary element of studying sexual violence, but rather one of its "defining aspects."

Some participants recalled occasions in which students, colleagues, and personal acquaintances had described their work as unimaginably challenging. Colleagues might dismiss rape as "too political" to study. Students might struggle individually or collectively when professors incorporated content on sexual violence into courses. Echoing Amy's comments, Max remarked that "my colleague teaches about drugs. You know, that's cool, that's fun, that's exciting. [Students think] my stuff's depressing." This comparison is striking. A course on drugs might well feature content on mass incarceration, addiction, systemic inequality—and nonetheless be regarded as more "cool" than "depressing." The same was not true for courses with units on rape.

The perception of sexual violence research as uniquely challenging contributed to feelings of isolation in scientific and other professional communities. Speaking of a recent collaboration, Miranda commented: "I just feel grateful to not be laboring alone on this issue. Because that was very much my experience [previously]. It's not that my colleagues were doing happy projects . . . I had colleagues studying human rights abuses, housing instability, hunger—difficult, heavy things. But I still think those things are somehow easier for people to talk to and discuss, particularly in academic contexts, without this kind of veil of silence that's wrapped around it." Colleagues who found rape exceedingly heavy might be unwilling or unable to have even informal discussions about participants' work, let alone offer to collaborate on projects. In this case, rape scholars often came to rely on one another for feedback and support.

The "veil of silence" among colleagues, as described by Miranda, contrasted sharply with ongoing disclosures of sexual victimization from students. However depressing students found her courses, Max received "four or five disclosures every semester." This was consistent with the experiences of several other participants; those with backgrounds in social work or crisis counseling sometimes spoke of a direct service component to their teaching. Yet those participants (and their colleagues) who taught courses in other presumably heavy areas, such as substance use or crime and deviance, did not necessarily hear disclosures of addiction or nonsexual victimization on a regular basis.

The original draft of my interview guide did not address care work. As a longtime antiviolence advocate and crisis counselor,[3] I recognized that self-care would be essential for rape researchers but did not appreciate its social dimensions or scientific value. This changed several interviews into the project, as participants began describing what seemed to be collective care work within science. I modified my interview guide to explore these matters in greater depth. I grew increasingly sure that, in addition to being an important personal practice, care work functioned as a social mechanism that sustained scholars through the intellectual, emotional, and professional challenges of producing scientific knowledge about rape.

Participants' narratives revealed that self-care was learned, and could be difficult to attempt without social support and guidance. Unfortunately, scientific environments were rarely conducive to this. Within academia, particularly in graduate school but also in faculty positions, individuals might feel pressured to distance themselves or maintain high productivity such that self-care seemed like a distraction or indulgence. Even scholars with backgrounds in advocacy, social work, clinical psychology, and other care providing fields might struggle to adapt their previous training to academic contexts. Kristen remarked:

> I had zero self-care in grad school. Zero. Which doesn't make sense, since I did advocacy work, and I promoted self-care constantly to people. I knew what it was. I said, "This is the best thing for you, this is how you do it." I think when people say, "Oh, do self-care," it's really bullshit to say that "it's easy to do" and "if we know how to do it, we're going to do it." Especially in grad school, right? . . . You've got to know what works for you, and you've got to give yourself time to do it. . . . I would always advocate for that, because I was horrible at it. I think it's just not how grad school is. . . .'Cause we think we've just got to keep hustling and keep going, and you've got no time for it.

Several participants echoed Kristen's concern that graduate students were pressured to ignore their well-being in favor of productivity and hastening timelines to graduation. This denigration of self-care aligns with positivist and masculinist norms within science. If scientists are presumed to be—or acquire legitimacy through appearing to be—detached observers, they should neither influence nor be influenced by objects of study. Agential realism offers an alternative framework (Barad 2007). Rather than viewing scientists as detached observers, it is possible to understand them as entangled within the phenomena they study. If researchers are themselves part of scientific processes, rather than outside them, there are scientific (as well as social and moral) reasons to take researchers' welfare into account.

Supportive colleagues might alleviate or counter the academic pressures that can stifle emotional labor. Whereas Kristen had engaged in "zero self-care" as a graduate student, this changed when she developed a mutually supportive relationship with another scholar of sexual violence:

> We were just texting today, like, "Wow, this is really hard." You know? And we kind of feel bad, we're worried about letting each other down. I'll say that, and she'll say, "Wow, no, I just took an hour break, because I just transcribed some notes and I feel sick." Right? And so, [it helps] to

have someone like that to say, "This is a lot, and let's be gentle with ourselves." Because most of the time, we're not, and we kind of need someone else to give us permission. So we give each other permission to kind of cool it, to care for ourselves, to be gentle, to go slowly.

When scholars feel obliged to "keep hustling and keep going," self-care may not function as a strictly individual process. It may not seem possible to slow down or prioritize our own well-being, even briefly. Kristen and her colleague were able to provide "permission" for one another to engage in self-care without feeling guilty or unprofessional. This made their individual and collaborative projects, and the work of studying rape in general, more sustainable for both of them. The shorter breaks and support work described here mitigated risks of burnout and abandoning the field.

In addition to countering the pressures of academia, scholars sometimes engaged in more direct communal care work such as proactively checking in with and monitoring one another. If someone seemed to immerse themselves too heavily in research, or seemed to be burning out, someone else might intervene. Wendy recalled struggling with a project on criminal victimization, and confiding in a friend and colleague who cautioned against becoming too engrossed in the work: "I was looking at rapes, murders, domestic violence, assaults. . . . It was horrible. And I was like, 'I want to really honor each woman that had to experience this.' And my friend was like, 'They're data points. Treat them as data points.' And I'm like, 'I can't. I literally can't.' So I just really had to be good about taking care of myself. And taking breaks. And telling my boss, like, I got to work on something else today." Although Wendy did not follow her friend's specific advice to "treat them as data points," she shared the concern that self-care was essential for completing the work. In larger projects with research assistants, she was "very clear, from interview forward, [that] you are going to take care of yourself. And if you're not, you can't work for me . . . because this is going to be really hard."

Leigh had also come to incorporate collective care processes into supervision, particularly when studying victimization:

It's hard to hear these stories, even though it's very rewarding. It does have an impact, and you want to be there fully for the person you're interviewing. So it's extremely important personally, and for the participants, you know, to do that. So I feel like I know how to do that.

But also, there's that group process. So you can't always know yourself. You have to check in with other people. And with my students, I've had a mentoring model where they can either talk to each other or they can talk in the group. I can't obviously pay for all their therapy, but you know, just making sure that they have the resources.

In this approach, Leigh and her students proactively sought the sort of feedback that Wendy's friend had provided, and developed a culture in which check-ins and self-assessments were integrated into their research practices.

Finally and perhaps most intuitively, researchers often simply turned to each other for emotional support. In interviews, this often came up in discussions that were initially unrelated to care work. When I asked about networking among sexual violence researchers, Brenda reflected: "I think you have to . . . professionally, but I think also emotionally, you have to. Which I'm sure, many other people, and as an advocate yourself [referring to me]. Just the heaviness of this material. And the sense of needing to share, needing to be able to debrief, needing to be able to talk about this. Because it's tough to do in your social circles." For those who encountered a "veil of silence" around sexual violence in academia, it was of tremendous value to connect with people who were engaged in similar work and could relate to their struggles. When I asked Miranda about collaboration, she spoke first of the intellectual and practical benefits of collective knowledge production, and then elaborated:

> The other piece of it is clearly, when you collaborate, then you have somebody to talk through all of the emotional garbage with. Which, when I was in graduate school, that was my partner. . . . [Eventually] I also started thinking about, how much of this can I take home? 'Cause there are ways that I could really sort of deal with this, and have clear boundaries, and I can be like a healthy, happy contributing member of my household. . . . And so having a collaborator—I think both of us wanted that from the outset. We get a lot of questions like, "Isn't it hard?" and I'm like, "It's a lot less hard when you have someone to talk to."

Amy shared similar experiences about connecting with a group of scholars in the field: "Finding them and being able to share both the research and also the personal cost of this stuff was a game changer. And was something that was a real turning point—being able to think about the research, but being able to share it with people who I felt like understood the day-to-day, because they were living it, too." As discussed earlier in this chapter, Amy had felt a sense of isolation and emotional struggle even relative to colleagues studying human rights abuses and other weighted subjects. Finding others in her field was a "game changer" not only in terms of intellectual possibilities, but also for connecting with people who "were living it, too."

CHOOSING THIS WORK

Engagement in rape research does not arise from nowhere. Personal dispositions and political orientations, exposure to victimization or aggression, public controversies and policy developments, and encounters with institutional prevention and response efforts may motivate a project or entire career in the field. Even scholars who seem to fall into this work might be better described as being drawn in. Graduate assistant positions, colleagues who seek particular skills or expertise, unexpected patterns in projects or careers that seem unrelated to violence—factors akin to what Dalton Conley describes as "not so random" differences in interpersonal networks and experiences—facilitate entry (2005, 137).

Choosing to study rape is not a singular or one-time process. Within and after individual projects or assignments, researchers must decide whether to remain immersed or even tangentially involved with the field. Although it is certainly not problematic to move among disciplines and industries, and I do not aim here to promote entry and persistence in sexual violence research for all scholars, it is valuable to explore the factors that encourage persistence and departure. These are critical social processes in science. Perhaps even more so for sexual violence research; the heaviness and social barriers unique to this work exacerbate the already substantial pressures of academic labor.

In addition to raising these concerns, I have argued here that two social mechanisms, mentoring and collective care work, sustain scholarship in sexual violence. For established researchers, concerns that sexual violence is a persistent social problem may compound with memories of harsh opposition such that recruiting and mentoring new people become urgent priorities. Graduate students and junior scholars may feel pressured to abandon the field altogether in the absence of supportive mentors. Finally, collective processes of care mitigate the numerous personal and professional challenges of studying rape.

CHAPTER 6

Dividends and Detriments of Dissent

INFIGHTING IS OFTEN regarded as a "kiss of death" for social movements. At best, dissent among organizers seems distracting; at worst, it might break coalitions down and foreclose hope of collective action. In *The Dividends of Dissent*, Amin Ghaziani (2008) put these assumptions to empirical scrutiny. He investigated the scope and consequences of infighting in social movements by tracing the histories of four queer marches on Washington—or rather, two lesbian and gay marches; one lesbian, gay, and bisexual march; and one lesbian, gay, bisexual, and transgender march. Dissent was pervasive. Ghaziani encountered numerous and tense conflicts concerning activists' conceptualizations of who "fit" within "the community," whose voices to feature at events, whether to prioritize assimilation with or disruption of social norms, and the extent to which ostensibly nonsexual identities such as race and disability shaped queer (or LG or LGB or LGBT) communities and therefore ought to inform community activism. Ultimately, Ghaziani argued that dissent was productive under some conditions. Far from being a kiss of death, in-group conflict could force activists to recognize and reconcile differences, and to design campaigns and collective platforms that better reflected the interests of diverse communities. A lack of argument might be reconceived as stagnation, or as the prioritization of dominant or privileged voices—for example, White, middle-class, gay and lesbian people without disabilities who sought to assimilate within mainstream society—over marginalized voices. Disagreement might be reconceived as a prerequisite to collective identity and strategy.

Scientific research and social movements comprise different domains. Nonetheless, these fields sometimes align or overlap, and are shaped by many of the same social forces. Like actors within social movements, scholars within what Frickel and Gross (2005) have theorized as "scientific/intellectual movements" engage in efforts to "gain adherents, win intellectual prestige, and ultimately acquire some level of institutional stability" (205). Leaders face pressure to build a sufficient following and institutional support base to ensure that their scientific goals do not perish when their careers or lives end (see chapter 5 for a discussion on the urgency of mentoring in sexual violence scholarship). All participants in a scientific/intellectual movement may contend with challenges from within and without, and develop varied or flexible discursive strategies for navigating them. Moreover, many activist processes described in *The Dividends of Dissent* apply to the scientific processes of selecting and prioritizing research questions, designing investigations, building professional networks and collaborations, pursuing funding and other resources, and interpreting and distributing findings. Similarities are particularly pronounced for the study of rape. Many scholars in this field have backgrounds in advocacy, and maintain those ties throughout their careers. Others find that studying sexual violence compels them toward social action. Even those who do not venture directly into activist work are apt to contend with others who do. Given these patterns, the study of rape will at times function simultaneously as a scientific/intellectual movement and a movement for social change. Whereas the activists in Ghaziani's work (2008) were united against a perceived common threat of heteronormativity, a threat which often sufficed to maintain commitments for collective action through periods of infighting, researchers in this project were united against a common threat of rape. Infighting has also been a constant and arguably sometimes productive mechanism in the field.

This chapter explores conflict in sexual violence research. Drawing on Ghaziani's depiction of common threats as unifying, participants' insights, and my own experiences as a sexual violence researcher, I have organized such conflict loosely into in-group dissent and out-group challenges. Out-group challenges often draw from the feminization of rape research discussed in previous chapters. This field of work is sometimes devalued within science for its association with feminist activism (an association that impacts feminist and nonfeminist scholars alike), and for its association with questions of social morality. Skeptical outsiders regularly depict rape researchers as unscientific or unproductive. Some go so far as to dissuade graduate students or junior scholars from choosing this work, or attempt to exert control over their research agendas and career trajectories. Scientists facing such conflict confront limited options. In some cases, people abandon the field. Others develop strategies to mitigate outsiders' challenges. Those invested in scientific credibility, particularly those whose feminist values motivate rape scholarship but who also embrace positivist understandings of proper or objective scientific inquiry, may engage in substantial efforts to establish and defend their credibility among peers. For example, a researcher might favor quantitative methodology or dispassionate writing styles in order to produce convincingly scientific works for publication. Alternatively, scientists who actively politicize their own and others' research might disinvest in outsiders' critiques, and focus instead on building and supporting a community of insiders. Although this last approach can be quite liberating, it risks a loss of status within the larger domains of science and academia.

In-group dissent concerns infighting among scholars of sexual violence. This might involve disagreements over what can and should be studied, what is publishable or presentable in specialist journals and conferences, and several concerns that parallel Ghaziani's observations about queer activism: disagreements regarding who "fits" within the category of "people affected by sexual violence," and who among them merits prioritization; whether scientists ought to politicize their work and actively seek to disrupt social norms, including norms within professional science; and the extent to which various identities and lived experiences, such as gender and race and disability, are relevant to the phenomenon of rape. Scientists whose work garners fears of misuse, or poses challenges to dominant scholars or widely accepted assumptions within sexual violence research, may ultimately abandon their efforts for fears of controversy or in-group pushback. In these instances, in-group conflict stifles innovation and forecloses lines of inquiry. Yet dissent can also be productive. Disagreements can push scholars to confront unsettled (and perhaps even impossible-to-settle) questions, and promote a scientific culture characterized by accountability and openness to change.

Out-Group Challenges

Sexual violence research occupies a contested position within science. Scholars with other specialties might question whether the study of sexual violence is scientific at all. Even those who perceive such work as scientific might question its intellectual or social value. Several participants in this project had faced such challenges. Often times, those with backgrounds in advocacy were dismissed as "applied" or "public" researchers whose work was presumed less rigorous than comparatively "pure" endeavors. Scholars who embraced feminist perspectives and methodologies were further dismissed as lacking objectivity by peers who perceived science and politics as wholly separate (or at least wholly separable) fields. Some participants connected this form of opposition with a general skepticism toward women and other socially marginalized actors within science and academia.

Out-group challenges often arose in graduate school, when students had yet to establish or publicly commit themselves to any particular lines of research. Students across disciplines might be dissuaded from projects that seemed insufficiently marketable or too overtly political to secure tenure-track positions at prestigious universities. Participants reported such dissuasion from both well-meaning, supportive advisors and overtly dismissive, hostile faculty. In her public health doctoral program, Alisa was warned that "sexual assault prevention is a very polarizing topic" and that she should wait until tenure to pursue it. Any work that seemed critical of institutional approaches to violence might render her unhireable. When applying to graduate school in philosophy, Jeff was repeatedly warned that "you shouldn't delve into [sexuality], because no one does that, and it's not going to be very marketable. So do something else." If scholars persisted in studying rape and did manage to secure faculty positions, these experiences lent urgency to the work of mentoring younger students. As discussed in chapter 5, Jenna was told by numerous professors that sexual violence was not a priority in public health during her graduate studies; it was not until she connected with a mentor who specialized in this area that she finally learned otherwise, and felt able to continue in her research.

Those who continued in the field often continued to face out-group opposition. Several participants had faced critics who spoke of sexual violence research as inherently unscientific. Studies pertaining to social controversies or human values were often discounted as "public" research. Such work was then presumed insufficiently rigorous and/or too ideological to comprise objective science. When speaking of psychological research on men's sexual aggression, Brian commented: "When one does research in an area such as this, particularly for perceived morals, dealing with sexual morality and violence, there's a certain attitude among some academics with it not being as important or legitimate as some other areas." These concerns reflect broader patterns in science, including social science as well as STEM fields, through which any work characterized as social or political is devalued relative to work characterized as purely technical (Cech 2013).

Some scholars, particularly those who favored qualitative or feminist approaches, connected out-group conflict with methodological hierarchies in science. Stephanie recalled facing challenges as a psychologist who did not pursue laboratory experiments:

> When I was younger and still coming through the ranks, there was still a very strong emphasis on doing very basic, theoretically driven, laboratory-based research. And what I was doing, there was theory there, but it was certainly not laboratory based. It was not through experiments. So it was like I wasn't true to the cannon. And people would make comments: "If you want to do this kind of work, you should go be a sociologist" or "You should go be a social worker. Go to public." So it was a disciplinary kind of thing. And that's not true of all psychology departments, I don't think it's true of the discipline as a whole. But that was my own personal sort of circumstances at that particular point in time.

Yet for all these concerns, shifting toward experimental psychology might not have solved the problem. Stephanie elaborated that her affiliation with women's studies was also an issue, and that "there were certain people in my field who didn't think that doing anything related to gender was really legitimate." Any investigations of violence against women might thus be dismissed as irrelevant to psychology. It was not merely engagement with "sexual morality and violence" as described by Brian, but affiliation specifically with women's studies and feminist politics that drew scientific opposition.

Such matters were not limited to psychology and public health. As discussed in previous chapters, Virginia expressed concerns that her fellow sociologists tended to "gloss over" matters of sexual violence in their own projects rather than take it seriously as a causal force in the reproduction of social inequalities. Kristen echoed these concerns when recalling the challenges she had faced during and after graduate school, and worried that people might be driven away from studying rape if they relied on others for validation and guidance: "You're so pressured to go here, to say this, and do something different, and something that's going to get you a job and get you published. If I had listened to everyone, I never would have been, I never would have done this work. People were just like, 'It's not going to get published, no one cares, it's like this niche field . . . you're not going to get published, or you're only going to get published in the really low journals.' Which, you know what, is true sometimes." Kristin elaborated that her experiences reflected problems within the larger production of sociological knowledge. She called for critical reflection across the discipline, and suggested that scholars in more marginalized fields persist in spite of out-group challenges:

> It's horrible, and our discipline has a lot of self-reflection I think it should go through. What to publish, who gets published, the classic sociology of knowledge. Like what kind of knowledge are we actually producing in the world? When is it helpful, when is it not helpful? So now we have public sociology, or public academia—which is really, in my opinion, a way to say, "Oh, you're doing that public stuff that doesn't matter as much as theoretical debates" or something. . . . I think you've got to just turn it off sometimes, and think about what is going to make you whole.

Jeff was similarly critical of intellectual policing in philosophy, and convinced that scholars of sexuality and sexual violence should be prepared to rely on themselves for encouragement. When I asked what advice he would give to an aspiring philosopher who wanted to follow in his footsteps, he remarked:

> This is a very small field, and there's definitely a lot of material that you could work with. And that you could try to focus on, and make it your

own thing. That could be adventurous. At the same time, because hardly anyone does this, and people in philosophy don't consider this a serious subject, you might be ridiculed. Or you might be seen with scorn because you're not doing "real philosophy." And I would just kind of give that student the warning that you will probably be admired and liked by your students, because students love this material. With people who already do this, you might be considered a good colleague to work with. Other philosophers, they may or may not take you seriously. Until they get to know you—then they will pay attention to your work. But initially, they may not think of you as a philosopher per se.

These and other participants connected skepticism toward sexual violence research with disciplinary values rather than apolitical notions of rigor or objectivity. The persistence of such skepticism meant that scholars of rape needed to prepare for credibility struggles, including challenges to their legitimacy as psychologists or philosophers or sociologists.

Some conflicts reflected broader political trends within the interdisciplinary field of sexuality studies. Regardless of whether they study rape, sexuality scholars often face immense personal challenges from colleagues (Irvine 2012). Researchers might be perceived as perverse or immoral for approaching sex/sexuality as worthy of academic attention. They might be accused of studying trivial rather than serious or scientific matters, of being problematically "obsessed" with sex, or of seeking to transform their own sexual lives and experiences into an academic career. They may be perceived as open to sharing any and all details about their personal sexual lives, or hearing the details of others' sexual lives, under the guise of discussing research interests (Chadwick 2019). The same is true for those who focus specifically on sexual violence.[1] Many participants shared that critics had challenged their moral character alongside their research agendas. Some had been asked repeatedly about their personal histories and political allegiances. In some cases, readers made assumptions about researchers' histories of sexual victimization or aggression, and engaged these (often false) assumptions when criticizing their work.

Several participants connected out-group opposition with (anti)feminist politics and widespread investment in maintaining what they perceived as a false notion of scientific detachment. Stephanie's previous comments on the devaluing of gender-related work in psychology speak to this. Reflecting on her career in antiviolence advocacy and academia, Brenda shared that "many would argue that [I do] biased research, and I'm not keeping my feminist ideology out of my research," though she quickly clarified that she "never spent much time entertaining those arguments." Like her peers quoted above, Brenda trusted her personal judgment and the judgments of more supportive colleagues over the objections of out-group critics.

Taking these concerns further, Clara observed that "you get some people in academia who are actually trying to dissuade women from studying this area of sexual violence." This had become evident to her during a grant-writing workshop in graduate school. Attendees were asked to bring a paragraph or two describing an upcoming project. During the workshop, everyone had a chance to review and critique each other's work with the aims of making general improvements and increasing each scholar's chances of securing external funding. When it was Clara's turn for critique, she recalled that the facilitator "really got aggressive" and seemed to fixate on her personal background: "It was almost like he wanted [me to say], 'I'm a rape victim myself, and that's why I'm so focused on this, and that's why I'm biased, and so hellbent on holding perpetrators responsible.' And I'm like, 'Yeah . . . I'm not sharing anything about that.'" When I asked whether other workshop participants faced such treatment, she said: "No. He's not asking the woman who's interested in autism why she's studying autism. You know? Why is this person studying . . . the experiences deaf people in psychotherapy, or why somebody is interested in chronic pain in old people? He was really focused on me." While Clara may have been the only workshop attendee to face suspicion and invasive questioning, she was far from the only participant in this study to have experienced that kind of pushback. Miranda suggested that the problem went far beyond dissuading women from studying rape, and rather concerned a broader skepticism toward marginalized scholars across disciplines:

> Some of this falls into that category of like, when women or queer people or people of color do research on women, queer people, or people of color, I think the term is "mesearch," right? People assume you are doing it because you have some kind of personal stake in it. Whereas when, you know, hetero cis White men study hetero cis White men, that's somehow normative and not marked by the kind of mesearch. Which, you know, now I'm strategizing—oh, do you study the presidency because you're a man and think you can relate?
>
> So that's part of it. And I think it's a way of invalidating people's research, by some standard of objectivity. Which, you know, I don't think it's possible to be objective. That's the tradition I'm trained in, and also as somebody who does espouse feminist methodology, I don't think that's the end goal either.

Just as Clara's peers had not faced accusations of bias for focusing on autism and chronic pain, Miranda's colleagues in comparatively socially privileged positions had not been accused of doing mesearch even when studying people within "their own" communities. Challenges seemed to arise based on who the researcher was, rather than what they studied.

In some instances, out-group conflict manifested as overt support for rape myths (Edwards et al. 2011; Suarez and Gadalla 2010) or hostility toward people (particularly women) who disclosed sexual victimization. Madeline described resistance from individuals "who challenge the whole reality of sexual violence against women." Clara recalled facing substantial pushback against a study of women's support-seeking behaviors after assault. As she understood it, her colleague "had a whole problem with, just even the idea that women don't lie about rape. He was really stuck on it." When she protested that this issue was irrelevant for that particular project—she was exploring the aftermath of sexual violence, not the veracity of reports—he insisted that he was "just a critical thinker." Another colleague had accused her of being "sexist towards women, because I'm just letting them off the hook . . . not holding them accountable for their actions that lead them to get raped." Brenda described a dramatic incident in which, after delivering a presentation on sexual violence in relationships, a man in the audience "quoted scripture to me and told me that he had the right to have sex with his wife on demand." For these and other scholars, ostensibly scientific criticisms of their work often read like antifeminist defenses of rape culture.

Consistent with the controversy over "one in four women" described in chapter 2, scholars who had studied the prevalence of sexual violence were routinely accused of overstating the problem. When presenting work on sexual violence in alcohol-serving establishments, Marion noted "defensiveness" from some men in the audience who argued that high rates of aggression in such spaces were mitigated by the fact that women patrons seemed to anticipate a risk of violence:

> They said, "Aren't women just asking for it then? If they know that they are going to experience that, and yet they choose to go to these places with loud music, indoor/outdoor seating, like they want that." And so it was a matter of having a conversation that somebody can want to go to an environment that is maybe sexually charged, or has some sort of sexual energy around it, without wanting sexual aggression or without wanting to experience sexual violence. And so that was interesting to me, to have that kind of "aren't they asking for it" attitude when they're looking at data.

Julia, on the other hand, had faced pushback regarding definitions. Critics of her research on campus sexual violence suggested that she restrict prevalence estimates to penetrative assaults rather than document a range of nonconsensual experiences, as these were more likely to constitute rape or sexual assault in criminal contexts:

> I certainly heard from some individuals who thought our definition was too broad, and that it meant that we were inflating sort of this notion that sexual violence is widespread on campus.
>
> And so my response has been, I had multiple responses. Some sort of technical, in that at this point we have some pretty good science on sexual violence research, and sort of know how to ask about these questions behaviorally. And I think that we need to be asking about a broad range of behaviors, because that's what's happening to our students. And that sexual violence happens on a continuum. And that certainly sexual assault/rape is a problem, but so too are other sort of forms of sexual violence that might be viewed as lesser or lower on that continuum. . . . I think that it does reflect this sort of lack of understanding that something that may not involve penetration, but is a form of sexual violence, can still have really negative consequences on our students.

Both of these scholars were accused of "inflating" the problem. In Marion's case, colleagues endeavored to shift responsibility toward women who "choose to go to these places" where they might experience sexual violence, rather than holding aggressive men accountable. According to this logic, even high rates of violence might be deemed unproblematic because women were "asking for it." Julia resisted hierarchical assumptions when documenting victimization, and was challenged for refusing to restrict prevalence estimates to assaults that might (legally) qualify as rape. The fact that she could isolate those incidents—that her survey design enabled her to calculate distinct estimates for "rape" and broader conceptualizations of "sexual violence"—did not necessarily satisfy her critics.

In-Group Dissent

In addition to out-group challenges, participants in this project regularly faced or learned about conflicts among sexual violence researchers. These did not concern whether rape could or should be studied scientifically, but rather how this might occur. The questions Kristen raised above regarding the sociology of knowledge, and the conditions of intellectual production within generalist journals and social science more broadly, had counterparts within specialist journals and smaller scholarly communities. Fears over potential "misuse" of research were particularly salient for scholars who studied the causes of sexual aggression and victimization. Gender politics were consistently fraught.

Amy expressed frustration with "ideological policing around things like how we talk about sexual violence . . . which things researchers are allowed to say, and which [they] are not." Well-established scholars' theoretical and methodological preferences might overshadow substantive contributions when evaluating the work of newer or less well-known scholars (Bourdieu 1975; Latour 1987). This often manifested in peer-review processes. Amy described one experience in which a collaborative project was rejected for publication on the grounds that it seemed too interdisciplinary for reviewers. Yet this logic seemed suspect, given that the journal itself was interdisciplinary:

> [We] got real pushback around things like, "What is the disciplinary framework here? You can't use case studies from different research methods." And this was from an interdisciplinary journal. And, you know, we had worked very hard to recognize and bridge things like the different disciplinary approaches . . . and the issues around research methods. It was frustrating to feel like people in the discipline were unwilling to get past those. What didn't always feel like intellectually significant questions, but more sort of policing around, "This is what research looks like, I'm comfortable and familiar with this, and I'm not really willing [to deviate]." And I'm not saying that they didn't really have interesting critiques that helped us do a better version of the article. But I think—I'll speak for myself—what I felt was that there was some ideological policing around discipline and method that, to me, missed the point of what we were talking about.

In some cases, Amy suspected that reviewers and editors were simply unwilling to support novel approaches from less established scholars. Other times, she thought that such criticisms belied a more concerning investment in silencing work that challenged scientific norms (including political norms within scientific research). Senior scholars and editors who felt unsettled or intellectually threatened by an argument might offer harsh and even detailed methodological criticisms to mask a more personal "rejection of the findings."

Adam also recalled facing opposition from scholars who seemed threatened by or politically opposed to his work. Although fellow biologists and other natural scientists were often responsive to his research, he had received criticism from scholars in social science and humanities fields who rejected the entire project of applying evolutionary theory to rape: "Some people again are saying, 'Well, you shouldn't think about humans as biological phenomena,' and that kind of thing." Adam insisted that developing a scientific understanding of sexual violence was a prerequisite to eliminating it, and that evolutionary theory comprised a powerful scientific resource for understanding human and nonhuman behavior, including sexual aggression. He remarked that a "non-biological" conceptualization of human beings was "pretty naïve, to say the least . . . basically, they're saying that humans are not alive. Because that's what biology means." Given this, he argued that naiveté or problematic ideologies, rather than scientifically informed criticism, must be driving the opposition. Although their disciplinary training and research agendas contrasted sharply, Max had faced similar pushback for investigating the causes of victimization:

> One has to be much more delicate when looking at predictive factors of victimization, because people get cranky, and assume that we're victim-blaming. And so I have done some of this research, you know, invariably you end up having to write something to the effect of, you know, "Predictors doesn't mean it's the person's fault." And if you don't—you know, we need to study this stuff to be able to prevent it. You always need some kind of "I'm really not blaming the victims, I swear," kind of comment in there. It's good to be aware of that, but you don't end up having to do that when you're studying offending.

Whereas biological/evolutionary accounts have been dismissed for absolving aggressors, criminological and psychological investigations of individual predictors of victimization have been portrayed as victim-blaming. Yet scholars in both lines of research might protest that their aim is to understand and ultimately eliminate sexual violence.

In chapter 3 on causal inquiries, I discussed fears of misuse surrounding some lines of research on sexual violence. Evolutionary approaches, as discussed by Adam above, comprised one example. Another concerned scholarship on the complexities of consent. Stacey and her collaborators had faced some accusations of reinforcing rape myths and mitigating aggressors' responsibility for their behavior:

> The piece about consent, too, is potentially controversial among sexual assault researchers. And this may be why there are not so many people doing it. . . . So many people's response to that is, "This is not a confusion about consent, this is people knowingly ignoring nonconsent." Which I would say is probably true in most cases. I mean, I think that is probably the case in most sexual assaults, someone is knowingly ignoring or not attending to consent cues.
>
> On the other hand, I do think at least an understanding of consent is the sort of basic minimum requirement for consensual sex. Like, you have to have a shared understanding to even begin to do it. And although I think probably [in] most cases, someone is explicitly ignoring consent, I think that there are probably some cases of miscommunication—see, that's a really controversial limb to go out on—but I think that that's

probably the case, that sometimes there's miscommunication. And at the very least, it can lead to less than ideal situations. Even if it's not the cause of things we would legally call rape. So that's a potentially controversial area.

As noted here, Stacey suspected that colleagues' dissent drove some people away from this line of research. Even those who believed that exploring sexual (mis)communication might be valuable, or who disputed conceptualizations of sexual violence as always characterized by "people knowingly ignoring nonconsent," might shy away for fear of attracting controversy.

Additional, or perhaps overlapping, dissent concerned researchers' treatment of gender within studies of rape. The in-group gender politics of sexual violence research are fraught, such that scholars who prioritize cisgender men's aggression toward cisgender women and scholars who prioritize other patterns or more gender-inclusive approaches often feel scrutinized and challenged by their peers. There seems to be no dominant collective position on this issue.

In the 1970s and 1980s, it was routine for scholars to approach sexual violence as a subset of men's violence toward women. Gender variance was not widely acknowledged in academic literature at this time, and it was consequently standard to use female/woman and male/man interchangeably. Those who studied anything aside from cisgender men's sexual violence toward cisgender women tended to qualify their terms. Researchers might refer to "male rape" when discussing male victimization, and speak simply of "rape" when discussing female victimization. The term "rapist" was often synonymized with "male rapist." Indeed, I noted no direct references to "female rapists" across all 1,313 abstracts and 84 full studies assessed for this project; sexually aggressive females were referred to as "female offenders" or "female perpetrators."

Many scholars of rape perceive cisgender men's aggression toward cisgender women as the most pervasive and urgent dimension of this social problem. However, they seem to have faced increasing pushback for this approach. When I asked whether she had experienced any conflicts or disagreements with scholars in the field, Madeline described facing "the most resistance" from "those that want to talk about male victims." When pursuing grant funding for a campus-based project, Jenna had initially intended to distribute separate surveys to male and female students that focused on aggression and victimization, respectively. She was advised that her chances of funding would improve considerably if she posed all questions to all participants. As discussed in chapter 2 on prevalence research, Rebecca had found public health professionals resistant to describing sexual violence as gender-based violence, which made collaboration with gender and women's studies scholars challenging. She further felt ongoing tension between her desire to produce and support inclusive, intersectional scholarship with her certainty that heterosexual, cisgender men's aggression toward heterosexual, cisgender women comprised the vast majority of (adult) sexual violence.

Yet for all these concerns, the field of rape research was far from embracing an altogether different approach. Scholars who favored gender-inclusive or gender-neutral approaches, or who prioritized same-sex violence, violence within or toward transgender communities, women's aggression, or men's victimization, also faced resistance from their peers. Gretchen, who had done some work on violence in queer communities, expressed frustration with "people who are just on opposite ends. Like women can never be violent . . . just people who say there's absolutely no parallel. And then other people say it's 100 percent the same." Stacey recalled hearing from "big names in the field" that "we shouldn't be attending to that because it really just draws attention away from the bigger problem of men perpetrators and women as victims." According to these critics, simply acknowledging other gendered patterns in rape might detract scientific attention from "the bigger problem."

Assumptions about gender and sexual violence intersected with assumptions about other dimensions of social position and lived experience. Age was particularly important when conceptualizing potential assailants and victims. Max spoke at length of criminologists' tendency to recognize the possibility of women's aggression in the context of child sexual abuse, but not adult sexual assault:

> I think that people think that a woman can physically control a child in a way that they don't think that a woman can physically control an adult. . . . I'm always sort of struck [by] . . . naiveté that women don't do these sorts of things. If you look, for instance—even the FBI definition only included women victims a few years ago, they only [recently] made it gender neutral. You didn't see any women offenders in FBI arrest data because they didn't even ask. They didn't even include it. So you know, some poor police officer in Philly or wherever that arrests a female for sexual assault, there's no place in the [Uniform Crime Reporting] system to include it. There wasn't up until a couple years ago. So it's not surprising people don't realize these things happen.

When it came to acknowledging adult men's experiences of victimization, Max suggested that misperceptions about sexual arousal and threat response might play a role:

> I think another big myth that plays into it as well—and again at the risk of being blunt and gross, well not gross, anatomically correct—is this

notion that if men are fearful, they can't stay erect. . . . There's tons of research that shows that there's excitation transfer. In other words, if you're really afraid or you're really excited, the blood's pumping everywhere. It's not deciding, like, "God, I'm afraid, heaven forbid the blood's pumping, but it's not going to go to my penis." That's not how it works. And I think if people had a better understanding of that, a better understanding of just the ways in which people can coerce people into doing things they don't want, I think that there would be much more understanding.

Another example is, even among female victims, we talk about fight or flight response. And most people don't think about, well, there's the whole freeze response, that you know, many victims freeze. People are finally starting to realize, "Oh yeah, women can freeze as a response to sexual violence." . . . So can men. You know, if I put a gun to your head and say, "Pull your pants down," you might freeze too. Or even if I'm just very hostile, or I shock you or surprise you, or put you in a situation where you don't expect it.

Not all scholars opposed gender-inclusive (or even gender-neutral) approaches, just as not all scholars opposed a strict emphasis on men's violence toward women. Participants who explored a range of gendered patterns in sexual violence broadly perceived an increasing openness to their work among in-group peers. Nonetheless, they continued to expect and face pushback.

Toward Productive Outrage and Kind Criticism

Is infighting a kiss of death for science? Or the scientific study of rape, specifically? Out-group and in-group conflict certainly comprise powerful mechanisms here. For every scholar who faces opposition in or after graduate school and chooses to persist, there may be one or several who change course. This might mean abandoning the study of sexual violence in favor of subjects deemed less political or controversial by fellow researchers, or moving away from scientific or scholarly pursuits altogether. Scholars might change course more subtly, shifting their focus within sexual violence studies as a means of circumventing protest. Someone might change their gendered approach, as described by Jenna; or decline to critically investigate controversial subjects such as consent, as described by Stacey.

Notwithstanding these mixed or detrimental outcomes, infighting among scientists and specifically among scholars of rape has its dividends. Several participants shared that conflicts and discouragement motivated them to persist. When recounting directives to avoid studying rape and other "polarizing" subjects until tenure, Alisa shared that such guidance "almost makes me want to do it more." Far from abandoning the field, she had worked to familiarize herself with the politics of higher education. Although she sometimes strategically broadened her focus to less overtly controversial matters such as sexual health or student welfare, she did not lose her passion for or commitment to addressing sexual violence. Even personal attacks and challenges might be reframed as fuel. Whereas her initial struggles "put me in molasses a little bit," Clara had come to believe that "when I get that kind of visceral reaction from a guy like that, I know I'm on the right track." She had learned to channel opposition into motivation. She responded to accusations of being "sexist toward women" for holding aggressors accountable, and repeated efforts to discount her research by reinforcing the very rape myths she sought to dismantle, with "moral outrage" that drove her work.

Under the right circumstances, infighting may also ensure that scholars continue to pose challenging questions and confront empirical uncertainties regarding the nature and scope of sexual violence. In-group gender politics offer a telling example. Although the vitriolic pushback described by some participants was regrettable and problematic, the struggle over how to engage gender in sexual violence research is a productive one. The struggle over whether to endorse patriarchy as the sole or principle (proximate) causal agent, or whether to incorporate other forces such as racism and poverty and ultimate causes such as human evolution, is likewise productive. Wendy touched on this when I asked about her vision for the field. She expressed that "we're not really honest enough about the limitations of our findings," and wished that she and her colleagues might be "more critical of one another, but in a kind way." Absent room for dissent among scholars, it will not be possible to produce or accept even "kind" criticism. Yet with sufficient openness, supportive and critical infighting might be as productive as working toward consensus.

CHAPTER 7

Conclusion

IN THE EARLY 1970s, as Susan Brownmiller researched for and wrote *Against Our Will*, she was repeatedly asked whether she had been raped. She repeatedly answered "no." The first edition opened with a personal statement on these encounters. Brownmiller shared that neither she nor her questioners seemed satisfied by such a brief, superficial exchange. She contemplated their persistent drive to discover (and probably critique) her motivations for studying rape, and wrote thoughtfully about her own shifting conceptualization of sexual violence and gendered power dynamics within and beyond the United States. She shared that years of work with feminist antiviolence activists transformed her from someone who met victimization stories with skepticism into someone who believed and advocated for survivors. Ultimately, Brownmiller concluded, she had written *Against Our Will* because she was "a woman who changed her mind about rape" (Brownmiller 1975, 9).

In the mid-2010s, as I researched for and wrote this book, few people asked after my history with violence. Yet I have struggled endlessly with whether, and to what extent, I might share it here. I have tried to balance my privacy aspirations with my gratitude for rich and open narratives like Brownmiller's (and numerous other scholars who have shared narratives of victimization within academic texts, such as Alcoff 2018 and Estrich 1987), and with my ongoing dismay at the scarcity of queer and transgender voices across more than a thousand scientific works. I have tried to think and feel reflexively. Feminist ideals have pulled me in both directions, pushing me to situate my own knowledge production while also reminding me that victims/survivors (should) carry full ownership of their own stories. Logistical and political concerns were likewise muddled. On one hand, disclosure might help me to get ahead of invasive questions, and control the narratives as much as possible. On the other hand, neither disclosure nor nondisclosure would provide sure defenses against the kinds of credibility challenges that sexual violence researchers (and activists) face. As Linda Alcoff (2018) has noted, speaking "as a survivor"—whether proclaiming that identification for myself, or having it imposed upon (or withheld from) me through others' understandings of my personal history—carries opportunities for political transformation and empowerment as well as "the realistic expectation that one's account will be met with skepticism . . . that telling will result in new humiliations" (148). At particularly indecisive times, I even tried to burden friends and colleagues with the decision. To their collective credit, most insisted that these decisions were mine to make, and that I faced no obligations in any direction.

Ultimately, it is the social and historical contingency of classification— including my and other researchers' capacity to locate the problem of rape within and outside of various bodies and spaces, and to engage such different conceptualizations and methodologies and audiences—that moves me to speak here. Have I been raped? Do I "count?" I said as much, in the opening chapter. And although that passage was initially composed for a feminist science studies conference, where I fully expected (and received) affirmation and trust, I chose to retain it for this writing.

I also chose to return to the question repeatedly, as a sort of intellectual exercise, throughout the work of publication searches and content analyses and interviews and meetings and endless drafting and rewriting. Now, asking myself more directly and after several years immersed in this project, I revise:

> Have I been raped? I believe so. Or maybe I believe that I have been raped somewhere between zero and three times at the time of this writing. It depends on who is asking, and who gets to decide with authority. It depends on what specific acts will count as rape, and whether gender identifications and enactments affect the perceptibility of assailants and victims/survivors. It depends on whether and how much my own perceptions matter, and how consistent those need to be. It depends on whether researchers or legislators or crisis counselors or activists have a say, and maybe even whether my (and my assailants') friends and relatives and other close observers have a say, and how their classifications measure up against my own narratives, and how much that matters. Rape is a complex phenomenon with numerous potential boundaries and conceptualizations, and my own history is no exception.

If Susan Brownmiller wrote as a woman who changed her mind about rape, perhaps I write here as a researcher and advocate—and also as a queer and transmasculine person with complex and sometimes shifting understandings of my own victimization history—who has faced a range of both changing and immoveable minds on the subject. I write as someone who does not perceive myself (or others) as socially unified. Even when assessing my own history, which is closer and more known to me than it would be to a fellow scientist, I produce different counts and enact different agential cuts at different moments. As identitarian articulations manifest and shift, I might approach this question as a sociologist, as a crisis counselor and advocate, as a queer person, as a White person, as a man, as a transgender person, as someone of Jewish ancestry, as an atheist, as an educator, as someone who was assigned female at birth and raised as a girl, as a middle-class person, as a (particular sort of) feminist, as someone who proudly claims survivorhood, as someone who resents being at all defined by others' violence toward me, as any combination of these and other identifications. I cannot produce a singular or innocent truth here.

CONCEPTUALIZING RAPE

Rape and other forms of sexual violence—and our ways of knowing, counting, accounting for, and responding to them—comprise intra-active phenomena. These objects of knowledge are inseparable from agencies of observation. All this is not to say that rape is imaginary or trivial. Rather, it means that an understanding of rape requires some understanding of the means through which it is perceived, and how various actors enact agential cuts to distinguish this object from the conditions that make it perceptible (and how even the same actor might enact different agential cuts in different moments). In scientific contexts, conceptualizing rape requires a consideration of the complex decision-making processes, disciplinary conventions, research instruments, theoretical and methodological approaches, funding and other resource constraints, collaboration and conflict, broader social contexts and historical events, personal dispositions, and more that contribute to the production of particular scientific knowledges. From a conventional positivist perspective, these dimensions of knowledge production are understood as separate from an external and preexisting object called "rape." From an agential realist perspective, the nature and scope of "rape," its causes and consequences, and the perceptibility of various acts and assailants and victims, shift through and alongside changes in the conditions of scientific knowledge production. These are not merely theoretical concerns. Given the capacity of research to inform social policy and public perceptions, decision-making and other processes in the production of scientific knowledge about sexual violence can have far-reaching consequences.

The study of rape comprises a vibrant and complex scientific field. Scholars of innumerable backgrounds have engaged questions regarding the scope, causes, and aftermath of this social problem, and taken a tremendous variety of approaches in doing so. Notwithstanding this variety, there have also been several patterns in knowledge production over the past four decades that merit (re)consideration. I will address two of them here. The first concerns a historical, if somewhat declining, dominance of psychological and psychiatric inquiry, and consequent reliance on individual-level understandings. The second concerns gendered precasting, and related controversy over whether to conceptualize rape as a component of (cisgender) men's violence against (cisgender) women or as a gender-neutral phenomenon. Addressing these patterns—with the aim of expanding scholarship and avenues for knowledge production, rather than replacing or superseding established work—complements a broader aim of engaging systemic and intersectional approaches in science and antiviolence work.

The Dominance of Psychological and Individual-Level Accounts

Many participants in this project described rape as an "interdisciplinary problem." In other words, knowledges and analytical resources across numerous fields—psychology, sociology, anthropology, criminology, criminal justice, social work, public health, biology, communications, medicine, philosophy, and interdisciplinary fields such as gender studies and cultural studies, to name but a few—have value for understanding and addressing sexual violence. At the same time, some researchers in this project criticized what they perceived as a dominance of psychological work in the field. I agree, based on my own analyses of scientific research. Psychological works comprised the bulk of the 1,313 scientific abstracts reviewed here. When I examined the top-cited causal and aftermath studies across four decades, psychology and psychiatry were better represented than any other disciplines, both in terms of study authors' backgrounds and journals' disciplinary affiliations. This pattern was so pronounced that particular lines of inquiry within psychology, such as investigations of PTSD symptomology and treatment after sexual victimization (in effects research), sometimes reached farther than non-psychological and interdisciplinary research combined.[1] Although interdisciplinary journals made the top ten in several instances, as did authors with backgrounds in other fields such as sociology and public health, psychological and psychiatric knowledges of rape seem to have reached farthest for more than forty years.

None of the participants in this study called for an end to psychological inquiries into rape, nor do I make any such proposal. The concerns raised here would likewise remain unaddressed if another discipline or scientific/ intellectual movement claimed "ownership" over the field.[2] Rather, I call for intellectual diversity. I call for an expansion regarding which knowledges are treated as the most credible, the most worthy of publication and citation. There is vast room for interdisciplinary collaboration, and for the inclusion and valuing of perspectives that emphasize interpersonal, institutional, and cultural dimensions of social problems in addition or alternative to the more individual dimensions prioritized in psychology. Multiple participants expressed an interest in exploring the capacity for sexual violence to arise from and contribute to systemic inequalities, and to consider the role(s) of various institutions such as schools and legislatures and courts in promoting or deterring rape. Psychological assessments of individual risk factors for aggression and victimization may complement systemic work—for example, a finding that women from low-income families face greater risk of victimization than women from middle-class families might motivate an investigation of sexual violence and class inequality, or into the prevention and support services available in schools from neighborhoods with varying economic resources—but micro-level analyses are insufficient for exploring such matters in depth. Scholars who study rape might work to incorporate a broader range of voices, and to read and cite work across disciplines. Those in disciplines such as sociology and anthropology that have been historically less represented in the field, or whose colleagues have tended to "gloss over" narratives of victimization and aggression, might reconceptualize sexual violence as a powerful and pervasive mechanism for maintaining social inequalities (Armstrong, Gleckman-Krut, and Johnson 2018; Collins 2004).

Some concerns around the dominance of psychology were not particular to that discipline, but rather to a more general interest in diversity of perspective. This was evident in participants' calls for novel or at least more varied lines of scientific inquiry, and frustration with what some perceived as needless replication or uncritical endorsement of particular institutional interventions. If individuals within and beyond science have overwhelmingly embraced bystander intervention campaigns or criminal prosecution or sexual assault forensic examinations without sufficient data—suggestions made by some participants in this project—this is surely not due to an emphasis on psychology. Neither is the problem of feeling "stuck" and unable to innovate a result of the dominance of psychology in the field. Singularity of perspective is more at issue. Whether scholars seek to refine bystander intervention programs or emphasize agentic sex education, whether they opt to reform existing legal practices or prioritize alternatives such as restorative justice conferencing, such efforts may benefit from a plurality of voices.

Precasting in Sexual Violence Research

Precasting, as I have theorized it here, occurs when scientists set boundaries regarding which actors may enact which statuses. This is distinct from simply making assumptions about study participants that may be reinforced or challenged in subsequent data collection and analysis, in that precasting forecloses lines of scientific inquiry. In the study of rape, the most high-stakes statuses concern those of actual and potential aggressors and victims. Scientists who suspect particular patterns in aggression and victimization may design a study with those patterns in mind, and intentionally or unintentionally ensure that the only perceptible rapes are those that confirm their assumptions.

Although precasting may occur along any number of dimensions, I have focused here on assumptions regarding gender and sexuality. These concepts are particularly salient when studying rape for at least two reasons. First and foremost, large-scale activism and scholarship to address sexual violence in the United States and Canada developed through feminist activism to address cisgender men's violence toward cisgender women, particularly (though not exclusively) in the context of heterosexual dating and partnerships. Second, throughout this project—including the quantitative analysis of 1,313 abstracts and close readings of 84 scientific studies— assumptions concerning gender and sexuality were more likely than assumptions concerning any other characteristic to be built into study designs through restrictive definitions and sampling frames. Scholars might disagree regarding the extent to which race and disability intersect with violence, but I have yet to encounter a study that excluded people of particular racial/ethnic backgrounds or people with(out) disabilities from enacting the status of victim or aggressor, or claimed to provide information regarding the general scope or causes or aftermath of sexual violence while restricting to a single-race or single-disability-status sampling frame.

Gendered precasting may take several forms in research on rape. All such forms have consequences for the production of scientific knowledge, as well as the development of antiviolence policy and interventions. At the level of sampling, scientists might decide from the outset to restrict a study of victimization to female-assigned women. This would not constitute precasting if researchers set out specifically to consider the nature and scope of female sexual victimization, or to design prevention and response measures specifically for this population; it is rather the conflation of "victim" with "cisgender female victim" that becomes problematic. Sexual victimization among all male-assigned people, and all female-assigned people who do not identify as women, are rendered imperceptible by such approaches.

Definitions and survey design provide further precasting opportunities. Researchers might embrace an overtly restrictive approach, as in the original Sexual Experiences Survey which asked women about victimization by men and asked men about aggression against women. Same-sex violence, violence by and against people with nonbinary gender identifications, women's sexual aggression, and men's sexual victimization are rendered imperceptible by such instruments. Even ostensibly inclusive approaches may contribute to precasting if survey designs are informed by dominant understandings of "real" or "typical" rape. This is evident in projects such as the National Intimate Partner and Sexual Violence Survey and Campus

Sexual Assault Study, which ask male and female participants about victimization while restricting "rape" to penetration by an assailant. As demonstrated in chapter 2, female-identified survivors of sexual violence are substantially more likely to report nonconsensual penetration by an assailant, whereas male-identified survivors are more likely to report nonconsensual envelopment by (or being made to penetrate) an assailant. Gender gaps in victimization narrow and expand depending on whether being made to penetrate is excluded or included within definitions of rape. Restricting rape to penetration by an aggressor makes it comparatively difficult for male-identified or male-assigned people to qualify as rape victims, even if it does not altogether preclude this possibility. Again, such scientific approaches only constitute precasting if the larger problem of rape or sexual violence is synonymized with cisgender men's sexual violence toward cisgender women—or, in its more subtle form, if "real" or "serious" or "severe" victimization is rendered synonymous with penetration by an aggressor, whereas envelopment or being made to penetrate an aggressor is relegated to a lower status. It is also important to recognize that these decisions reach beyond the realm of science. Press coverage of prevalence research often focuses on statistics for rape rather than theoretically "lesser" experiences such as sexual assault or unwanted sexual contact. Training manuals for antiviolence advocates often incorporate these figures directly, without delving into definitional subtleties.

Gender politics are particularly fraught in the study of sexual violence. This was evident in many of the conversations I had with scholars regarding their own approaches in research and advocacy (where applicable), as well as broader conflicts within the field between two seemingly polarized camps: scientists who believed that there was absolutely nothing gendered about sexual violence, and that all research should embrace gender-neutral approaches; and scientists who believed that the real problem of/behind sexual violence was masculinity or patriarchy, and that any discussion of anything aside from (presumably heterosexual and cisgender) men's violence against (presumably heterosexual and cisgender) women was a politically suspect and dangerous distraction. As with many analytical binaries, these rather extreme positions did not necessarily reflect many scholars' actual perspectives. Nonetheless, this sense of polarization was constraining regardless of individuals' personal conceptualizations and scientific approaches.

Can this tension be resolved? And should it be? Dissent can be productive in science, including dissent regarding how best to approach gender and sexuality in the study of rape. Yet precasting is counterproductive. Precasting forecloses scientific inquiry, and treats empirical uncertainties as resolved matters unworthy of investigation. The opposite of precasting is not neutrality, so much as openness or inclusivity. I believe that the concept of gender inclusivity is of value here, not necessarily to eliminate disputes or provide

a definitive true or truest answer to the question of gender and sexual violence, but rather to resolve the sort of false binary described above. A
gender-inclusive approach would presume that people of all genders and
sexualities may experience sexual victimization and commit acts of sexual
aggression. At the same time, such an approach would not necessarily presume that gender was irrelevant to sexual violence, or that aggression and
victimization were distributed equally across all genders and sexualities, nor
would it demand gender neutral theoretical and methodological decisions.

When designing a study of rape, scholars might critically assess gendered and other dimensions of sampling and study design as an intellectual
and ethical practice. We might ask ourselves a series of questions—who am
I regarding as a potential assailant, victim, or bystander? What variables and
levels of analysis have I included? What is perceptible here? What am I prioritizing or making most visible? Where am I (not) locating the problem?
What ethico-onto-epistemologies am I embracing or rejecting?—and seek
to account for our choices. In asking such questions, we should attempt to
consider a broad range of personal and systemic factors, and be open to new
ideas and information. It is not problematic to design and conduct a study
that focuses solely on heterosexual, cisgender men's sexual aggression
toward heterosexual, cisgender women. It is problematic to assume that this
pattern in sexual violence is the only pattern, or the only pattern that
matters. It is not problematic to conduct a study of campus-based prevention at a predominantly White and middle-class urban university. It is problematic to assume that the successes and struggles in such spaces and
populations apply seamlessly to all campuses, and to render the abstract
notion of "college student" synonymous with "White, middle-class student
at an urban university." When we design gender-specific and otherwise
restrictive projects, we should be prepared to explain why, and to consider
the impact of the partial knowledges we produce. We should recognize our
and other scientists' (constrained) agency in selecting definitions, embracing
quantitative or qualitative or mixed methods approaches, selecting or
designing research instruments, building and employing sampling frames,
selecting research sites, analyzing data, and presenting our work to individuals and institutions within and beyond science and academia.

Such matters are not strictly theoretical or even strictly scientific. Rape
is a pervasive social problem. Its causes and consequences are diverse and
variable, transcending individual, interpersonal, institutional, and cultural
dimensions of human life. Scientific knowledge shapes public understandings and institutional prevention and response efforts in a range of domains
including criminal justice, legislation, medicine, labor, news and nonfictional
media, fictional media, and social services. In the United States, years of
grassroots activism were unable to achieve what a single statistical

figure—"one in four women"—accomplished practically overnight (Gavey [2005] 2018; Jhally 1994; Koss, Gidycz, and Wisniewski 1987; Rutherford 2017). But that figure did more than establish rape as a widespread problem. That figure established rape as a heterosexual problem. That figure established rape as an adolescent and young adult—or more specifically, a college and university—problem. That figure established rape as gendered, characterized by men's violence toward women. That figure indicated that patriarchy—but not necessarily racism or homophobia or classism or ableism—was a driving force behind sexual violence in the United States. Law and policy responses were informed by all of these messages. Grassroots organizing was informed by all of these messages. Feminist activists and academics, along with others who did not necessarily claim feminist identities but were nonetheless compelled to address men's sexual violence toward women after learning that rape was a widespread problem, prioritized addressing and reforming sexist logics within criminal statutes, police investigation practices, prosecutorial decision making, trial procedures, and campus adjudication procedures.

For all these innovations, many individuals and populations and spaces were left out. Perhaps more concerning is the fact that many of those rendered imperceptible through "one in four women"—not to mention much of the dominant sexual violence scholarship and activism since then—experience elevated rates of sexual violence and substantially restricted access to social support. In focusing exclusively on gender, and approaching "women" as a coherent or perhaps even monolithic group, researchers may also inadvertently reinforce (or at least fail to challenge) oppressive ideals that contribute to or stem from sexual violence. What does it mean, for example, to approach sexual violence as a race-neutral phenomenon? Numerous studies over numerous decades have revealed that Black, Latinx, and Native American and Indigenous women experience higher rates of sexual violence than White women (Black et al. 2011; Breiding et al. 2014; Deer 2015; Koss, Gidycz, and Wisniewski 1987). As Danielle McGuire (2010) has documented, Black civil rights activists approached sexual violence as a priority issue decades before the emergence of national-scale activism against rape in the United States and Canada. Ten years before "one in four women" established rape as a widespread social problem in popular consciousness, the Combahee River Collective's *Black Feminist Statement* connected the legacy of White male slaveholders' violence toward Black female slaves with contemporary racist and sexual oppression in the United States (Combahee River Collective [1977] 2006). More recently, Patricia Hill Collins' (2004) *Black Sexual Politics* connected legacies of sexual violence toward Black female slaves and lynching of Black male slaves to contemporary controlling images. Stereotypes of Black women as insatiable temptresses render them

socially acceptable targets for violence, and undermine these women's credibility if and when they disclose victimization. Stereotypes of Black men as
dangerously sexually aggressive—particularly toward White women—make
it socially acceptable to approach Black men as predatory, credible as rapists
but never as victims/survivors. Sarah Deer (2015) has drawn attention to
centuries of Native American activism to address White European men's
violence toward Native women. Scientific research that approaches rape as a
race-neutral issue may inadvertently obscure these legacies. State officials who
draw on such work may embrace race-neutral approaches and decline to support policies and interventions tailored to addressing violence in communities
of color—particularly in non-campus spaces. White activists and service providers may fail to partner or ally with people in Black, Native and Indigenous,
and other racial and ethnic minority communities when designing interventions and outreach materials. Ultimately, women of color may find themselves erased and unsupported as survivors of sexual violence.

Yet even these critical intersectional feminist interventions have often
approached sexual violence as a heterosexual and predominantly patriarchal
(and White supremacist) phenomenon. Women's sexual aggression toward men,
and any violence beyond what Gayle Rubin has theorized as the "charmed
circle" of normative sexuality ([1984] 1993, 13) are often rendered imperceptible. Violence toward and against transgender and gender-nonconforming
people is likewise rendered imperceptible. This has consequences. Prevention and response curricula rightly train boys and men to recognize and
avoid perpetrating sexist behaviors, including sexual aggression toward girls
and women. Less often are boys and men trained to avoid perpetrating sexual violence toward each other, or to consider themselves as actual or potential targets of rape. Simultaneously, women and girls are trained to recognize
themselves as potential targets of men and boys' violence, but not as targets of
women and girls' violence or as potential aggressors (Levine 2017; McMahon
and Banyard 2012; Taylor et al. 2012). As sociologist Susan pointed out in
this study, people who have experienced same-gender assaults may be less
likely to identify as rape survivors, and thus less likely to pursue and receive
rape crisis services, than women who have been assaulted by men. If the
providers of such services are trained to understand rape as a problem of men's
violence toward women, they may be unprepared to adequately support
anyone whose experience is different. This is all the more concerning given
that queer and transgender communities report substantially elevated rates of
sexual violence (Griner et al. 2020; Rothman, Exner, and Baughman 2011;
Stotzer 2009; Walters, Chen, and Breiding 2013).

Scientists, as human beings immersed in human societies and institutions, may both influence and be influenced by public perceptions of rape.
Regarding the former, it would be unfair and unreasonable to hold

scientists fully accountable for others' use of their work. We have little, if any, control over the life trajectories of our own publications. It is sometimes unavoidable that key findings, methodologies, and arguments will be overly simplified or altogether misrepresented by other actors in various contexts (including by other scientists). Yet I argue that it is possible, even ethically necessary, to incorporate questions about the social impact of research into the everyday work of doing science—particularly for work that engages questions of social morality, violence, and systemic inequities, as is the case with studying rape. It is already standard practice to raise questions about the scholarly contributions of our projects. Many scholars, myself included, routinely confront these questions within our own writing as a means of establishing the value of our work (and increasing our chances of publication, due to widespread emphases on innovation and uniqueness in peer-reviewed outlets). Questions about potential social contributions should likewise be engaged as standard practice. When submitting prevalence studies to academic journals, for example, researchers might consider the potential reach of the statistics therein. They might engage the sort of foundational questions described above, and consider the potential effects of their choices, on public as well as scientific knowledges. When composing paper titles and abstracts, researchers might think critically about the potential reception by and impact upon a range of audiences—particularly given that titles and abstracts of published works are often broadly and freely accessible, whereas access to full manuscripts is more restricted—and consider the main takeaways for public and practitioner audiences as well as their academic peers. On the rare occasions when we are asked to serve as experts for public or nonacademic professional audiences (perhaps appearing on a news program, or speaking with advocates or police), we might work to emphasize key arguments or findings and proactively address potential misinterpretations or misuses of our work within these domains.

What, then, of the capacity for scientists (and our research) to be influenced by broader social perspectives? This is neither avoidable, nor inherently concerning. To be "influenced" is not necessarily to be ruled or without agency. On the other hand, to be completely cut off from social conceptualizations of rape—if such a thing were possible—would mean missing out on the insights of community activists and practitioners. It would mean working to maintain ignorance of (or detachment from) the social conditions that might be prioritized in scholarship concerned with social change, such as widespread victim-blaming attitudes or discriminatory practices in criminal justice systems. Several participants in this project pointed to historical events and perspectives as motivation for choosing to study rape (see chapter 5). Several high-profile scholars have pointed to public disputes over the nature of sexual consent and sexual violence as driving forces behind their projects (e.g., Muehlenhard 2011; R. Thornhill and Palmer 2000). Moreover, the history of sexual violence scholarship owes a great deal to a far longer history of grassroots and institutionalized activism (Alcoff 2018; Combahee River Collective 1977; Deer 2015; McGuire 2010; Senn 2011). Yet, just as it would be inaccurate to suggest that any and all social influence is harmful, it would be inaccurate to suggest that any and all social influence is beneficial. The perception of rape as a hetero-sexual problem, for example, predates "one in four women." This perception informed Koss and colleagues' research on the scope of rape, before their work went on to inform public and institutional understandings for decades. I do not pretend to have a solution to such matters. However, as I elaborate further below, an agential realist approach (Barad 2007) is promising here. It is productive for researchers to recognize that we are entangled within phenomena, and subject to a range of influences throughout the work of doing science. As several participants in this project noted, collaborative work, thoughtful criticism, and openness to criticism are valuable practices for engaging diverse perspectives and recognizing our own assumptions as researchers (and human beings).

SOCIAL MECHANISMS

Science studies scholars have long argued that science is a social domain, and that cultural and interpersonal forces guide the production of scientific knowledge and the distinguishing of fact from falsehood (Barad 2007; Bourdieu 1975; Epstein 1996; Haraway 1997; Jasanoff 2005; Jordan-Young 2011; Latour 1987; Rutherford 2017; Shapin and Schaffer [1985] 2011; Waidzunas 2012; Waidzunas 2015). My claims to that effect are hardly novel. Several of the social forces documented in this project—the involvement of actors who are not trained as scientists, credibility struggles within and across disciplines, the tendency to devalue work associated with social or political matters—are well established in the science studies literature (Cech 2013; Epstein 1996; Latour 1987; Waidzunas 2015). Nonetheless, some aspects of the scientific study of rape documented here offer contributions to that literature. One contribution concerns the fact that rape research occupies a feminized and contested status within science, which has implications for the particular in-group and out-group conflicts faced by professionals in the field. Another concerns care work as a social mechanism within science.

Contested Legitimacy and Multifaceted Credibility Struggles

Much of the literature in science studies emphasizes science, technology, engineering, and mathematics (STEM) fields, many of which are dominated by cisgender (and often White, highly educated, middle-class) men, and many of which are often perceived as apolitical by insiders (e.g., Barad

2007; Cech 2013; Epstein 1996; Jordan-Young 2011; Shapin and Schaffer [1985] 2011). Even if science studies scholars politicize physics and chemistry, physicists and chemists may claim to engage in detached and objective work, seeking and retrieving external knowledges rather than producing them through social practices. Even if science studies scholars argue that physics and chemistry research carry moral implications, physicists and chemists may claim detachment from moral concerns and sole investment in seeking "pure" truths.

Few sexual violence researchers are STEM professionals. Many have backgrounds in social science fields, which are less prestigious and less masculine-dominated. Many embrace political affiliations, aligning with feminist or queer or antiracist aims as a part of their scientific work. All contend with unavoidably value-laden subjects. In other words, even scholars in fields such as evolutionary psychology, who may well reject the notion that their research on rape is political or social in character, must navigate contentious political landscapes as they conduct and publish their work (Dreger 2015). Many scientists who study rape do so with consciously feminist and social justice aims, which can cause personal and professional tension for those who also adhere to or regularly confront positivist epistemologies.

The participants in this study faced out-group and in-group challenges that I suspect are particular to more overtly political scientific fields. Outsider critics have at times dismissed sexual violence research as inherently unscientific. Those who believe that science and social issues are altogether separate (or at least separable), or that feminist or other value-driven work cannot comprise real science, are particularly apt to pose such credibility challenges. Consequently, scientists who study rape must be prepared to defend the scientific character of their work, and perhaps their own legitimacy as scientists, in addition to facing the sort of methodological and theoretical challenges common to scientific criticism. When Neil Gilbert and Katie Roiphe sought to challenge the veracity of "one in four women," they did more than criticize Mary Koss's methods. They attacked her credibility as a statistical researcher. They portrayed Koss and her supporters as corrupted by "rape crisis feminism," driven by problematic ideological concerns to the point of producing bad science (Gilbert 1991; Gilbert 1992; Jhally 1994; Roiphe [1993] 1994, 70; Rutherford 2017). When Christina Hoff Sommers (2012) sought to challenge the veracity of "one in five women," in reference to the Center for Disease Control's National Intimate Partner and Sexual Violence Survey, she accused CDC scholars of engaging in "careless advocacy research" rather than rigorous scientific analysis. These critics rejected the very premise of feminist science. They expressed skepticism toward any scholarship in the field of sexual violence research, wary that such work was apt to be politically contaminated from the outset.

Field insiders rarely make such claims. These scholars have already endorsed the project of studying sexual violence, and either accepted such work as (at least potentially) legitimately scientific or disinvested in such categorizations. Yet the connection of sexual violence with social morality remains a source of conflict. Insiders continue to dispute the boundaries of acceptable research. Concerns over scientific legitimacy give way to concerns over misuse. Researchers are held accountable for the political and moral implications of their work, including intended and unintended consequences. It is telling that a colleague once likened Charlene Muehlenhard's (2011) research on token resistance to research on the atomic bomb—the latter being an unquestionably scientific project with permanent and devastating global consequences.

These struggles comprise two sides of the same coin. Overtly political and value-laden scientific work carries the dual risks of credibility challenges and dismissals over perceived scientific (il)legitimacy from colleagues beyond one's field of specialization, and character challenges and moral attacks from field insiders.

Care Work in Science

Many of the social processes emphasized in science studies literature—credibility struggles, competition, intellectual opportunities, evidentiary hierarchies, the distribution of power and other resources, opportunities for advancement and funding—align with masculine-coded skills and practices, such as acquiring and demonstrating superior technical knowledge. Yet more feminine-coded processes, such as emotional labor and interpersonal communication, also play a role. In this project, care work emerged as a crucial social mechanism in the production of scientific knowledge about sexual violence, as well as the maintenance of an engaged and active scholarly community.

Feminist science studies scholars have worked tirelessly to demonstrate that gendered and sexual logics inform the production of scientific knowledge, as well as scholarship within the field of science studies (Barad 2007; Haraway 1989; Haraway 1997; Harding 1995; Jordan-Young 2011). In proposing care work as a social mechanism, I offer a further feminist intervention to this literature. Care work is a collective and powerful process within science. Scholars in any scientific or scholarly field may face substantial emotional challenges; sexual violence work is particularly heavy, even perhaps in comparison with other difficult subjects such as wartime violence and substance use. Those who study rape may rely on one another to offer formal or informal "permission" to engage in self-care, and to find effective strategies for supporting themselves and others in their work. Moreover, scientific collaborations in this field are characterized by intellectual and emotional processes that cannot be disentangled. The care work of sharing and hearing narratives of struggle is connected with the analytical work of documenting and assessing narratives of personal victimization and institutional responses to violence.

STUDYING RAPE AS AN AGENTIAL REALIST

Scientific research on rape, like scientific research more broadly, is a human enterprise. Such research is shaped by the social conditions that produce it, including entanglements among researchers, funding agencies, cultural values, and "target" populations within phenomena. These realities do not indicate a need to abandon science, or to dismiss scientists as irrelevant or harmful to the work of addressing rape. Scholars such as Donna Haraway, Karen Barad, and Sandra Harding have proposed epistemologies that engage love and respect for science alongside critical attention toward the conditions that produce and preclude scientific knowledges (Barad 2007; Haraway 1988; Haraway 1997; Harding 1995; Harding 1986). Situated knowledge and strong objectivity provide alternatives to the "god tricks" (Haraway 1988, 587) of viewing from nowhere and apolitical relativism. Agential realism facilitates critical engagement with the ethical, ontological, and epistemological perspectives within and surrounding scientific work, as well as the entanglement of researchers and research instruments with the objects they study.

Following these feminist scholars of science, I end here with a call for agential realist perspectives in the study of rape. Rather than accept detached objectivity as the ideal and most credible standard, I argue that agential realism facilitates more comprehensive and more credible scientific inquiry. Such scholarship engages entanglements among observers and objects of study, recognizes discreet "objects" and "findings" as products of particular agential cuts, provides for the recognition of scholars' and participants' welfare within scientific ethics, and approaches scientific facts critically without equating "socially produced" with "imaginary" or "false." These are not deficits. These are strengths.

While agential realist insights may well apply to all social scientific enterprises (Barad, herself, has focused primarily on STEM fields to date), scholarship on rape is a particularly powerful place to begin. Scientists and activists who work on this issue are well equipped to challenge normative conceptualizations of truth. Research on rape trauma syndrome and PTSD (Burgess and Holmstrom 1974a; Ullman et al. 2007), for example, has long provided tools to challenge victim-blaming attitudes in public and criminal justice contexts. Memory gaps and self-doubt have been recast as markers for rather than against credibility. Scientists have demonstrated (and continue to demonstrate) that rape is often experienced as traumatic, that trauma impacts memory formation, and that a victim/survivor's struggle to recall specific details may just as well serve to bolster their narrative—consensual, nontraumatic sexual encounters simply do not produce the same difficulties that traumatic assaults do. A similar logic applies here. Rather than accept that scientific truth relies on detached and apolitical observation, scholars of rape should pursue and demand better science.

Interview Guide

THIRTY-ONE PEOPLE were interviewed for this project. Our conversations focused on their individual experiences as sexual violence scholars, perceptions of historical and contemporary work in the field, and the social dimensions of studying sexual violence. Interviews were semistructured, in that I used the questions below as a general guide. If conversations developed in different directions, or if participants seemed particularly interested or disinterested in discussing various subjects, I followed their lead. With the exception of questions regarding the emotional aspects of studying sexual violence, which I added partway through the project (see chapter 1), I used the following interview guide throughout.

Tell me a bit about your work.

What led you to focus on rape as a researcher?

Generally speaking, how would you define rape? How would you define consent? Has any of this changed over the course of your career?

I'd like to hear about some of the work you've done in this area. Is there a specific project or publication you would like to discuss? [If not, mention one or more specific works.]

What was the goal of this research? Were you surprised by any of the findings? If you had a chance to repeat this study, would you do anything differently? Broadly speaking, how was your work received? How did others, in and out of your field, react?

Have you looked to any particular institutions—criminal law, or rape crisis centers for example—in designing and conducting your research?

Have you collaborated with other people in studying rape?

How have you found (or been found by) collaborators? Can you tell me a bit about how that went? Did you have similar understandings of what rape was, what research questions

to pose, and how to answer them? Did you and your co-
researchers have any disagreements?

Have you had conflicts or pushback from other scholars in this area?
Anyone you've directly collaborated with? Any conflicts with
other scientists, perhaps people who have disagreed with
your work, or whose work you have challenged?

I'm also interested in hearing about people that influenced your
work, but are not necessarily scientists. Can you think of anyone in other fields who has made a difference?

Have you pursued grant funding? If so, how have you approached
that? Have you used different approaches for different funding
agencies?

Sexual violence can be a difficult subject to study. Over the course of
your career, have there been emotional components, or maybe
emotional challenges, in your work? Have you engaged in any
sort of self-care?

What advice would you give to a young scholar who was thinking
about entering this field?

What recommendations do you have for future scholarly work in
this area?

Is there anything else that I should have asked, or mentioned, to
understand your work in this area?

ACKNOWLEDGMENTS

THIS PROJECT has been wonderful and challenging throughout, and I am indebted to many for their support along the way. Rayna, you have been so incredible throughout these years. You have talked through every version of this project with me, every frustration and triumph, even every ill-timed side project, notwithstanding your own absurdly demanding workload(s). I simply could not have done this without you. Ben (S.), you have helped me stay engaged and excited about this work and have been a brilliant and thought-provoking partner in intellectual curiosity. Tasia, you have always been and shall remain my partner in survival. Even though we get far too little time together, and I was (and remain) reluctant to spend what time we have hashing through academic matters, our friendship was central to this work. Spencer, you'll never get to read this, but your love and support were a part of it, too.

I am continually grateful for the wisdom and compassion of antiviolence advocates. It is my hope to never approach sexual violence as a purely academic object, or through the lens of a would-be detached observer confined to the academy. My background in and ongoing connections to advocacy help me remember what is at stake here.

This project began as a dissertation, and I owe much to my committee. Tom, Laura, and Pablo, thank you for pushing me to consider my own assumptions and to produce strong and reflexive scholarship without ever making me doubt myself or the legitimacy of this effort. Laura, I owe you further gratitude for encouraging me to transform that dissertation into a book, and for offering guidance and compassion throughout the process. There have, of course, been other professors who bear mention here. Rujuta, Judith, Omar, Rachel, and Robin, I can't imagine having reached this point without you. Since joining the faculty at Stockton, I have also been grateful for the support of many wonderful colleagues, including (but not limited to) Deeanna, Loretta, Ian, and Jen.

So many others have kept me going throughout this project, sometimes when I reached out and sometimes when they mysteriously figured out that I was struggling. Addya, Ariel, LilyDean, Hannah, Mimi, Jamie, Brad, Yasha, Ben (R.), Tuck, and Matt—and there are almost certainly others I'm forgetting. Thank you all.

Notes

Chapter 1 Introduction

1. Large-scale, national organizing against rape emerged through large-scale, national feminist activism in the United States and Canada in the 1960s and 1970s. However, it is important to note that marginalized communities in these nations began publicly challenging sexual violence centuries earlier. For example, legal scholar and activist Sarah Deer (2015) has written extensively about early Native American activism against White colonist men's sexual violence toward Native women and connects present activism with that legacy. Danielle McGuire (2010) has written extensively about civil rights activists' efforts to address White men's violence against Black women, including Rosa Parks's work as an antiviolence investigator and organizer as early as the 1940s.

2. To be clear, Rutherford did devote considerable attention to the historical and political context of research, including the various ideological concerns held by researchers. However, her primary focus—as indicated through engagement with a "social life of methods" approach—was on the ontological politics of the sexual assault survey. This project extends her analyses with a more central focus on the social processes within scientific research, and the intra-active relationships described by Barad (1998; 2007).

3. Throughout this project, I use the terms "victim," "survivor," and "victim/survivor" interchangeably to refer to people who have experienced sexual violence. I also use the terms "aggressor," "perpetrator," and "assailant" interchangeably to refer to people who have committed acts of sexual violence. Some of this variation reflects variation across the academic fields addressed within this study, as well as variation among professional fields such as antiviolence advocacy and law enforcement. It should be noted that there is considerable disagreement in scholarly and advocacy domains (Alcoff 2018; Gavey [2005] 2018; Martin 2005) regarding how best to refer to people who have experienced or committed sexual violence. In my own work as an advocate, I have known colleagues who found the term "victim" to be inherently negative and demeaning, and colleagues who found the term "survivor" to be overly positive or politicized through associations with feminist organizing. I have also provided support to individuals who embraced and rejected all these terms. The fluidity (or perhaps inconsistency) of my language in this text is meant to reflect this range of positions and identifications, and to avoid taking a normative stance regarding how people who experience violence should identify or be identified by others.

4. Woolgar and Pawluch (1985) make a similar point in their piece on ontological gerrymandering, and ultimately call for reflective and transparent scholarship rather than an "end" to the practice.

CHAPTER 2   LOCATING THE PROBLEM

1. This has since changed. As of 2012, the FBI definition of rape expanded to allow for the possibility that men and women might qualify as assailants or victims, although the current definition remains restricted to penetration by an assailant.

2. As discussed in Rutherford (2017), Koss had originally included direct questions as a reliability check. She soon discovered that many women who reported experiences that legally qualified as rape answered "no" when asked directly whether they had ever been raped. This led her to develop the concept of "hidden" rape victims.

3. Although many think of adrenal responses as characterized by "fight or flight," tonic immobility or "freezing" is also a common response to actual and perceived threats—particularly threats of sexual violence (see TeBockhorst, O'Halloran, and Nyline 2015).

4. This is a bit of a dramatization—it might be more accurate to suggest that all participants would receive the identity question, but that identity-based responses would only matter for individuals who answered "no" to all experience questions.

5. I should note that I, myself, have done this. My first journal publication explored the prevalence of peer sexual victimization and aggression in middle school, and recognized underreporting but not overreporting as a potential limitation (Levine 2017).

6. Based on my own content analysis, I might add that studies of perpetration rarely incorporate any measures for sexual orientation. It is also rare for such investigations to regard women of any sexuality as potential assailants.

7. Following Annemarie Mol's analysis in *The Body Multiple: Ontology in Medical Practice* (2002), rape might be conceptualized as having varying ontological statuses that are enacted differently within and across phenomena—as characterized by multiplicity, rather than singularity. The ontological status of rape, in this sense, would depend on the composition of and agential cuts enacted within different phenomena. Scholars who approach rape as therapeutic and scholars who approach rape as legal or criminal may not always agree regarding which incidents of human behavior qualify as rape; which individuals qualify as victims or perpetrators; or the scope, causes, and consequences of rape more broadly; even if they ostensibly study "the same" object.

8. It is also worth noting that this analytical strategy attributes rape to sexuality, at least in part, given the assumption that rapists target the objects of their sexual desire.

CHAPTER 3   ACCOUNTING FOR RAPE

1. It should be noted that Dreger, herself, has been a controversial figure in academia and activism. Trained as a historian of science, she worked alongside activists at the Intersex Society of North America for several years before delving into conflicts surrounding research on transgender lives and experiences. The former efforts earned her considerable praise among intersex, queer, and transgender activists and scholars; the latter efforts have led to numerous condemnations of her work. She details this history in the book referenced here, *Galileo's Middle Finger*. It is not my intention to take any particular stance on Dreger's research or politics regarding intersex communities, trans communities, or sexual violence in this book; rather, I draw on her overview of the controversy surrounding *A Natural History of Rape* and the conversations she reports having with Craig Palmer.

2. In addition to a lack of evidence of misuse, there is evidence that "miscommunication theory" has contributed to scholarly and programmatic efforts to challenge rape culture. Muehlenhard and others' research on token resistance, and the complexities of sexual communication, has been incorporated into rape prevention programs focused on male responsibility and female empowerment (Senn 2011).

3. Notably, such concerns are not restricted to research on sexual violence. Other fields in which matters of scientific fact entangle with matters of social injustice, particularly those in which policy implications are often featured in publications, may draw harsh scrutiny across scientific and public domains. Tolwinski (2019) provides an engaging overview of controversies in developmental neuroscience. A subfield of scholars have investigated the capacity of early experiences, particularly the poverty and adversity, to affect brain development. Scholarly and public opponents of this work have raised concerns that any research distinguishing between "poor brains" and "affluent brains" may be (mis)used to advance racist/eugenicist projects. Much like Thornhill and Palmer, developmental neuroscientists have often countered that such criticism stems from a fundamental misunderstanding of biology, and that their research serves the goal of ending racialized poverty.

4. I am indebted here to Steven Epstein's (1996) analysis in *Impure Science*, in which he demonstrated that the link between HIV and AIDS became established in the scientific literature, often presented without qualifications, long before empirical data had sufficiently verified that link. Scientific consensus preceded the evidence.

5. In such models, "power" is complexly proposed as a motivation, resource, and outcome of sexual violence. Aggressors are regarded as individuals who seek to exert power over others, and use sexual violence as a means of exerting that power and taking control. This suggests that aggressors must also be people who have access to power, either in the sovereign (power that is held/carried) or strategic (power that is accessed within encounters, and operates through bodies) sense (Foucault 1982). Ongoing acts of sexual violence also contribute to a culture in which people who are perceived or perceive themselves as potential victims (e.g., cisgender women) are socialized to be fearful and take ongoing pains to avoid risk, whereas people who are perceived or perceive themselves as potential aggressors (e.g., cisgender men) are socialized to feel entitled and superior.

CHAPTER 4   INVESTIGATING THE AFTERMATH

1. This does not mean that no definitional work occurred, but rather that any efforts to distinguish victims from nonvictims would have been carried out by other institutional actors such as crisis counselors and hospital staff. Criteria might still be as simple or vague as "anyone who pursues a sexual assault forensic exam counts as a victim" or "anyone who calls a rape crisis center for support around their personal history counts as a victim," but again, these would be decisions made by professionals at these institutions and then passed along indirectly to researchers.

2. Although I can only speculate about the processes that led researchers to focus on various subjects over time, this turn to cisgender female rape victims in PTSD and depression research coincided with investigations of these psychological outcomes in cisgender male war veterans. It is likely that broader trends in psychological research, and the recognition that PTSD was limited neither to cisgender men nor to war veterans in particular, influenced psychological research on the aftermath of rape.

Chapter 5 Choosing to Study Rape

1. As shown in the interview guide (see appendix), I asked all participants about what led them to study sexual violence. I did not ask about personal experiences of victimization or aggression, or sexual violence within their social networks and local communities. Some participants did share such information (i.e., explicitly stating that they were or were not survivors of sexual violence), but only on their terms and not always in the response to this question. I do not provide an estimate here of the proportion of participants who disclosed being victims/survivors, nor do I attempt to estimate the proportion who were (given that nondisclosure indicates nothing about status). Moreover, I do not theorize a general causal mechanism between victimization and choosing this work. If/when personal encounters with violence appear in the section on "pathways into the field," it is because participants, themselves, connected those experiences with the decision to study rape.
2. Although this perception was shared by several participants—including some who lamented a general decline in recent years, and others who expressed excitement for what seemed to be a contemporary resurgence in sexual violence research—my own quantitative content analysis found a steady increase in scientific journal publications. Not only has the overall count of relevant publications increased in each decade since 1975, but so too have the publication frequencies in all assessed subfields (quantification, causality, effects, evaluation, and theory/methods). That being said, it is likely that more specialized lines of research, such as the evaluation of rape law reform or assessment of pornography as a causal factor in sexual aggression, have declined or risen and fallen at various times. Quantitative trends in publications are also insufficient for exploring Cynthia and others' concerns about "needless" replication or a general unwillingness to take risks and develop new lines of scientific inquiry.
3. I began this project with ten-plus years of experience in sexual assault and domestic violence crisis counseling. Once I began researching sexual violence fulltime, I stopped doing direct service as a part of my own self-care, but maintained active ties to the activist/advocacy community and engaged in other forms of antiviolence work such as public education and volunteer training.

Chapter 6 Dividends and Detriments of Dissent

1. These issues were central to my own dissertation process (research which eventually led to this book project). When preparing the first draft of my proposal, I encountered a faculty reader who hyper-focused on my transgender identity, and suggested that I was "leveraging" this identity to justify a project centered on "the rape of transpeople" (I have discussed this in more detail in a previous publication on benevolent transphobia; Levine 2018a). Further challenges arose after the proposal stage. Although I was fortunate to have a tremendously supportive committee, my advisor and I were concerned that I might face personal questions or judgments when seeking approval from the Institutional Review Board for the interview part of this project. We went so far as to conduct preparatory role plays. My advisor, embodying a discriminatory board member, asked me a series of invasive and offensive questions under the guise of critiquing the research. We continued this practice until I felt prepared to handle such questions appropriately, without jeopardizing my chances of approval.

CHAPTER 7 CONCLUSION

1. See Fassin and Rechtman's *An Inquiry into the Condition of Victimhood* (2009) for a critical examination of the historical construction and deployment of trauma as a concept and presumed consequence of violence. It should be noted that the dominance of psychological trauma-based conceptualizations of sexual violence has varied consequences across time, space, and community. In *Therapeutic Nations: Healing in an Age of Indigenous Human Rights*, Dian Million (2013) provides a decolonial feminist critique of "Aboriginal 'wounded' subjectivity" and the impact of psychological, medicalized, and neoliberal discourses of trauma on Indigenous communities.

2. To borrow from interview participant Miranda's analysis, this would occur if sexual violence were to shift within dominant research inquiries from a "therapeutic object" to a "public health object," as one example. The main concern here is that sexual violence not be regarded as singular, but rather as comprised of individual, interpersonal, and systemic dimensions; and of transcending the scope of inquiry within any single academic field or intellectual movement.

References

Abbey, Antonia. 2011. "Alcohol's Role in Sexual Violence Perpetration: Theoretical Explanations, Existing Evidence, and Future Directions." *Drug and Alcohol Review* 30(5): 481–489.

Abbey, Antonia, Pam McAuslan, and Lisa Thomson Ross. 1998. "Sexual Assault Perpetration by College Men: The Role of Alcohol, Misperception of Sexual Intent, and Sexual Beliefs and Experiences." *Journal of Social and Clinical Psychology* 17(2): 167–195.

Abbey, Antonia, Michele R. Parkhill, Renee BeShears, A. Monique Clinton-Sherrod, and Tina Zawacki. 2006. "Cross-Sectional Predictors of Sexual Assault Perpetration in a Community Sample of Single African American and Caucasian Men." *Aggressive Behavior* 32(1): 54–67.

Abbey, Antonia, Lisa Thomson Ross, Donna McDuffie, and Pam McAuslan. 1996. "Alcohol and Dating Risk Factors for Sexual Assault among College Women." *Psychology of Women Quarterly* 20(1): 147–169.

Abel, Gene G., David H. Barlow, Edward B. Blanchard, and Donald Guild. 1977. "The Components of Rapists' Sexual Arousal." *Archives of General Psychiatry* 34(8): 895–903.

Acker, Joan. 1990. "Hierarchies, Jobs, Bodies: A Theory of Gendered Organizations." *Gender and Society* 4(2): 139–158.

Alcoff, Linda Martín. 2018. *Rape and Resistance.* Newark, NJ: Polity.

Anderson, Ben. 2014. *Encountering Affect: Capacities, Apparatuses, Conditions.* Farnham, UK: Ashgate.

Anderson, Linda A., and Susan C. Whiston. 2005. "Sexual Assault Education Programs: A Meta-Analytic Examination of their Effectiveness." *Psychology of Women Quarterly* 29(4): 374–388.

Armstrong, Elizabeth A., Miriam Gleckman-Krut, and Lanora Johnson. 2018. "Silence, Power, and Inequality: An Intersectional Approach to Sexual Violence." *Annual Review of Sociology* 44:99–122.

Armstrong, Elizabeth A., Laura Hamilton, and Brian Sweeney. 2006. "Sexual Assault on Campus: A Multilevel, Integrative Approach to Party Rape." *Social Problems* 53(4): 483–499.

Atkeson, Beverly M., Karen S. Calhoun, Patricia A. Resick, and Elizabeth M. Ellis. 1982. "Victims of Rape: Repeated Assessment of Depressive Symptoms." *Journal of Consulting and Clinical Psychology* 50(1): 96–102.

Bachman, Ronet, Raymond Paternoster, and Sally Ward. 1992. "The Rationality of Sexual Offending: Testing a Deterrence/Rational Choice Conception of Sexual Assault." *Law and Society Review* 26(2): 343–372.

Barad, Karen. 1998. "Getting Real: Technoscientific Practices and the Materialization of Reality." *differences* 10(2): 87–128.

———. 2007. *Meeting the Universe Halfway: Quantum Physics and the Entanglement of Matter and Meaning*. Durham, NC: Duke University Press.

Beaulieu, Emily, Amber E. Boydstun, Nadia E. Brown, Kim Yi Dionne, Andra Gillespie, Samara Klar, Yanna Krupnikov, Melissa R. Michelson, Kathleen Searles, and Christina Wolbrecht. 2017. "Women Also Know Stuff: Meta-level Mentoring to Battle Gender Bias in Political Science." *Political Science and Politics* 50(3): 779–783.

Bergen, Raquel Kennedy. 1996. *Wife Rape: Understanding the Response of Survivors and Service Providers*. Thousand Oaks, CA: SAGE.

Bevacqua, Maria. 2000. *Rape on the Public Agenda: Feminism and the Politics of Sexual Assault*. Boston: Northeastern University Press.

Black, Michele C., Kathleen C. Basile, Matthew J. Breiding, Sharon G. Smith, Mikel L. Walters, Melissa T. Merrick, Jieru Chen, and Mark R. Stevens. 2011. *The National Intimate Partner and Sexual Violence Survey: 2010 Summary Report*. Atlanta: National Center for Injury Prevention and Control, Centers for Disease Control and Prevention.

Bourdieu, Pierre. 1975. "The Specificity of the Scientific Field and the Social Conditions of the Progress of Reason." *Social Science Information* 14(6): 19–47.

Breiding, Matthew J. 2015. "Prevalence and Characteristics of Sexual Violence, Stalking, and Intimate Partner Violence Victimization—National Intimate Partner and Sexual Violence Survey, United States, 2011." *American Journal of Public Health* 105(4): e11–e12.

Breiding, Matthew J., Sharon G. Smith, Kathleen C. Basile, Mikel L. Walters, Jieru Chen, and Melissa T. Merrick. 2014. "Prevalence and Characteristics of Sexual Violence, Stalking, and Intimate Partner Violence Victimization—National Intimate Partner and Sexual Violence Survey, United States, 2011." *Morbidity and Mortality Weekly Report: Surveillance Summaries* 63(8): 1–18.

Brownmiller, Susan. 1975. *Against Our Will: Men, Women, and Rape*. New York: Ballantine Books.

Burgess, Ann Wolbert, and Lynda Lytle Holmstrom. 1974a. "Rape Trauma Syndrome." *American Journal of Psychiatry* 131(9): 981–986.

———. 1974b. *Rape: Victims of Crisis*. Bowie, MD: R.J. Brady.

———. 1979. "Adaptive Strategies and Recovery from Rape." *American Journal of Psychiatry* 136(10): 1278–1282.

Burnam, M. Audrey, Judith A. Stein, Jacqueline M. Golding, Judith M. Siegel, Susan B. Sorenson, Alan B. Forsythe, and Cynthia A. Telles. 1988. "Sexual Assault and Mental Disorders in a Community Population." *Journal of Consulting and Clinical Psychology* 56(6): 843–850.

Burt, Martha R. 1980. "Cultural Myths and Supports for Rape." *Journal of Personality and Social Psychology* 38(2): 217–230.

Butler, Judith. (1990) 2006. *Gender Trouble: Feminism and the Subversion of Identity*. New York: Routledge.

Calhoun, Lawrence G., James W. Selby, and Louise J. Warring. 1976. "Social Perception of the Victim's Causal Role in Rape: An Exploratory Examination of Four Factors." *Human Relations* 29(6): 517–526.

Campbell, Rebecca. 2002. *Emotionally Involved: The Impact of Researching Rape*. New York: Routledge.

Campbell, Rebecca, Adrienne E. Adams, Sharon M. Wasco, Courtney E. Ahrens, and Tracy Sefl. 2010. "'What Has It Been Like for You to Talk with Me Today?':

The Impact of Participating in Interview Research on Rape Survivors." *Violence against Women* 16(1): 60–83.

Campbell, Rebecca, Sharon M. Wasco, Courtney E. Ahrens, Tracy Sefl, and Holly E. Barnes. 2001. "Preventing the 'Second Rape': Rape Survivors' Experiences with Community Service Providers." *Journal of Interpersonal Violence* 16(12): 1239–1259.

Cardi, Coline, and Geneviève Pruvost. 2015. "Thinking Women's Violence." *History of the Present* 5(2): 200–216.

Cech, Erin A. 2013. "Ideological Wage Inequalities? The Technical/Social Dualism and the Gender Wage Gap in Engineering." *Social Forces* 91(4): 1147–1182.

Cech, Erin A., and Heidi M. Sherick. 2015. "Depoliticization and the Structure of Engineering Education." In *International Perspectives on Engineering Education*, 203–216. Cham, Switzerland: Springer International.

Chadwick, Sara B. 2019. "Dispatches from the Unlikeliest of Labs: Dispatch #5, as a Woman Doing Sex Research." Psychology's Feminist Voices. *Standpoints*. Retrieved June 4, 2020. http://feministvoicesblog.com/2019/03/12/dispatches-from-the-unlikeliest-of-labs-5/.

Check, James V. P., and Neil M. Malamuth. 1983. "Sex Role Stereotyping and Reactions to Depictions of Stranger versus Acquaintance Rape." *Journal of Personality and Social Psychology* 45(2): 344–356.

Clarke, Adele E. 1998. *Disciplining Reproduction: Modernity, American Life Sciences, and the Problems of Sex*. Berkeley: University of California Press.

———. 2004. *Situational Analysis: Grounded Theory after the Postmodern Turn*. Thousand Oaks, CA: SAGE.

Coker, Ann L., Patricia G. Cook-Craig, Corrine M. Williams, Bonnie S. Fisher, Emily R. Clear, Lisandra S. Garcia, and Lea M. Hegge. 2011. "Evaluation of Green Dot: An Active Bystander Intervention to Reduce Sexual Violence on College Campuses." *Violence against Women* 17(6): 777–796.

Collins, Harry. 1975. "The Seven Sexes: A Study in the Sociology of a Phenomenon or the Replication of Experiments in Physics." *Sociology* 9(2): 205–224.

Collins, Patricia Hill. 2004. *Black Sexual Politics: African Americans, Gender, and the New Racism*. New York: Routledge.

Combahee River Collective. (1977) 2006. "A Black Feminist Statement." In *Encyclopedia of African-American Culture and History*, 2493–2498. New York: Macmillan Reference USA.

Conley, Dalton. 2005. *The Pecking Order*. New York: Vintage Books.

Cook, Sarah L., Christine A. Gidycz, Mary P. Koss, and Megan Murphy. 2011. "Emerging Issues in the Measurement of Rape Victimization." *Violence against Women* 17(2): 201–218.

Corrigan, Rose. 2013. *Up against a Wall: Rape Reform and the Failure of Success*. New York: NYU Press.

Crawford, Mary. 1995. *Talking Difference: On Gender and Language*. London: SAGE.

Daly, Kathleen, and Brigitte Bouhours. 2010. "Rape and Attrition in the Legal Process: A Comparative Analysis of Five Countries." *Crime and Justice* 39(1): 565–650.

Davies, Michelle, Paul Rogers, and Lisa Whitelegg. 2009. "Effects of Victim Gender, Victim Sexual Orientation, Victim Response and Respondent Gender on Judgements of Blame in a Hypothetical Adolescent Rape." *Legal and Criminal Psychology* 14(2): 331–338.

Deer, Sarah. 2015. *The Beginning and End of Rape: Confronting Sexual Violence in Native America*. Minneapolis: University of Minnesota Press.

Deitz, Sheila R., Karen Tiemann Blackwell, Paul C. Daley, and Brenda J. Bentley. 1982. "Measurement of Empathy toward Rape Victims and Rapists." *Journal of Personality and Social Psychology* 43(3): 372–384.

Dreger, Alice. 2015. *Galileo's Middle Finger: Heretics, Activists, and One Scholar's Search for Justice.* New York: Penguin.

Dunbar, Robin. 2000. "Human Coercion." Review of *A Natural History of Rape: Biological Bases of Sexual Coercion*, by Randy Thornhill and Craig T. Palmer. *Trends in Ecology and Evolution* 15(10): 427.

Edwards, Katie M., Jessica A. Turchik, Christina M. Dardis, Nicole Reynolds, and Christine A. Gidycz. 2011. "Rape Myths: History, Individual and Institutional-Level Presence, and Implications for Change." *Sex Roles* 65(11): 761–773.

Ehrlich, Susan Lynn. 2001. *Representing Rape: Language and Sexual Consent.* New York: Routledge.

Ellis, Carolyn, and Leigh Berger. 2003. "Their Story/My Story/Our Story: Including the Researcher's Experience in Interview Research." In *Postmodern Interviewing*, edited by Jaber F. Gubrium and James A. Holstein, 157–183. Thousand Oaks, CA: SAGE.

Emerson, Robert M., Rachel I. Fretz, and Linda L. Shaw. 2011. *Writing Ethnographic Fieldnotes.* Chicago: University of Chicago Press.

Epstein, Steven. 1996. *Impure Science: AIDS, Activism, and the Politics of Knowledge.* Berkeley: University of California Press.

———. 2006. "The New Attack on Sexuality Research: Morality and the Politics of Knowledge Production." *Sexuality Research and Social Policy* 3(1): 1–12.

Eschholz, Sarah, and Lynne M. Vieraitis. 2004. "Race-Specific Gender Equality and Rape: A Further Test of the Feminist Hypothesis." *Critical Criminology* 12(2): 195–219.

Espeland, Wendy Nelson, and Mitchell L. Stevens. 2008. "A Sociology of Quantification." *Archives of European Sociology* 49(3): 401–436.

Estrich, Susan. 1987. *Real Rape: How the Legal System Victimizes Women Who Say No.* Cambridge, MA: Harvard University Press.

Fassin, Didier, and Richard Rechtman. 2009. *The Empire of Trauma: An Inquiry into the Condition of Victimhood.* Princeton, NJ: Princeton University Press.

Fassin, Éric. 2007. "Sexual Violence at the Border." *differences* 18(2): 1–23.

Feild, Hubert S. 1978. "Attitudes toward Rape: A Comparative Analysis of Police, Rapists, Crisis Counselors, and Citizens." *Journal of Personality and Social Psychology* 36(2): 156–179.

Fisher, Bonnie S. 2009. "The Effects of Survey Question Wording on Rape Estimates: Evidence from a Quasi-Experimental Design." *Violence against Women* 15(2): 133–147.

Flax, Jane. 1992. "The End of Innocence." In *Feminists Theorize the Political*, edited by Judith Butler and Joan W. Scott, 445–463. New York: Routledge.

Foa, Edna B., Ulrike Feske, Tamera B. Murdock, Michael J. Kozak, and Paul R. McCarthy. 1991. "Processing of Threat-Related Information in Rape Victims." *Journal of Abnormal Psychology* 100(2): 156–162.

Foa, Edna B., Chris Molnar, and Laurie Cashman. 1995. "Changes in Rape Narratives during Exposure Therapy for Posttraumatic Stress Disorder." *Journal of Traumatic Stress* 8(4): 675–690.

Foa, Edna B., Barbara Olasov Rothbaum, David S. Riggs, and Tamera B. Murdock. 1991. "Treatment of Posttraumatic Stress Disorder in Rape Victims: A Comparison between Cognitive-Behavioral Procedures and Counseling." *Journal of Consulting and Clinical Psychology* 59(5): 715–723.

Follette, Victoria M., Melissa A. Polusny, Anne E. Bechtle, and Amy E. Naugle. 1996. "Cumulative Trauma: The Impact of Child Sexual Abuse, Adult Sexual Assault, and Spouse Abuse." *Journal of Traumatic Stress* 9(1): 25–35.

Ford, Torrey M., Michelle G. Liwag-McLamb, and Linda A. Foley. 1998. "Perceptions of Rape Based on Sex and Sexual Orientation of Victim." *Journal of Social Behavior and Personality* 13(2): 253–263.

Foucault, Michel. 1982. "The Subject and Power." *Critical Inquiry* 8(4): 777–795.

Fox, Nick J., and Pam Alldred. 2016. *Sociology and the New Materialism: Theory, Research, Action.* Thousand Oaks, CA: SAGE.

Frazier, Patricia, Amy Conlon, and Theresa Glaser. 2001. "Positive and Negative Life Changes Following Sexual Assault." *Journal of Consulting and Clinical Psychology* 69(6): 1045–1055.

Frickel, Scott, and Neil Gross. 2005. "A General Theory of Scientific/Intellectual Movements." *American Sociological Review* 70(2): 204–232.

Frith, Hannah. 2009. "Sexual Scripts, Sexual Refusal, and Rape." In *Rape: Challenging Contemporary Thinking*, edited by Miranda Horvath and Jennifer Brown, 99–121. Cullompton, Devon, UK: Willan.

Frith, Hannah, and Celia Kitzinger. 1997. "Talk about Sexual Miscommunication." *Women's Studies International Forum* 20(4): 517–528.

Gavey, Nicola. (2005) 2018. *Just Sex? The Cultural Scaffolding of Rape.* New York: Routledge.

Ghaziani, Amin. 2008. *The Dividends of Dissent: How Conflict and Culture Work in Lesbian and Gay Marches on Washington.* Chicago: University of Chicago Press.

Gidycz, Christine A., Christie Nelson Coble, Lance Latham, and Melissa J. Layman. 1993. "Sexual Assault Experience in Adulthood and Prior Victimization Experiences." *Psychology of Women Quarterly* 17: 151–168.

Gidycz, Christine A., Kimberly Hanson, and Melissa J. Layman. 1995. "A Prospective Analysis of the Relationships among Sexual Assault Experiences." *Psychology of Women Quarterly* 19(1): 5–29.

Gilbert, Neil. 1991. "The Campus Rape Scare," *Wall Street Journal*, June 27, A14.

———. 1992. "Realities and Mythologies of Rape." *Society* May/June: 4–10.

Girshick, Lori B. 2002. "No Sugar, No Spice: Reflections on Research on Woman-to-Woman Sexual Violence." *Violence against Women* 8(12): 1500–1520.

Godin, Benoit, and Yves Gingras. 2002. "The Experimenters' Regress: From Skepticism to Argumentation." *Studies in History and Philosophy of Science* 33(1): 137–152.

Golding, Jacqueline M. 1994. "Sexual Assault History and Physical Health in Randomly Selected Los Angeles Women." *Health Psychology* 13(2): 130–138.

Goodman, Lisa A., Stanley D. Rosenberg, Kim T. Mueser, and Robert E. Drake. 1997. "Physical and Sexual Assault History in Women with Serious Mental Illness: Prevalence, Correlates, Treatment, and Future Research Directions." *Schizophrenia Bulletin* 23(4): 685–696.

Griner, Stacey B., Cheryl A. Vamos, Erika L. Thompson, Rachel Logan, Coralia Vásquez-Otero, and Ellen M. Daley. 2020. "The Intersection of Gender Identity and Violence: Victimization Experienced by Transgender College Students." *Journal of Interpersonal Violence* 35(23–24): 5704–5725.

Groth, A. N., and A. W. Burgess. 1980. "Male Rape: Offenders and Victims." *American Journal of Psychiatry* 137(7): 806–910.

Groth, A. N., A. W. Burgess, and L. L. Holstrom. 1977. "Rape: Power, Anger, and Sexuality." *American Journal of Psychiatry* 134(11): 1239–1243.

Haag, Patricia. 1996. "'Putting Your Body on the Line': The Question of Violence, Victims, and the Legacies of Second-Wave Feminism." *differences* 8(2): 23–65.

Halberstam, Jack. 2011. *The Queer Art of Failure*. Durham, NC: Duke University Press.

Haraway, Donna. 1988. "Situated Knowledges: The Science Question in Feminism and the Privilege of Partial Perspective." *Feminist Studies* 14(3): 575–599.

———. 1989. *Primate Visions: Gender, Race, and Nature in the World of Modern Science*. New York: Routledge.

———. 1997. *Modest_Witness@Second_Millennium.FemaleMan©_Meets_OncoMouseTM: Feminism and Technoscience*. New York: Routledge.

Harding, Sandra. 1986. *The Science Question in Feminism*. Ithaca, NY: Cornell University Press.

———. 1995. "'Strong Objectivity': A Response to the New Objectivity Question." *Synthese* 104(3): 331–349.

Henrich, Joseph, Steven J. Heine, and Ara Norenzayan. 2010. "The Weirdest People in the World?" *Behavioral and Brain Sciences* 33(2–3): 61–83.

Hines, Denise A., Jessica L. Armstrong, Kathleen Palm Reed, and Amy Y. Cameron. 2012. "Gender Differences in Sexual Assault Victimization among College Students." *Violence and Victims* 27(6): 922–940.

Hochschild, Arlie Russell. (1989) 2003. *The Second Shift: Working Families and the Revolution at Home*. New York: Penguin.

———. (1983) 2012. *The Managed Heart: Commercialization of Human Feeling*. Berkeley: University of California Press.

Holstein, James A., and Jaber F. Gubrium. 2003. "Active Interviewing." In *Postmodern Interviewing*, edited by Jaber F. Gubrium and James A. Holstein, 67–80. Thousand Oaks, CA: SAGE.

hooks, bell. (1984) 2000. *Feminist Theory: From Margin to Center*. Cambridge, MA: South End.

Human Rights Watch. 2001. *No Escape: Male Rape in U.S. Prisons*. New York: Human Rights Watch.

Humphrey, John A., and Jacquelyn W. White. 2000. "Women's Vulnerability to Sexual Assault from Adolescence to Young Adulthood." *Journal of Adolescent Health* 27(6): 419–424.

Irvine, Janice M. 2012. "Can't Ask, Can't Tell: How Institutional Review Boards Keep Sex in the Closet." *Contexts* 11(2): 28–33.

Janoff-Bulman, Ronnie. 1979. "Characterological versus Behavioral Self-Blame: Inquiries into Depression and Rape." *Journal of Personality and Social Psychology* 37(10): 1798–1809.

Jasanoff, Sheila. 2004. "Ordering Knowledge, Ordering Society." In *States of Knowledge: The Co-production of Science and Social Order*, edited by Sheila Jasanoff, 13–45. New York: Routledge.

———. 2005. *Designs on Nature: Science and Democracy in Europe and the United States*. Princeton, NJ: Princeton University Press.

Jhally, Sut, ed. and writer. 1994. *The Date Rape Backlash*. DVD. United States: Media Education Foundation.

Jordan-Young, Rebecca. 2011. *Brain Storm: The Flaws in the Science of Sex Differences*. Cambridge, MA: Harvard University Press.

Kaufman, A., P. Divasto, R. Jackson, D. Voorhees, and J. Christy. 1980. "Male Rape Victims: Noninstitutionalized Assault." *American Journal of Psychiatry* 137(2): 221–223.

Kilpatrick, Dean G., Patricia A. Resick, and Lois J. Veronen. 1981. "Effects of a Rape Experience: A Longitudinal Study." *Journal of Social Issues* 37(4): 105–122.

Kilpatrick, Dean G., Lois J. Veronen, and Patricia A. Resick. 1979. "The Aftermath of Rape: Recent Empirical Findings." *American Journal of Orthopsychiatry* 49(4): 658–669.

Kimerling, Rachel, and Karen S. Calhoun. 1994. "Somatic Symptoms, Social Support, and Treatment Seeking among Sexual Assault Victims." *Journal of Consulting and Clinical Psychology* 62(2): 333–340.

Koss, Mary P. 1985. "The Hidden Rape Victim: Personality, Attitudinal, and Situational Characteristics." *Psychology of Women Quarterly* 9(2): 193–212.

———. 1993. "Detecting the Scope of Rape: A Review of Prevalence Research Methods." *Journal of Interpersonal Violence* 8(2): 198–222.

Koss, Mary P., Antonia Abbey, Rebecca Campbell, Sarah Cook, Jeanette Norris, Maria Testa, Sarah Ullman, Carolyn West, and Jacquelyn White. 2007. "Revising the SES: A Collaborative Process to Improve Assessment of Sexual Aggression and Victimization." *Psychology of Women Quarterly* 31(4): 357–370.

Koss, Mary P., Thomas E. Dinero, and Cynthia A. Seibel. 1988. "Stranger and Acquaintance Rape: Are There Differences in the Victim's Experience?" *Psychology of Women Quarterly* 12(1): 1–24.

Koss, Mary P., Christine A. Gidycz, and Nadine Wisniewski. 1987. "The Scope of Rape: Incidence and Prevalence of Sexual Aggression and Victimization in a National Sample of Higher Education Students." *Journal of Consulting and Clinical Psychology* 55(2): 162–170.

Koss, Mary P., and Cheryl J. Oros. 1982. "Sexual Experiences Survey: A Research Instrument Investigating Sexual Aggression and Victimization." *Journal of Consulting and Clinical Psychology* 50(3): 455–457.

Krakow, Barry, Michael Hollifield, Lisa Johnston, Mary Koss, Ron Schrader, Teddy D. Warner, Dan Tandberg, et al. 2001. "Imagery Rehearsal Therapy for Chronic Nightmares in Sexual Assault Survivors with Posttraumatic Stress Disorder: A Randomized Controlled Trial." *Journal of the American Medical Association* 288(5): 537–545.

Krebs, Christopher P., Christine H. Lindquist, Tara D. Warner, Bonnie S. Fisher, and Sandra L. Martin. 2007. *The Campus Sexual Assault (CSA) Study*. Research Triangle Park, NC: RTI International.

———. 2009. "College Women's Experiences with Physically Forced, Alcohol- or Other Drug-Enabled, and Drug-Facilitated Sexual Assault before and since Entering College." *Journal of American College Health* 57(6): 639–649.

Latour, Bruno. 1987. *Science in Action: How to Follow Scientists and Engineers through Society*. Cambridge, MA: Harvard University Press.

Legerski, Elizabeth Miklya, and Marie Cornwall. 2010. "Working-Class Job Loss, Gender, and the Negotiation of Household Labor." *Gender and Society* 24(4): 447–474.

Levine, Ethan. 2017. "Sexual Violence among Middle School Students: The Effects of Gender and Dating Experience." *Journal of Interpersonal Violence* 32(14): 2059–2082.

———. 2018a. "Becoming a Transgender Failure: Speciation, Benevolent Transphobia, and the Persistence of Binary Gender." *Women and Language* 41(1): 39–61.

———. 2018b. "Engaging the Community: Building Effective Partnerships in Sexual Violence Prevention." *Journal of Applied Social Science* 12(2): 82–97.

———. 2018c. "Sexual Scripts and Criminal Statutes: Gender Restrictions, Spousal Allowances, and Victim Accountability after Rape Law Reform." *Violence against Women* 24(3): 322–349.

Lloyd, Elisabeth A. 2001. "Science Gone Astray: Evolution and Rape." *Michigan Law Review* 99(6): 1536–1559.

Loh, Catherine, Christine A. Gidycz, Tracy R. Lobo, and Rohini Luthra. 2005. "A Prospective Analysis of Sexual Assault Perpetration." *Journal of Interpersonal Violence* 20(10): 1325–1348.

Lonsway, Kimberly A., and Louise F. Fitzgerald. 1994. "Rape Myths: In Review." *Psychology of Women Quarterly* 18:133–164.

———. 1995. "Attitudinal Antecedents of Rape Myth Acceptance: A Theoretical and Empirical Reexamination." *Journal of Personality and Social Psychology* 68(4): 704–711.

Madigan, Lee, and Nancy M. Gamble. 1991. *The Second Rape: Society's Continued Betrayal of the Victim.* New York: Macmillan.

Malamuth, Neil M. 1981. "Rape Proclivity among Males." *Journal of Social Issues* 37(4): 138–157.

Malamuth, Neil M., Scott Haber, and Seymour Feshbach. 1980. "Testing Hypotheses Regarding Rape: Exposure to Sexual Violence, Sex Differences, and the 'Normality' of Rapists." *Journal of Research in Personality* 14(1): 121–137.

Mamo, Laura. 2007. *Queering Reproduction: Achieving Pregnancy in the Age of Technoscience.* Durham, NC: Duke University Press.

Mancl, Karen, and Katrina Lee. 2016. "Mentoring East Asian Women Science and Engineering Faculty." *Ohio Journal of Science* 116(2): 28–33.

Martin, Patricia Yancey. 2005. *Rape Work: Victims, Gender, and Emotions in Organization and Community Context.* New York: Routledge.

Martin, Patricia Yancey, and Robert A. Hummer. 1989. "Fraternities and Rape on Campus." *Gender and Society* 3(4): 457–473.

Martin, Sandra L., Neepa Ray, Daniela Sotres-Alvarez, Lawrence L. Kupper, Kathryn E. Moracco, Pamela A. Dickens, Donna Scandlin, and Ziya Gizlice. 2006. "Physical and Sexual Assault of Women with Disabilities." *Violence against Women* 12(9): 823–837.

Matthews, Nancy A. 1994. *Confronting Rape: The Feminist Anti-rape Movement and the State.* New York: Routledge.

McCaul, Kevin D., Lois G. Veltum, Vivian Boyechko, and Jacqueline J. Crawford. 1990. "Understanding Attributions of Victim Blame for Rape: Sex, Violence, and Foreseeability." *Journal of Applied Social Psychology* 20(1): 1–26.

McFarlane, Judith, Ann Malecha, Kathy Watson, Julia Gist, Elizabeth Batten, Iva Hall, and Sheila Smith. 2005. "Intimate Partner Sexual Assault against Women: Frequency, Health Consequences, and Treatment Outcomes." *Obstetrics and Gynecology* 105(1): 99–108.

McGuire, Danielle L. 2010. *At the Dark End of the Street: Black Women, Rape, and Resistance—a New History of the Civil Rights Movement from Rosa Parks to the Rise of Black Power.* New York: Alfred A. Knopf.

McMahon, Sarah. 2010. "Rape Myth Beliefs and Bystander Attitudes among Incoming College Students." *Journal of American College Health* 59(1): 3–11.

———. 2014. "Measuring Bystander Attitudes and Behavior to Prevent Sexual Violence." *Journal of American College Health* 62(1): 58–66.

McMahon, Sarah, and Victoria L. Banyard. 2012. "When Can I Help? A Conceptual Framework for the Prevention of Sexual Violence through Bystander Intervention." *Trauma, Violence, and Abuse* 12(1): 3–14.

Miller, Mark W., and Patricia A. Resick. 2007. "Internalizing and Externalizing Subtypes in Female Sexual Assault Survivors: Implications for the Understanding of Complex PTSD." *Behavior Therapy* 38(1): 58–71.

Million, Dian. 2013. *Therapeutic Nations: Healing in an Age of Indigenous Human Rights.* Tucson: University of Arizona Press.

Mohler-Kuo, Meichun, George W. Dowdall, Mary P. Koss, and Henry Wechsler. 2004. "Correlates of Rape while Intoxicated in a National Sample of College Women." *Journal of Studies on Alcohol* 65(1): 37–45.

Mol, Annemarie. 2002. *The Body Multiple: Ontology in Medical Practice.* Durham, NC: Duke University Press.

Morrison, Shannon, Jennifer Hardison, Anita Matthew, and Joyce O'Neil. 2004. *An Evidence-Based Review of Sexual Assault Preventive Intervention Programs.* Research Triangle Park, NC: RTI International.

Mosher, Donald L., and Ronald D. Anderson. 1986. "Macho Personality, Sexual Aggression, and Reactions to Guided Imagery of Realistic Rape." *Journal of Research in Personality* 20:77–94.

Muehlenhard, Charlene L. 2011. "Examining Stereotypes about Token Resistance to Sex." *Psychology of Women Quarterly* 35(4): 676–683.

Muehlenhard, Charlene L., and Lisa C. Hollabaugh. 1988. "Do Women Sometimes Say No When They Mean Yes? The Prevalence and Correlates of Women's Token Resistance to Sex." *Journal of Personality and Social Psychology* 54(5): 872–879.

Muehlenhard, Charlene L., Terry P. Humphreys, Kristen N. Jozkowski, and Zoe D. Peterson. 2016. "The Complexities of Sexual Consent among College Students: A Conceptual and Empirical Review." *Journal of Sex Research* 53(4–5): 457–487.

Muehlenhard, Charlene L., and Melaney A. Linton. 1987. "Date Rape and Sexual Aggression in Dating Situations: Incidence and Risk Factors." *Journal of Counseling Psychology* 34(2): 186–196.

Muehlenhard, Charlene L., and Marcia L. McCoy. 1991. "Double Standard/Double Bind: The Sexual Double Standard and Women's Communication about Sex." *Psychology of Women Quarterly* 15(3): 447–461.

Muehlenhard, Charlene L., Zoe D. Peterson, Terry P. Humphreys, and Kristen N. Jozkowski. 2017. "Evaluating the One-in-Five Statistic: Women's Risk of Sexual Assault While in College." *Journal of Sex Research* 54(4–5): 549–576.

Muehlenhard, Charlene L., and Carie S. Rodgers. 1998. "Token Resistance to Sex: New Perspectives on an Old Stereotype." *Psychology of Women Quarterly* 22(3): 443–463.

Mulla, Sameena. 2014. *The Violence of Care: Rape Victims, Forensic Nurses, and Sexual Assault Intervention.* New York: NYU Press.

Murphy, Michelle. 2006. *Sick Building Syndrome and the Problem of Uncertainty.* Durham, NC: Duke University Press.

Olsen, Frances. 1984. "Statutory Rape: A Feminist Critique of Rights Analysis." *Texas Law Review* 63(3): 387–432.

Oudshoorn, Nelly. 2003. *The Male Pill: A Biography of a Technology in the Making.* Durham, NC: Duke University Press.

Palmer, Craig T. 1988. "Twelve Reasons Why Rape Is Not Sexually Motivated: A Skeptical Examination." *Journal of Sex Research* 25(4): 512–530.

———. 1991. "Human Rape: Adaptation or By-Product?" *Journal of Sex Research* 28(3): 365–386.

Palmer, Craig T., D. N. DiBari, and S. A. Wright. 1999. "Is It Sex Yet? Theoretical and Practical Implications of the Debate over Rapists' Motives." *Jurimetrics* 39(3): 271–282.

Palmer, Craig T., and Randy Thornhill. 2003. "Straw Men and Fairy Tales: Evaluating Reactions to 'A Natural History of Rape.'" *Journal of Sex Research* 40(3): 249–255.

Pattani, Aneri. 2018. "As Kavanaugh Hearings Stir Sexual Trauma Survivors' Memories, Crisis Centers Are Ready." *The Inquirer*, September 27. https://www.inquirer .com/philly/health/christine-blasey-ford-brett-kavanaugh-sexual-assault-crisis -centers-20180927.html.

Payne, Diana L., Kimberly A. Lonsway, and Louise F. Fitzgerald. 1999. "Rape Myth Acceptance: Exploration of Its Structure and Its Measurement Using the Illinois Rape Myth Acceptance Scale." *Journal of Research in Personality* 33(1): 27–68.

Peterson, Zoe D., and Charlene L. Muehlenhard. 2007. "Conceptualizing the 'Wantedness' of Women's Consensual and Nonconsensual Sexual Experiences: Implications for How Women Label Their Experiences with Rape." *Journal of Sex Research* 44(1): 72–88.

Pfohl, Stephen. 1977. "The 'Discovery' of Child Abuse." *Social Problems* 24(3): 310–324.

Pitts-Taylor, Victoria. 2016. *The Brain's Body: Neuroscience and Corporeal Politics*. Durham, NC: Duke University Press.

Porter, Theodore. 1995. *Trust in Numbers: The Pursuit of Objectivity in Science and Public Life*. Princeton, NJ: Princeton University Press.

Primé, Dominic R., Bianca L. Bernstein, Kerrie G. Wilkins, and Jennifer M. Bekki. 2015. "Measuring the Advising Alliance for Female Graduate Students in Science and Engineering." *Journal of Career Assessment* 23(1): 64–78.

Proctor, Robert N. 2008. "Agnotology: A Missing Term to Describe the Cultural Production of Ignorance (and Its Study)." In *Agnotology: The Making and Unmaking of Ignorance*, edited by Robert N. Proctor and Londa Schiebinger, 1–33. Stanford, CA: Stanford University Press.

Reilly, Steve. 2015. "Tens of Thousands of Rape Kits Go Untested across USA: Exclusive Nationwide Count by USA Today Reveals Abandoned Rape Evidence." *USA Today*, July 30. https://www.usatoday.com/story/news/2015/07/16/untested -rape-kits-evidence-across-usa/29902199/.

Resick, Patricia A., Pallavi Nishith, Terri L. Weaver, Millie C. Astin, and Catherine A. Feuer. 2002. "A Comparison of Cognitive-Processing Therapy with Prolonged Exposure and a Waiting Condition for the Treatment of Chronic Posttraumatic Stress Disorder in Female Rape Victims." *Journal of Consulting and Clinical Psychology* 70(4): 867–879.

Resick, Patricia A., and Monica K. Schnicke. 1992. "Cognitive Processing Therapy for Sexual Assault Victims." *Journal of Consulting and Clinical Psychology* 60(5): 748–756.

Resick, Patricia A., Lauren F. Williams, Michael K. Suvak, and Candice M. Monson. 2012. "Long-Term Outcomes of Cognitive-Behavioral Treatments for Posttraumatic Stress Disorder among Female Rape Survivors." *Journal of Consulting and Clinical Psychology* 80(2): 201–210.

Rice, Marnie E., and Grant T. Harris. 1997. "Cross-Validation and Extension of the Violence Risk Appraisal Guide for Child Molesters and Rapists." *Law and Human Behavior* 21(2): 231–241.

Roiphe, Katie. 1991. "Date Rape Hysteria." *New York Times*, November 20, A27.

———. (1993) 1994. *The Morning After: Sex, Fear, and Feminism on Campus.* Boston, MA: Back Bay.

Rothbaum, Barbara Olasov, Millie C. Astin, and Fred Marsteller. 2005. "Prolonged Exposure versus Eye Movement Desensitization and Reprocessing (EMDR) for PTSD Rape Victims." *Journal of Traumatic Stress* 18(6): 607–616.

Rothbaum, Barbara Olasov, Edna B. Foa, David S. Riggs, Tamera Murdock, and William Walsh. 1992. "A Prospective Examination of Post-traumatic Stress Disorder in Rape Victims." *Journal of Traumatic Stress* 5(3): 455–475.

Rothman, Emily F., Deinera Exner, and Allyson L. Baughman. 2011. "The Prevalence of Sexual Assault against People Who Identify as Gay, Lesbian, or Bisexual in the United States: A Systematic Review." *Trauma, Violence, and Abuse* 12(2): 55–66.

Rothman, Emily, and Jay Silverman. 2007. "The Effect of a College Sexual Assault Prevention Program on First-Year Students' Victimization Rates." *Journal of American College Health* 55(5): 283–290.

Rubin, Gayle. (1984) 1993. "Thinking Sex: Notes for a Radical Theory on the Politics of Sexuality." In *The Lesbian and Gay Studies Reader*, edited by Henry Abelove, Michele Aina Barale, and David M. Halperin, 3–44. New York: Routledge.

Russell, Diana E. H. 1975. *The Politics of Rape: The Victim's Perspective.* New York: Stein and Day.

Rutherford, Alexandra. 2017. "Surveying Rape: Feminist Social Science and the Ontological Politics of Sexual Assault." *History of the Human Sciences* 30(4): 100–123.

Ryan, Kathryn. 2011. "The Relationship between Rape Myths and Sexual Scripts: The Social Construction of Rape." *Sex Roles* 65(11): 774–782.

Schauben, Laura J., and Patricia A. Frazier. 1995. "Vicarious Trauma: The Effects on Female Counselors of Working with Sexual Violence Survivors." *Psychology of Women Quarterly* 19(1): 49–64.

Schwaneberg, Robert. 2006. "Study Finds Rape of Inmates Relatively Rare in New Jersey." *New Jersey Star-Ledger*, October 5. Retrieved September 7, 2016. Available at https://www.thebodypro.com/article/study-finds-rape-inmates-relatively-rare -new-jersey.

Scully, Diana, and Joseph Marolla. 1984. "Convicted Rapists' Vocabulary of Motive: Excuses and Justifications." *Social Problems* 31(5): 530–544.

Senn, Charlene Y. 2011. "An Imperfect Feminist Journey: Reflections on the Process to Develop an Effective Sexual Assault Resistance Programme for University Women." *Feminism and Psychology* 21(1): 121–137.

Seto, Michael. 2000. Review of *A Natural History of Rape: Biological Bases of Sexual Coercion*, by Randy Thornhill and Craig T. Palmer. *Animal Behavior* 60(5): 705–707.

Shapin, Steven. 1995. "Cordelia's Love: Credibility and the Social Studies of Science." *Perspectives on Science* 30(1): 12–45.

Shapin, Steven, and Simon Schaffer. (1985) 2011. *Leviathan and the Air Pump: Hobbes, Boyle, and Experimental Life.* Princeton, NJ: Princeton University Press.

Shotland, R. Lance, and B. A. Hunter. 1995. "Women's 'Token Resistant' and Compliant Sexual Behaviors Are Related to Uncertain Sexual Intentions and Rape." *Personality and Social Psychology Bulletin* 21(3): 226–236.

Sigurvinsdottir, R., and S. E. Ullman. 2015. "The Role of Sexual Orientation in the Victimization and Recovery of Sexual Assault Survivors." *Violence and Victims* 30(3): 636–648.

Simon, William, and John Gagnon. 1986. "Sexual Scripts: Permanence and Change." *Archives of Sexual Behavior* 15(2): 97–120.

————. (1973) 2005. *Sexual Conduct*. New Brunswick, NJ: Aldine Transaction.

Sommers, Christina Hoff. 2012. "CDC Study on Sexual Violence in the U.S. Over-states the Problem." *Washington Post*, January 27. https://www.washingtonpost.com/opinions/cdc-study-on-sexual-violence-in-the-us-overstates-the-problem/2012/01/25/gIQAHRKPWQ_story.html.

Spohn, Cassia, and Julie Horney. 1992. *Rape Law Reform: A Grassroots Revolution and Its Impact*. New York: Plenum.

Sprecher, Susan, Elaine Hatfield, Anthony Cortese, Elena Potapova, and Anna Lev-itskaya. 1994. "Token Resistance to Sexual Intercourse and Consent to Unwanted Sexual Intercourse: College Students' Dating Experiences in Three Countries." *Journal of Sex Research* 31(2): 125–132.

Star, Susan Leigh. 1989. *Regions of the Mind: Brain Research and the Quest for Scientific Certainty*. Stanford, CA: Stanford University Press.

Star, Susan Leigh, and Anselm Strauss. 1999. "Layers of Silence, Arenas of Voice: The Ecology of Visible and Invisible Work." *Computer Supported Cooperative Work* 8(1): 9–30.

Stockman, Jamila K., Jacquelyn Campbell, and David D. Celentano. 2010. "Sexual Violence and HIV Risk Behaviors among a Nationally Representative Sample of Heterosexual American Women: The Importance of Sexual Coercion." *Journal of Acquired Immune Deficiency Syndrome* 53(1): 136–143.

Stotzer, Rebecca L. 2009. "Violence against Transgender People: A Review of United States Data." *Aggression and Violent Behavior* 14(3): 170–179.

Suarez, Eliana, and Tahany M. Gadalla. 2010. "Stop Blaming the Victim: A Meta-analysis on Rape Myths." *Journal of Interpersonal Violence* 25(11): 2010–2035.

Tang-Martinez, Zuleyma, and Mindy Mechanic. 2001. Review of *A Natural History of Rape: Biological Bases of Sexual Coercion*, by Randy Thornhill and Craig T. Palmer. *American Anthropologist* 103(4): 1222–1223.

Taylor, Bruce, Nan D. Stein, A. R. Mack, T. J. Horwood, and F. Burden. 2012. *Experimental Evaluation of a Youth Dating Violence Prevention Program in New York City Middle Schools, 2009–2010*. Ann Arbor, MI: Inter-university Consortium for Political and Social Research.

TeBockhorst, Sunda Friedman, Mary Sean O'Halloran, and Bair N. Nyline. 2015. "Tonic Immobility among Survivors of Sexual Assault." *Psychological Trauma* 7(2): 171–178.

Thompson, Charis. 2007. *Making Parents: The Ontological Choreography of Reproductive Technologies*. Cambridge, MA: MIT Press.

Thornhill, Nancy Wilmsen, and Randy Thornhill. 1990a. "Evolutionary Analysis of Psychological Pain Following Rape I: The Effects of Victim's Age and Marital Status." *Ethology and Sociobiology* 11(3): 155–176.

————. 1990b. "Evolutionary Analysis of Psychological Pain Following Rape II: The Effects of Stranger, Friend, and Family Member Offenders." *Ethology and Sociobiology* 11(3): 177–193.

————. 1990c. "Evolutionary Analysis of Psychological Pain Following Rape III: The Effects of Force and Violence." *Aggressive Behavior* 16(5): 297–320.

————. 1991. "Evolutionary Analysis of Psychological Pain Following Rape IV: The Effect of the Nature of the Sex Act." *Journal of Comparative Psychology* 105(3): 243–252.

Thornhill, Randy, and Craig T. Palmer. 2000. *A Natural History of Rape: Biological Bases of Sexual Coercion*. Cambridge, MA: MIT Press.

Thornhill, Randy, and Nancy Wilmsen Thornhill. 1983. "Human Rape: An Evolu-tionary Analysis." *Ethology and Sociobiology* 4(3): 137–173.

Tillman, Shaquita, Thema Bryant-Davis, Kimberly Smith, and Alison Marks. 2010. "Shattering Silence: Exploring Barriers to Disclosure for African American Sexual Assault Survivors." *Trauma, Violence, and Abuse* 11(2): 59–70.

Timmermans, Stefan, and Steven Epstein. 2010. "A World of Standards but Not a Standard World: Toward a Sociology of Standards and Standardization." *Annual Review of Sociology* 36(1): 69–89.

Tjaden, Patricia, and Nancy Thoennes. 2000. *Full Report of the Prevalence, Incidence, and Consequences of Violence against Women*. Washington, DC: United States Department of Justice.

Tolwinski, Kasia. 2019. "Fraught Claims at the Intersection of Biology and Sociality: Managing Controversy in the Neuroscience of Poverty and Adversity." *Social Studies of Science* 49(2): 141–161.

Travis, Cheryl Brown, ed. 2003. *Evolution, Gender, and Rape*. Cambridge, MA: MIT Press.

Ullman, Sarah E. 1996. "Social Reactions, Coping Strategies, and Self-Blame Attributions in Adjustment to Sexual Assault." *Psychology of Women Quarterly* 20(4): 505–526.

———. 2010. *Talking about Sexual Assault: Society's Response to Survivors*. Washington, DC: American Psychological Association.

Ullman, Sarah E., and Henrietta H. Filipas. 2001. "Predictors of PTSD Symptom Severity and Social Reactions in Sexual Assault Victims." *Journal of Traumatic Stress* 14(2): 369–389.

Ullman, Sarah E., Henrietta H. Filipas, Stephanie M. Townsend, and Laura L. Starzynski. 2005. "Trauma Exposure, Posttraumatic Stress Disorder, and Problem Drinking in Sexual Assault Survivors." *Journal of Studies on Alcohol* 66(5): 610–619.

Ullman, Sarah E., Stephanie M. Townsend, Henrietta H. Filipas, and Laura L. Starzynski. 2007. "Structural Models of the Relations of Assault Severity, Social Support, Avoidance Coping, Self-Blame, and PTSD among Sexual Assault Survivors." *Psychology of Women Quarterly* 31(1): 23–37.

Vila, Pablo. 2017. "Music, Dance, Affect, and Emotions: Where We Are Now." In *Music, Dance, Affect, and Emotions in Latin America*, edited by Pablo Vila, 1–38. Lanham, MD: Lexington.

Waidzunas, Tom. 2012. "Young, Gay, and Suicidal: Dynamic Nominalism and the Process of Defining a Social Problem." *Science, Technology, and Human Values* 37(2): 199–225.

———. 2015. *The Straight Line: How the Fringe Science of Ex-Gay Therapy Reoriented Sexuality*. Minneapolis: University of Minnesota Press.

Waidzunas, Tom, and Steven Epstein. 2015. "'For Men, Arousal Is Orientation': Bodily Truthing, Technosexual Scripts, and the Materialization of Sexualities through the Phallometric Test." *Social Studies of Science* 45(2): 187–213.

Walters, Mikel L., Jieru Chen, and Matthew J. Breiding. 2013. *The National Intimate Partner and Sexual Violence Survey (NISVS): 2010 Findings on Victimization by Sexual Orientation*. Atlanta: National Center for Injury Prevention and Control, Centers for Disease Control and Prevention.

Warr, Mark. 1985. "Fear of Rape among Urban Women." *Social Problems* 32(3): 238–250.

Warshaw, Robin. (1988) 1994. *I Never Called It Rape*. New York: Harper Perennial.

White, Bradley H., and Sharon E. Robinson Kurpius. 2002. "Effects of Victim Sex and Sexual Orientation on Perceptions of Rape." *Sex Roles* 46(5): 191–200.

White House Council on Women and Girls. 2014. *Rape and Sexual Assault: A Renewed Call to Action*. Washington, DC: White House Council on Women and Girls.

Whitman, Charlene. 2012. *Rape and Sexual Assault Analyses and Laws: Current as of July 2012.* Washington, DC: AEquitas.

Whittier, Nancy. 2009. *The Politics of Child Sexual Abuse: Emotion, Social Movements, and the State.* New York: Oxford University Press.

Williams, Linda S. 1984. "The Classic Rape: When Do Victims Report?" *Social Problems* 33(4): 459–467.

Wolff, Nancy, Cynthia L. Blitz, Jing Shi, Ronet Bachman, and Jane A. Siegel. 2006. "Sexual Violence inside Prison: Rates of Victimization." *Journal of Urban Health* 83(5): 835–848.

Wolfthal, Diane. 2001. Review of *A Natural History of Rape: Biological Bases of Sexual Coercion,* by Randy Thornhill and Craig T. Palmer. *Journal of the History of Sexuality* 10(2): 343–346.

Wolitzky-Taylor, Kate B., Heidi S. Resnick, Jenna L. McCauley, Ananda B. Amstadter, Dean G. Kilpatrick, and Kenneth J. Ruggiero. 2011. "Is Reporting of Rape on the Rise? A Comparison of Women with Reported versus Unreported Rape Experiences in the National Women's Study-Replication." *Journal of Interpersonal Violence* 26(4): 807–832.

Woodward, Kathleen. 1999. "Statistical Panic." *differences* 11(2): 177–203.

Woolgar, Steve, and Javier Lezaun. 2013. "The Wrong Bin Bag: A Turn to Ontology in Science and Technology Studies?" *Social Studies of Science* 43(3): 321–340.

Woolgar, Steve, and Dorothy Pawluch. 1985. "Ontological Gerrymandering: The Anatomy of Social Problems Explanations." *Social Problems* 32(3): 214–227.

Wyatt, Gail Elizabeth. 1992. "The Sociocultural Context of African American and White American Women's Rape." *Journal of Social Issues* 48(1): 77–91.

Yodanis, C. L. 2004. "Gender Inequality, Violence against Women, and Fear: A Cross-National Test of the Feminist Theory of Violence against Women." *Journal of Interpersonal Violence* 19(6): 655–675.

INDEX

Note: Page numbers in *italics* refer to illustrative matter.

About the Author

Ethan Czuy Levine is an assistant professor of criminal justice and victimology and victim services at Stockton University. His research focuses on interpersonal violence, gender, and the production of knowledge, and has been published in numerous peer-reviewed outlets. Outside of academia, Levine is a consultant, advocate, and award-winning speaker on interpersonal violence and lesbian, gay, bisexual, transgender, queer, and other sexual and gender minority (LGBTQ+) communities. He has more than ten years' experience supporting survivors of sexual and domestic violence. This has included direct service work, such as staffing crisis hotlines, medical accompaniment, court accompaniment, police department accompaniment, and supporting survivors and their children in shelters, as well as education and outreach for diverse community and professional audiences.

Available titles in the Critical Issues in Crime and Society series: